Reason and Human Good
in Aristotle

Reason and Human Good in Aristotle

John M. Cooper

Hackett Publishing Company
Indianapolis

Preface to the paperback edition and
Index Locorum and List of Works Cited
copyright © 1986 by John M. Cooper

Printed in the United States of America

For further information, please address

Hackett Publishing Company, Inc.
P.O. Box 44937
Indianapolis, Indiana 46204

Library of Congress Cataloging-in-Publication Data

Cooper, John M. (John Madison), 1939–
    Reason and human good in Aristotle.

        Reprint. Originally published: Cambridge, Mass.:
Harvard University Press, 1975.
        Includes bibliographical references and indexes.
        1. Aristotle—Contributions in ethics.   2. Reason
—History.   3. Ethics, Ancient.   I. Title.
B491.E7C66   1986   171'.3   86-19468
ISBN 0-87220-022-1 (pbk.)

Reprinted by arrangement with Harvard University Press

Copyright © 1975 by the President and Fellows of Harvard College
All rights reserved
Second printing 1977
Library of Congress Catalog Card Number 74-30852
ISBN 0-674-74952-9
Printed in the United States of America
Publication of this book has been aided by a grant from the
Andrew W. Mellon Foundation

For M. C. C.

Contents

Preface to Paperback Edition

In the eleven years since this book was first published, talented scholars and philosophers have been drawn in remarkable numbers to the study of ancient philosophy, and especially Greek moral philosophy. An unprecedented outpouring of books and articles on the moral philosophies of Socrates, Plato, Aristotle, and the major Hellenistic philosophers has permanently altered for the better our understanding of each of these philosophies. Not only have many difficult points of detail been subjected to searching and illuminating examination; our increased grasp of the whole history of philosophical ethics in Greece has put us now in a good position, perhaps for the first time, to achieve a balanced, historically responsible understanding of the central and distinctive contributions to moral thought of each of the Greek ethical theories. Naturally enough, Aristotle, in many ways the pivotal figure in this history, as well as a continuing influence on current work in ethical theory, has been a major focus of study in recent years. Correspondingly great progress has been made in our understanding of his moral theory.

Accordingly, if I were writing this book anew today, there is much that I would write differently, even in places where I continue to be satisfied with the correctness of my analysis and presentation of Aristotle's views. But on one central topic (dealt with in chapter III of the book), I would make major changes: this concerns the place of contemplative study in the best human life according to Aristotle and the relation of the theory of *eudaimonia* or human flourishing in book X of the *Nicomachean Ethics* to that presupposed in the earlier books. I am no longer convinced that the "life of the intellect" that Aristotle champions in book X, recommending it as a god's life that some few human beings, as well, can live, is not also a life of moral virtue—of close and deep attachment to family, friends and fellow-citizens, without regard to whether they too are capable of leading this intellectually most satisfying, god-like life. I now see new possibilities for interpreting what Aristotle says about *eudaimonia* in book X of the *Ethics* so that it fully coheres with his theory of the moral virtues in the middle books and with his preliminary consideration of the human good in book I.[1]

This book continues to be a principal resource for discussion of this and a number of other aspects of Aristotle's moral philosophy that have attracted the liveliest interest among philosophers in recent years. I hope that the publication of this paperback edition will make it easier for everyone, particularly students, to find their way into this, one of the most exciting fields of current research in philosophy.

I would like to thank Brian Rak for preparing the List of Works Cited and the Index Locorum, which have been added for this edition.

J.M.C.

Princeton, New Jersey
June 1986

---

[1] See "Contemplation and Happiness: A Reconsideration," forthcoming in *Synthese* for 1987.

Preface

The modern European languages contain more commentaries on the *Nicomachean Ethics* than on any other work of Aristotle. Moreover, readers of English are the best provided for of all: we have four full commentaries, those of Grant, Stewart, Burnet, and Joachim, as well as commentaries on the fifth book by Jackson and on the sixth by Greenwood. In addition, several good books furnish the English reader with extensive and detailed accounts of the contents of the *Ethics* and evaluations of its leading ideas. The recent appearance of W. F. R. Hardie's comprehensive and careful study, *Aristotle's Ethical Theory* (1968), has significantly increased this literature. When one adds the comparable, though rather less profuse, materials in French and German one plainly has a formidable array of resources for the study of the *Ethics*. Embarrassed by such riches serious students of Aristotle's moral philosophy may understandably want to know what contribution the essay which follows aspires to make to the understanding and appreciation of Aristotle's views on moral subjects.

I have not attempted a critical survey of Aristotle's moral philosophy as a whole. I have instead concentrated on the two chief aspects of its theoretical backbone: his theories of practical reasoning and human flourishing (as I render that omnipresent but elusive Greek notion, *eudaimonia*). For Aristotle the fundamental component of any moral outlook is a conception of what it is to flourish, while it is by practical reasoning that, in his view, human beings do, or ought to, work out how best to implement such a conception in their daily lives. Hence his views on what in general a moral virtue is, which states of character are the virtuous ones, and what attitudes the virtuous person adopts toward himself, toward other persons and toward nonhuman things, all depend directly on his central theories of practical reasoning and human flourishing. Anyone who wishes to understand Aristotle's views on such fundamental questions of moral philosophy must start with a study of these more central theories.

But it is my experience that standard books and commentaries are not very helpful on these issues. It is not so much that they are mistaken in what they do say (though as a matter of fact many of them are) as that they do not, for the most part, give any clear, comprehensive, and consistent account at all of Aristotle's views on these topics. Partly this is because Aristotle himself is notably inexplicit, or seems to waver, at crucial junctures. For his commentators, understandably desiring to attribute to their author just what his texts clearly show him to have held, and nothing more, characteristically do little else than report his actual assertions. Thus the predilection for scholarly safety prevents them from following out far enough the implications of what he does say. The result is that the standard sources do not attempt to work out in adequate detail the over-all theory lying behind Aristotle's analyses of moral virtue, practical intelligence (*phronēsis*), and the other leading components of his moral theory. It is this essential task that I undertake in this essay. In doing so, I have not hesitated to risk following out Aristotle's ideas considerably beyond the point at which conventional interpretations leave off; while at the same time I have tried to show that if the relevant texts are read carefully and sensitively enough there is far more solid evidence of a conventional kind than one might have anticipated in support of the interpretations that I develop by this method.

In discussing Aristotle's moral theory one of course has in mind first and foremost the *Nicomachean Ethics*. But this is not our only source. For, as is well-known, there are two other full-scale works on ethics in the *Corpus Aristotelicum,* the *Eudemian Ethics* and the *Magna Moralia.* There has been much scholarly debate about these other treatises, and on many questions connected with them there is no consensus among competent scholars. It is, however, generally agreed (though not always on the same grounds) that the *Eudemian Ethics* is a genuine work of Aristotle, composed considerably earlier than the *Nicomachean.* And on the status of the three books of the *Nicomachean Ethics* (V-VII) that our manuscripts record as belonging also to the *Eudemian* there is now substantial, though not universal, agreement that they were originally written for the *Eudemian Ethics* but were revised by Aristotle for inclusion in the *Nicomachean.* The *Magna Moralia,* on the other hand, is generally agreed not, at least in its present form, to have been written by Aristotle at all. Recently, however, Franz Dirlmeier[1] has argued for the authenticity of its content, and I have tried to show elsewhere, on substantially different grounds from his, that this conclusion cannot be avoided, at least for significant parts of the treatise.[2] The *Magna Moralia* seems to report in someone else's hand lectures of Aristotle's on ethics that were delivered well before the composition of the *Eudemian Ethics,* and it therefore represents the earliest version of Aristotle's moral theory. Hence in attempting to understand those aspects of Aristotle's philosophy that I deal with I turn frequently to these other treatises—to the *Eudemian Ethics* without qualms, to the *Magna Moralia* with the necessary circumspection. A proper understanding of the *Eudemian Ethics* is essential for the assessment of Aristotle's theories of practical reasoning and human flourishing in the *Nicomachean Ethics;* but the *Magna Moralia* has its contribution to make as well.

---

[1] *Aristoteles, Magna Moralia, übersetzt und kommentiert* von Franz Dirlmeier (Berlin: Akademie-Verlag, 1962).

[2] "The *Magna Moralia* and Aristotle's Moral Philosophy" *American Journal of Philology* 94 (1973), 327-349.

In working out my ideas and writing this book I have incurred many debts, personal and other, beyond those recorded in the footnotes. I am indebted to G.E.L. Owen, whose work has been a model for me of what scholarly rigor and philosophical subtlety together can accomplish in the study of ancient texts. I owe much also to John Rawls, for the example he has provided of the fruitfulness of systematic thinking on moral subjects, as well as for his personal encouragement over many years. I received helpful comments on early drafts of various parts of the book from B. J. Diggs, G. B. Matthews, Thomas Nagel, Wilfrid Sellars, J. J. Thomson, J. D. Wallace, and L. K. Werner. I profited from suggestions of Annette Baier, M. F. Burnyeat, Terence Irwin, and J. B. Schneewind on the penultimate draft of the manuscript. The detailed and excellent criticisms of Burnyeat and Irwin forced me to rethink many of my ideas about Aristotle and, in some cases, to formulate and argue them afresh. This published version is immeasurably better for the criticism and advice of all these people than I could otherwise have made it. I am conscious, however, that my way of understanding and presenting Aristotle's moral theory remains at many places and in various respects open to reasonable objection; another person setting out to write a book on the same subject would certainly place different emphases and discover other connections of ideas. What I hope to offer is a way of reading the relevant portions of Aristotle's ethical writings that is as philosophically coherent and as deeply rooted in the texts as any comparable alternative is likely to be.

Debts of another kind are owed to the Department of Philosophy at Harvard for support from the George Santayana Fellowship fund, and to the University of Illinois at Urbana-Champaign, where I wrote the first draft of much of the book as a Fellow of its Center for Advanced Study in 1969-70. The helpfulness and congeniality of the Center's staff and of its Director, David Pines, and the friendship of the other Fellows were an inestimable benefit to me during that time.

Pittsburgh, Pennsylvania   J.M.C.
May 1975

Reason and Human Good in Aristotle

Deliberation, Practical Syllogisms, and Intuition

1. Introduction

Aristotle's views on moral reasoning are a difficult and much disputed subject. Aristotle is himself partly to blame for some of the disputes and misunderstandings among his interpreters. To begin with, he never attempts to discuss moral reasoning as such, but always instead focuses on practical reasoning in general, treating moral reasoning as a species of this wider genus, without bothering to examine its special features. And, what is worse, he never illustrates his views on practical reasoning by reference to pieces of specifically moral thinking: he never gives examples in which the principles of some moral virtue figure as reasons for doing some action, or where some moral value is being pursued. His examples tend to fall into two other categories, ordinary prudential reasoning, on the one hand, and, on the other, what might be called technical thinking—the sort of thinking which doctors or generals engage in when faced in their professional capacities with practical problems. Though Aristotle concentrates on these particular categories of practical thinking, especially on technical reasoning, he implies that the theory of deliberation which he constructs from them is meant to apply to moral reasoning as well, and this has disgruntled many of his interpreters. For according to his official theory of deliberation, deliberation *seems* always to consist in working out the means, in particular situations or types of situations, of achieving given, relatively concrete ends; and though this may fit well enough the

1

doctor's or the general's deliberations, it seems not an entirely suitable model for moral reasoning. Moral reasoning, as some of his critics bluntly put the matter, must consist, at least in part, in the recognition of the rightness of certain courses of action not as *means* to some end or ends. For where actions are undertaken as means their value is completely derivative, being a function of the value of the end being pursued; whereas actions done on moral grounds—because courage, or justice, or temperance, or some other moral virtue requires them—are, as such, regarded as possessed of "intrinsic value." The assimilation of moral reasoning to technical deliberation, with its means-ends structure, seems to preclude Aristotle's recognition of this distinctive feature of moral thinking.

On the other hand, Aristotle sometimes (*NE* VI 2 1139b1-4, 1140b1-7)[1] distinguishes between "acting" (*praxis*) and "making" (*poiēsis*, which includes the professional activities of doctoring, marshaling an army, and the others from which Aristotle's examples in his official account of deliberation in the third book are drawn), precisely on the ground that in acting, but not in "making," the thing done is an end in itself and not merely a means to some further end. Noticing this, and thinking that Aristotle's important insight in this later passage really cannot be taken account of within his official theory of deliberation, based as it obviously is primarily on technical deliberation, D. J. Allan has argued in an influential article[2] that Aristotle's maturest (and best) thoughts on the nature of moral reasoning are not contained in book III at all. For these we must look to the sixth and seventh

---

[1] See also II 4 1105a32, where Aristotle makes it a condition of moral action that the agent should choose (προαιρούμενος) his actions for themselves (δι'αὑτά). (Throughout text and notes I refer to the *Nicomachean Ethics* as *NE*, to the *Eudemian Ethics* as *EE*, and to the *Magna Moralia* as *MM*. In citations of the *NE*, I follow the chaptering found in the Oxford Translation, which coincides with that marked by Roman numerals in the Oxford Classical Text.)

[2] D. J. Allan, "The Practical Syllogism," in *Autour d'Aristote* (Louvain: Publications universitaires de Louvain, 1955), pp. 325-340.

books, where, according to Allan, Aristotle introduces the so-called "practical syllogism": such syllogisms, Allan thinks, exemplify two patterns, only one of which mentions an action as a means of achieving an end. The other pattern names an action as an instance of a rule, and it is by treating moral thinking as exemplifying this second type of practical syllogism that Allan thinks Aristotle can accommodate his insight that there is an "intrinsic value" in actions done for moral reasons. For this second pattern seems to be exemplified when one returns someone's lost property not as a means to getting the reward money, but because one adheres to some rule requiring that action; and this is at least an important first step toward the recognition of an "intrinsic value" in certain actions, since it permits the possibility that one might perform a particular action not because one expected good consequences to result from it but just because some accepted rule required it.

Of course, as Allan does not remark, it is not enough merely to distinguish between ends-means and rule-instance patterns of practical thinking. What after all is the status of these accepted rules on which in the latter type of case the agent acts? It is certainly possible that someone should employ a rule-instance practical syllogism and yet not thereby recognize any "intrinsic value" in the action he performs. A shopkeeper, for example, who rigidly adheres to a rule of honesty solely on the ground that it is the safest means of making a regular and sufficient income certainly does not see anything intrinsically good in his acts of fair-dealing. Quite the contrary: he adopts this rule only because it is a means to certain ends he is aiming at, and neither the rule nor the actions it enjoins have any value for him other than what they derive from their relation to these ends. It therefore appears that even if Allan is right, and the theory of the practical syllogism is the means by which Aristotle hoped to make room in his theory of practical thinking for the recognition by moral agents of an "intrinsic value" in their moral actions, Aristotle could not achieve this purpose without in addition giving an

account of the validity of moral rules that treats them as
something other than policies adopted to advance given ends.
And it is a formidable difficulty for Allan that Aristotle seems
throughout the *Ethics*, and not merely in the book III account of
deliberation, to think of the principles of the virtues as themselves
arrived at by deliberation[3]—the very process which, on Allan's
account, is patterned on the sort of means-ends reasoning which
necessarily assigns to the means no intrinsic value. If, according
to Aristotle, the principle or principles of, say, just action are decided on by deliberation, in which justice is seen as a means to
some further end, Allan's appeal to rule-instance practical syllogisms does nothing to remove the apparent inconsistency between
Aristotle's theory of deliberation and his occasional recognition of
a value inherent in moral actions themselves and not derived from
their relation to other desired ends. Clearly, if we are to avoid
finding Aristotle inconsistent in this matter we will have to
reconsider his theory of deliberation, hoping that perhaps the
means-ends pattern to which he assimilates deliberation can be
interpreted broadly enough so that, in regarding a virtue as a
"means," one may after all still be attributing "intrinsic value"
to it.

This possibility is enhanced by the observation that not even in
the sixth book is there any definite statement about, or any
example of, specifically moral practical syllogisms. There are only
two passages which might be taken to give concrete illustrations:[4]
one of these talks about the necessity to eat light meats if one is to
be healthy (1141b18 ff), while the other (1142a20-23) contrasts
two types of ignorance, exemplified by ignorance that all water

---

[3] Thus the φρόνιμος, who knows how and why to act virtuously (1107a1-2),
is constantly represented as an expert at deliberation (see, e.g., VI 5 1140a25ff),
and the σκοπός to which he is said to look in fixing what the virtuous mean is
(1138b21-25) is surely an end (εὐδαιμονία) to which virtue is somehow
regarded as a "means." See below pp. 49ff, and n. 63, on the role of deliberation in establishing the major premises of practical syllogisms.

[4] I do not myself think they are meant to illustrate the theory of the practical syllogism at all. See below, pp. 27ff.

that weighs heavy is bad and ignorance that "*this* weighs heavy." So however exactly one interprets these passages there is precisely the same problem here as in book III: while professedly interested especially in moral reasoning, Aristotle does not tell us how to apply what he says about other types of case to moral examples. We must be careful, then, not to leap to any hasty conclusion about how his theories of deliberation and practical syllogism are to be construed when applied to specifically moral thinking. Allan seems sure that the third book account does not apply at all well to moral examples, and must be supplemented by the addition of the theory of the practical syllogism from the sixth book before moral thinking is adequately provided for. But since Aristotle gives no explicit directions in either place about how his theories are to apply to moral thinking, the evaluation of these claims must await an examination *in extenso* of such indications as there may be of how the application is meant to be effected. It is surprising that no one has yet attempted to construct a detailed account of Aristotle's theory of moral thinking by working out fully the implications of what he says about other types of case. One of my main objects in this chapter will be to do this.

There is a second difficulty caused by Aristotle's way of expounding his theory. An account of practical thinking might be either a theory about how practical conclusions, and the actions expressing them, are arrived at, or a theory about how conclusions and actions (however arrived at) can be justified, or at any rate explained; or it might be both of these. There is no doubt that Aristotle, both in connection with the practical syllogism and in his analysis of deliberation (*bouleusis*), speaks mostly in terms of a procedure for determining, rather than for explaining or justifying, a course of action. The English word "deliberation" refers to a process of working out what to do, given certain interests, aims, and principles of action, together with relevant facts about the situation to be affected; and this is equally true of the Greek *bouleusis*, with its suggestion of debate in council (*boulē*). Aristotle's discussion bears very clear marks of this usage. Thus he relies very heavily in book III on an analogy between deliberation and geometrical analysis: but analysis is problem-solution, so if deliberation is like analysis it must be a matter of figuring out what to do.[5]

Despite these plain facts about deliberation, and about Aristotle's treatment of it, it is difficult to regard Aristotle's theory of deliberation as merely or exclusively an account of a method for discovering what to do. For deliberation is called for principally or only in difficult or delicate cases, where the facts are complicated, or their bearing on the interests or principles in question is not easy to assess, or where a very great deal hangs on the decision's being correct, and so on. Certainly, cases of routine action do not call for deliberation.[6] Furthermore, many overt decisions are reached without going through any sort of calculation (at least none that is explicit). I may hesitate before saying what I think and decide not to hold back, but without reaching this decision by doing any calculating. Hence one would expect a theory of deliberation to be quite limited in scope, dealing neither with all intentional actions, nor even with all decisions, but only with those where, for one reason or another, the agent takes time to weigh the matter systematically before acting. This limitation would be particularly serious because many moral decisions are certainly arrived at without deliberation: when I decide not to steal a book, when momentarily tempted, or defend myself from attack on the ground that courage requires me to do so, I need not deliberate about what to do. Yet Aristotle defines moral virtue as a disposition to choose (*proairetikē*) certain types of actions,[7] and defines choice (*proairesis*) in turn as what is determined by deliberation (1112a15). From this it follows that actions

[5] See also Aristotle's references to variations of speed in deliberation (1142b26-27, cf. 2-5) and his definition of deliberation as a form of searching (ζήτησις, 1141a32).

[6] Cf. *NE* III 1112b2, *EE* II 10 1226a33-b2 (We don't deliberate about how to make an R when setting ourselves to write one).

[7] *NE* II 6 1106b37; cf. II 4 1105a31-32.

chosen by a virtuous person for moral reasons are all of them done after deliberation. And since Aristotle appears normally to count all virtuous actions of virtuous agents as chosen, the result is that on his view an enormous number of actions which do not seem to be preceded by any explicit calculation turn out to be done after deliberation.[8] If "deliberation" in this context refers to a process of explicit calculation, then Aristotle would seem to hold that moral decisions are much more excogitated than in general they are.

Now one might attempt to resist this conclusion by the plea that not all the deliberation that leads to an action need be carried on immediately before the action is itself done: a person can have deliberated quite some time back what to do in a certain type of

[8] Aristotle sometimes seems to hold that not all actions done by a moral agent on moral grounds are done by "choice" (κατὰ προαίρεσιν). Thus he remarks generally that τὰ ἐξαίφνης are ἑκούσια but not κατὰ προαίρεσιν (1111b9-10), presumably on the ground that where there has not been time for prior consideration there is no προαίρεσις (1135b8-11). And at 1117a17-22 he says that it is a surer sign of courage that one acts bravely in unexpected emergencies than where there is time to think through what to do: spur-of-the-moment braveries more clearly derive from a firm character (ἀπὸ ἕξεως), since foreseen dangers might be faced from "choice," after figuring the pros and cons (τὰ προφανῆ μὲν γὰρ κἂν ἐκ λογισμοῦ καὶ λόγου τις προέλοιτο, a20-21), rather than from courage. This passage seems to mark a distinction between non-"chosen" (ἀπροαίρετα), but nonetheless courageous, acts of a courageous person, and non-courageous acts that are, however, deliberated and "chosen" (evidently as means to some nonmoral end, perhaps self-preservation, rather than διὰ τὸ καλόν). Aristotle does not, however, generally speak of προαίρεσις, as these passages might seem to indicate, only where there is explicit calculation. According to his normal usage, any act of a virtuous person, even a "sudden" one, in which he acts διὰ τὸ καλόν, will be reckoned to be κατὰ προαίρεσιν: thus at 1105a31-32 he makes it a condition of an action's being virtuously done that the agent should choose (προαιρούμενος) it, and choose it for its own sake, and in *Met.* E1 1025b24 he asserts without qualification the identity of τὸ πρακτόν with τὸ προαιρετόν (and cf. *NE* 1139a31, πράξεως μὲν οὖν ἀρχὴ προαίρεσις). In the light of these and other such passages it seems permissible to interpret the remarks about courage just cited not as implying that spur-of-the-moment braveries are not "chosen," but only that, being expressions of a courageous ἕξις, they are not "calculated" in the pejorative sense of the word.

situation, and then all that is necessary for him to decide what to do is to recognize that he is in such a situation. But though this is true, and something that Aristotle, as we shall see, wants to insist upon, it still seems too much to claim that all actions done by virtuous persons for moral reasons are done after deliberation. For even with this clarification, Aristotle would have to maintain that the calculations *were* actually performed at some time: that, for example, the courageous man at some time actually works out policies for various types of situation where there is threat of danger, and adopts these policies, quite explicitly, as the outcome of a process of deliberation. And not only does this seem a false general account of the virtuous man's adoption of the policies in which his virtue expresses itself, but Aristotle's own theory of moral development seems to suggest a quite different, and indeed more plausible, view. Aristotle holds that we become just (etc.) by being repeatedly made to act justly (etc.) (*NE* II 2-4). Now, though he is not careful to say so, this process of training is not the purely mechanical thing it may at first glance seem: since he emphasizes that the outcome of the training is the disposition to act in certain ways, knowing what one is doing and choosing to act that way (1105a30-32), the habituation must involve also (though Aristotle does not explain how it does so) the training of the mind.[9] As the trainee becomes gradually used to acting in certain ways, he comes gradually to understand what he is doing and why he is doing it: he comes, to put it vaguely, to see the point of the moral policies which he is being trained to follow, and does not just follow them blindly. Now because this sort of under-standing is arrived at gradually, it seems obviously wrong to say that the virtuous man's adoption of his virtuous policies is founded on an explicitly deliberated decision. His commitment to them, and his reasons for accepting them, would seem, in general, to be merely implicit in his attitudes and his outlook on life.

[9] Compare *NE* VI 13 1144b1-17 on the difference between "natural" and "full and proper" (κυρία) virtue; see also 1144b26-28.

Thus I think, first, that it would be wrong to say that all moral decisions are actually deliberated, and, second, that to attribute this view to Aristotle would clash with his theory of moral development. But even if not every moral decision is reached by deliberation, there does seem to be a weaker connection between decision and deliberation, and it is worthwhile asking whether Aristotle may not really have intended to assert this connection instead of the more problematic one just discussed. For it might be said that though the virtuous person does not, in general, arrive at his moral policies by any process of deliberation, he must, on demand, be able to defend his acceptance of them, however he may in fact have become committed to them: if his commitment involves knowing what he is doing and why he is doing it, he must be able, to some considerable degree, to explain and even to justify himself (since, on Aristotle's view, virtue entails "practical wisdom" and this entails *knowing* what conduces to a good life). Now when one has reached a decision by explicit deliberation, the process of defending or explaining it will take the form of reconstructing the course of deliberation by which one arrived at it: the deliberation contains one's reasons for acting. Similarly, it might be said, even when there has actually been no deliberation, the attempt to explain what one has done will take the form of setting out a course of deliberation by which one *might* have decided to do what one has done, and which contains the reasons one actually had in acting as one did. That is to say, if a person does have reasons for acting, they will, when produced, constitute a deliberative argument in favor of the decision actually made; hence one can regard that argument as lying behind and supporting the decision even though it was not actually gone through in advance. In this hypothetical guise, then, deliberation might be said to lie behind every moral decision, even those not actually reached by explicit calculation.

Aristotle's insistence that moral decisions are all of them "choices" (*proaireseis*), and therefore supported by deliberation, can be defended, then, provided one understands by this only that moral decisions are always backed by reasons which, when made explicit, constitute a deliberative argument in favor of the decision. Insofar as those are one's reasons it is *as if* one had deliberated and decided accordingly (even if one actually did no deliberating at all). It would seem that only if one interprets Aristotle in this way can one make his account of moral decision cohere with his theory of moral development. This means that though in analyzing deliberation itself he speaks constantly in terms of a process of discovering what to do, when he comes to make use of the notion of deliberation in his account of specifically moral decision he thinks of it at least partly in the hypothetical way I have suggested. Thus what is presented as a theory of how decisions are reached also serves as a theory of how decisions, however reached, can be explained and justified.

With these complications in mind we can now turn to consider Aristotle's account of deliberation and its intended application to moral reasoning.

2. Nonmoral Practical Reasoning

Aristotle's theory of deliberation[10] is superficially very simple. Deliberation, according to Aristotle, takes the form of figuring out the best way within one's power, given the prevailing circumstances, of achieving some end which one has made an object of pursuit. In his official account of deliberation in the third book of the *Nicomachean Ethics* Aristotle compares deliberation to the analysis of a geometrical figure, apparently[11] in connection with a problem of construction, where the problem is set by the specification of the figure to be produced, and the solution is reached by

[10] The theory is expounded in *NE* III 3, *EE* II 10 and *MM* I 17 1189a1-b25. The three accounts agree in fundamentals; I shall concentrate mostly on the *Nicomachean* version.

[11] Thus Ross in the note *ad loc.* to his translation. That it is a problem in construction seems guaranteed by the reference to γένεσις (1112b24), a word not aptly applied directly to a proof except where construction is involved.

the progressive analysis of the given figure into simpler figures until something is reached which one knows how to construct.

Three points call for immediate comment. Just as, in the geometrical case, the problem is not set by means of analysis but is presupposed by the analysis and gives it its point and direction, so in deliberation too: "We do not deliberate about the ends but about what bears on the ends" (*NE* III 3 1112b11-12).[12] Furthermore, again like the geometrical case, Aristotle thinks here of deliberation as restricted to weighing actions in the light of a single end in each case: the political advocate's end is to persuade the assembly to adopt a certain measure, and he proceeds singlemindedly in his task (1112b15-20), figuring out how, as easily and effectively as possible, to succeed in this. There is no sign of awareness on Aristotle's part of the necessity of taking into account the effect of proposed actions on other ends one may have, besides the one principally in question.[13] A doctor, for example, may be able to cure a patient, but only at great risk to his own life; or perhaps the most effective, but not the only, means involves great risk of his own infection; but the necessary weighing of his professional end of curing people against his pri-

---

[12] This view seems to be one to which Aristotle was led early on in his philosophizing: see *Rhet.* I 2 1362a18-19 and *MM* I 17 1189a8-9 and 24-31 (formally concerned with προαίρεσις but the application to βούλευσις is evident). See also *EE* II 10 1226b10-12.

[13] Allan suggests ("The Practical Syllogism," p. 336), and Gauthier-Jolif adopt (*Ethique à Nicomaque*, Louvain: Publications universitaires de Louvain, 1958-1959, *ad loc.*) the view that in referring at 1142b22-26 to the false reasoning (ψευδεῖ συλλογισμῷ) by which one attains some good end, Aristotle has in mind the decision to pursue some end by an immoral means. So interpreted, this passage might be regarded as an expression on Aristotle's part of the need to assess the bearing of one's actions on more than one end. Describing the reasoning in such a case as *false* seems a bit inappropriate, however; and doubtless what Aristotle has in mind is rather the situation where one does something one ought to have done, but for the wrong reason. E.g., one avoids some water on the ground that it is stagnant and therefore bad, which, however, it is not; yet it has arsenic in it, so one has achieved a good nonetheless. See Hardie, *Aristotle's Ethical Theory* (Oxford: Clarendon Press, 1968), p. 242, and my discussion below p. 45.

vate end of maintaining his own life (the kind of circumstance
which would seem to be of the essence of deliberation as *we*
understand it) seems to find no room in Aristotle's scheme.

Finally, Aristotle comments on how long this process must go
on: he says that the process of calculation continues until the
agent has "brought the starting-point back to himself"
(1113a5-6).[14] He does not here explain his meaning, but he
evidently implies at least that deliberation is incomplete until the
agent has noted some action that he himself can perform by
which he can begin to realize his purpose. But he is sometimes
taken to imply more than this, namely, that no decision—at least
none that can be put into effect without supplementary deliberation—is reached until the agent has attained the stage of taking
notice of some action that he can perform *then and there* as a
means of achieving his end.[15] The difference between these two
interpretations is important, as we shall see more fully later. On
the first, Aristotle would be saying that a course of deliberation
must remain abortive unless and until the agent discovers something he (knows he) can do, perhaps on the spot but perhaps,
instead, at some appropriate time and place later on, but that
once this is achieved no further calculation is called for. The
decision to perform the action in question is the final outcome of
the deliberative process. On the second interpretation, deliberation always extends right into the situation in which action is first
undertaken in pursuit of the end; no course of deliberation is
finally concluded until the agent calculates what currently present
objects, explicitly referred or pointed to, need to be manipulated,
and in what way, at that very moment, as a means to fulfillment
of his plan.

---

[14] See also *EE* II 10 1226b12-13, 1227a17, *Met.* Z 7 1032b9.

[15] Gauthier plainly adopts this view in his account of human action according to Aristotle (see his summary statement, *Ethique à Nicomaque*,
pp. 211-212); the judgment that this, here before me, is an effective means
to my end "*clot* la délibération et fait du moyen sur lequel il porte le *dernier
moyen* découvert par la délibération" (p. 212, his italics).

An example may help to bring out the point at issue between these two interpretations. An examining doctor may reach the conclusion that what ails a patient is an excess of body temperature caused by an internal imbalance of elements, which can best be cured by the administration of an emetic in midafternoon. On the first interpretation his deliberation about the case may be complete at this point: he decides to give the patient an emetic in midafternoon, tells him to come back then, and goes on to the next patient. When the time comes he carries out this decision by looking among his medicines, selecting the emetic, and giving it to the patient to drink. None of these subsequent actions calls for or involves further calculation; they are straightforward matters of routine undertaken in effecting the conclusion reached previously by deliberation. But on the second interpretation the morning's decision is only a preliminary outcome of a process of deliberation that is picked up again in the afternoon. For when the time for action comes, further calculation is necessary: "I must give this man an emetic; this (pointing) is an emetic; so I must give him *this*." At this point, but not before, the deliberation has yielded its final outcome and action begins. On this interpretation Aristotle holds that deliberation must continue until a decision is reached to act upon or with currently present, explicitly referred to, individual persons and things. His comment that deliberation continues until the agent "brings the starting point back to himself" seems, in context, to suggest this interpretation, since in discussing deliberation in the third book Aristotle plainly has always in mind the situation where a person is thinking out what to do on the spot. In that situation, "bringing the starting point back to oneself" naturally suggests explicitly noticing what one can do to or with objects then and there present, to begin to effect one's purpose.

There are, then, three prominent theses that, on a first reading, Aristotle might seem to commit himself to in the third book. First, ends are never deliberated about; deliberation only concerns ways of attaining ends that are adopted in some other way.

Second, in deliberation one always concentrates on a single end at a time, no provision being made for deliberation where the weighing of conflicting ends is called for. And, third, deliberation to be productive must connect the end being pursued to ways of acting upon individual objects within the agent's environment. On all three of these points, I think, Aristotle does not mean what he might be taken to say, and most of my discussion in the remainder of this section will be devoted to arguing that this is so. First, as to deliberation about ends.

It is clear on reflection, I think, that Aristotle does not hold that no end anyone pursues is deliberated about and chosen (*proaireton*) by him, or that, in general, the adoption of ends is not subject to explanation and justification. The truth is rather that, according to Aristotle, each person has some end or ends which he has not adopted by deliberation, but he may nonetheless have other ends the pursuit of which he can explain: this he can do by showing that they contribute to some one of his fixed ends. A fixed end is itself never deliberated about at all, and the subordinate ends, when deliberated about, are treated not as ends, but as "means" to higher, fixed ends. So while it is true that no end, *as such*, is deliberated about, it is not true that none of the things that people pursue as ends is subject to deliberative explanation and justification. Aristotle's theory does not drastically restrict the range of matters on which we can deliberate.

That this is so can be seen from the following considerations. First, Aristotle holds that the various practical sciences in which he finds paradigms of deliberation—medicine, rhetoric, statesmanship (*NE* 1112b12-15), generalship (*EE* 1227a11-13, 20), and so on—exhibit a hierarchical ordering (*NE* I 1-2). Rhetoric and generalship are subordinate to statesmanship (1094b3), and generalship has other crafts subordinate to it (1094a12-13). Both the lower crafts and the "more architectonic" sciences have the same means-end structure: each has its own end (health, persuasion, victory, the production of bridles) in the light of which it orders each of its various operations. Yet, when a craft is subordinate to a higher capacity, its end is pursued also for the sake of the higher capacity's end (*toutōn gar* [*tōn telōn*] *charin kakeina* [*ta telē*] *diōketai*, 1094a15-16). Thus, the bridle-maker performs his various tasks with a view to making bridles, but also, through that end, for the sake of military victory, the end of generalship; likewise, the actions which the general directs for the sake of victory he also, through that end, directs for the sake of the well-being of his city, which is the end of the statesman. This means that though the practitioners of the military crafts, for example, do not deliberate about their professional ends, these are subject to deliberation: it is the users of bridles,[16] and ultimately the generals who direct them, who determine what kind of bridles are best, namely, those that are best suited to the kind of riding cavalrymen have to do, and they determine this by deliberation. The general deliberates about what the bridle-maker is to make, while the bridle-maker deliberates only about how to make it. The general also presumably decides when and how much the bridle-maker is to practice his craft: the requirements of the army with a view to winning a victory, which it is the general's job to figure out, will therefore determine both what the bridle-maker is to make and in what numbers he is to make them.

Thus what is an end in one practical context, and so not deliberated about there, is a means in another, where it is subject to deliberation. Now, so far I have only shown that this is the case where practical contexts differ because different professional persons, or at any rate different professions, are involved. But essentially the same account can be given for a single person's deliberation. Aristotle thinks that for each person there is,[17] or ought to be,[18] some single end which he constantly pursues and which is the ultimate object being pursued even in his pursuit of other things. His constant pursuit of this ultimate end does not,

[16] Cf. Plato, *Cratylus* 390b.
[17] *NE* I 2 1094a18-22.
[18] *EE* I 2 1214b6-11.

as we shall see in a moment, rule out his having other ends as well—that is, other things desired for their own sake; it entails only that any such end is at the same time pursued as a means to the ultimate end. About this conception of an ultimate end I shall have much more to say in the next chapter, where I shall consider what Aristotle thinks the correct ultimate end to pursue is. For the moment it is enough to note that Aristotle identifies it with *eudaimonia*, or human flourishing (1095a14-20), so that the end which a person pursues as ultimate will constitute his idea of what it is for a human being to flourish: anyone who followed Aristotle's suggestion (*EE* I 2 1214b8) and made "honors or reputation or wealth or intellectual cultivation" his ultimate end would thereby show that he thought that to flourish is to live out one's days heaped with honors, or to maintain the best and most widespread reputation possible, or to make as much money as one can, or to become as cultivated as possible. Now Aristotle is quite explicit in holding that, in the pursuit of these or other such conceptions of flourishing, a man may have other ends besides his ultimate one: he says (1097b2) that "we choose honors and pleasure and intelligence and every excellence both for themselves (for we would choose each of them even if nothing issued from them), but we also choose them for the sake of flourishing, on the assumption that we will flourish through them." That is to say, other things may be pursued as ends provided that at the same time they are pursued as means to whatever end is ultimate. So these subordinate ends can be deliberated about by considering whether they will contribute to the attainment of whatever end is ultimate; and therefore the pursuit of them can be explained, and hopefully justified, by reference to the ultimate end, to which they serve also as "means."

Now presumably neither a doctor's professional end of curing people nor a general's professional end of winning victory is by either man pursued as ultimate. Typically, each person will have a conception of flourishing with which his professional end is connected in such a way that in pursuing his profession he is at the same time pursuing his ultimate end. Presumably, also, he will have subordinate ends other than his professional one; what these are will depend in part at least on his conception of flourishing, but in any man's life there will undoubtedly be some other ends besides that involved in his work which his ultimate end will license him to pursue. In his official account of deliberation, Aristotle artificially isolates one side of a man's life, his work, from his other ends and from his conception of flourishing, and in doing so he makes the process of deliberation appear much more narrowly focused on a single end than in his opinion it really is. Thus, if in doing his job, a doctor is pursuing also some ultimate end beyond that of curing people, it may very well be that that further end is not best achieved, under some conditions, by attempting to cure the patient. Pursuit of his ultimate end may instead dictate acting so as to protect his own life (to revert to my former example). Again, if a man has other ends besides a professional one, and all of these are subordinate to a single ultimate end, then in considering how to achieve his professional end in a particular situation he may very well opt for something less than the most effective means to that end. After all, it is his ultimate end that he is pursuing in the first instance, and he must choose always the most effective means to *this* end. It is easy to see that pursuit of his ultimate end may require choosing the *less* effective means to a given subordinate end—for example, if he has other subordinate ends as well, and there is some degree of conflict between the given end and one of these, the correct balance may be struck by acting so that the given end is less fully or less certainly achieved than it might have been, while at the same time the other end is more fully or more certainly achieved than it might have been. Thus, for example, a doctor takes the less effective means of curing his patient because of the greater risk the more effective means involves of infecting himself with disease.

In this way it can be seen that Aristotle's theory that an agent's choices ought to be so structured that, though he may have several different ends, nonetheless some one end is treated as ultimate, makes it necessary to qualify the account of deliberation which he sketches in the third book of the *Nicomachean Ethics* and elsewhere. Ends can be deliberated about and chosen as means to a higher end (and ultimately as means to the highest end). Two or more ends can conflict, and when they do the conflict is resolved by looking to a higher end (and ultimately to the highest end) to see which end is to be preferred, how far the requirements of the one are to be allowed to interfere with the pursuit of the other, and so on. Just as the general, by looking to his professional end, defines the ends of the subordinate military crafts and determines how many bridles, saddles, and so on, are to be produced, and where and when, so the individual by consulting his ultimate end determines what subordinate ends to adopt and how to balance them against one another in cases of partial or total conflict. When the theory of the ultimate end is taken into account, Aristotle's dictum that we deliberate about means only and never about ends becomes: we never deliberate about ends *as such*, but may do so when considering them as alternative means to higher ends. And given that all ends other than a person's ultimate end are considered by him as means to that end, all his ends, except one, will be subject to deliberative examination. The ultimate end itself is beyond deliberation and therefore beyond the kind of justification that deliberation can provide. Later on (section 4 below) I will consider how one can decide which end to adopt as ultimate, if this cannot be decided by deliberative reasoning.

So much, then, for two of the three points on which Aristotle's apparent doctrine in book III needs expansion and qualification. He does, after all, recognize that we can and do deliberate about what ends to pursue, and his theory does make room for deliberation in which the claims of different ends are weighed against one another. I will turn in a moment to the third point, which concerns the place at which deliberation is complete and action can begin. But it will be convenient, now that we have explicitly before us a full account of the structure of deliberation according to Aristotle, to consider first how far, and in what ways, Aristotle is committed to means-ends reasoning as the only form of deliberation. I have already argued that there is room in Aristotle's theory for the weighing of ends (namely, by considering them in the light of a higher end); but the question I now want to raise concerns the relation of what Aristotle (in his translators' English) calls means to their ends, even when only one end is in question.

In the foregoing discussion I have followed without comment the general practice of translators and commentators, and have spoken of deliberation as the working out of means to given ends. It is important to notice, however, that the Greek expression *ta pros ta telē*, translated "means," covers more than just means:[19] it signifies "things that contribute to" or "promote" or "have a positive bearing on" an end. Thus the Greek expression does not suggest, as the English word "means" perhaps does, that an end must be some distinct object or event or state of affairs causally produced by whatever serves as a "means" to it. Petitioning the governor, for example, might be a means of obtaining a pardon for a condemned prisoner; and it could be described in Greek as something done *pros* the end of obtaining the pardon. But equally, presenting a letter to the governor could be described as something that one does *pros* the end of petitioning for the pardon; and I take it that it would be eccentric to describe presenting a letter as a *means* to the end of petitioning the governor: it is what, in this case, the petitioning consists in, and not something that leads up to it or that brings it about. Again, if one's end is a complex one—say, to get a hat and a coat—the achievement of part of the end (getting a coat) can be said to be something which is *pros* the complex end. Now in the third book, as elsewhere, Aristotle's examples tend to fall into the pattern of means, strictly speaking, to ends: for example, he mentions (1112b25) money as something necessary for the attainment of an end; and the ends he mentions (health, persuasion, military victory) are of such a

---

[19] This is noted also by Hardie, *Aristotle's Ethical Theory*, p. 256.

kind that anything done for the sake of them would almost have to be regarded as something that might cause them to come about. On the other hand, there is evidence, even in the discussion of deliberation in *Nicomachean Ethics* III, that the broader application of the expression *ta pros ta telē* is to be insisted upon in interpreting Aristotle's theory.

First of all, there is the analogy Aristotle draws between deliberation and the analysis of a problem of geometrical construction (1112b20-24). In the geometrical case that Aristotle seems to have in mind, the first step taken in order to construct the figure will be the production of part of the figure being aimed at, and not a preliminary move bringing about or enabling the construction itself. For example, a many-sided figure may have been analyzed into its constituent triangles, and then the first step in the construction, the drawing of a triangle, will be the construction of part of the many-sided figure itself.[20] If deliberation is like this, then among the things done that "contribute to" an end will be the production of some of its parts.

This point is made explicit in a passage of the *Metaphysics* where Aristotle is obviously setting out the same theory of deliberation as we find in *Nicomachean Ethics* III: here, too, as in the *Nicomachean Ethics*,[21] he emphasizes that in making or producing anything there are two parallel processes, the "thinking" (*noēsis*) and the "doing" (*poiēsis*), the first step in the doing being the last stage of the thinking (1032b15-17). He gives an example: "I mean, e.g., if a man is to be healthy he must have his elements in balance. And what is it to have his elements in balance? This. And this will come about if he is heated. But what is that? This. And this exists potentially; it is immediately within the power of [the doctor]" (1032b18-21). He goes on to maintain (26-29) that in such a case some stage among those mentioned will be the production of a part of the end being aimed at: thus, he says, perhaps heat is a part of health (*meros tēs hugieias*), or else it produces something, whether immediately or at several removes,

---

[20] I believe G. E. L. Owen first drew my attention to this fact.
[21] See also *EE* II 11 1227b32-33.

which is. This is to say that the first stage of the analysis consists in determining some part of health which is lacking in the patient, to produce which will be a way of making him healthy.[22] No distinction is made between the step of rubbing the patient (b26) to make him warm and that of balancing his elements (if that is the relevant part of health) to make him healthy. Both are regarded as among *ta pros to telos*.

It should also be noticed that in this example Aristotle twice introduces steps in the analysis which consist in (something like) defining the "means" arrived at in the previous step: balancing his elements is necessary in order to make him healthy, but we need to know what that is before discovering a means of producing it (and likewise for the next stage, making him warm). Since in the analysis each step is regarded as a way of achieving its predecessor, this means that bringing about whatever it is that balancing his elements consists in must be regarded as a way of bringing about (that is, as something *pros*) the balancing. The whole chain of reasoning can be set out thus: to make this man healthy one must balance his elements; to do that one must do so and so (whatever it is that balancing consists in); to do that one must heat him up; to do that one must do such and such (whatever heating him consists in); and to do that one must rub his skin. The inclusion of the definition or analysis of something among the stages of deliberation can be seen also in the briefer statement of the same example earlier in the chapter (1032b6-8): "Health is produced by a man by the following course of thought: since *this* is health, *that*, e.g., balance, must exist if health is to exist, and if this (in turn) is to exist heat is necessary." Here the first stage of the deliberation is to take note of what the end,

---

[22] Ross in his notes *ad loc.* (*Aristotle's Metaphysics*, Oxford: Clarendon Press, 1924) exercises himself over what he takes to be the disparity between what Aristotle says about the production of health and what he goes on to say about the building of a house, where the pre-existent parts are material parts (the bricks). But the fact that in some cases the parts are the materials does not mean that they must be such in all; the health example is perfectly in order as it stands.

health, consists in; and it is by way of producing this that the man is to be made healthy.

It is clear, then, from these passages that in describing deliberation as the discovery of "means" to ends Aristotle includes among "means" not only means properly speaking, i.e., causal conditions, but also (1) constituent parts and (2) the results of defining what something consists in. Long ago, L. H. G. Greenwood, in the introductory essay to his edition of *Nicomachean Ethics* VI,[23] introduced a distinction between what he called "external," or "productive," means and "constituent," or "component," means, the former being causal conditions while the latter are parts of wholes rather than proper means to ends. With the exception of one passage (1144a3-6) Greenwood thought that Aristotle, in speaking of means and ends, always had explicitly in mind external means. The passages just considered show that some such relation as that which Greenwood intended under his heading of "constituent means" (even if one might object that his terminology abuses the English word "means") was a constant and even quite explicit part of Aristotle's conception of ends and what "contributes" to them. This fact will turn out to be very important when we come to consider the relation, as Aristotle conceives it, between morally virtuous activities and the ultimate end of *eudaimonia*, and in working out Aristotle's account of the deliberation by which general moral principles are applied to particular types of situation. Given that deliberation, on Aristotle's theory, is not restricted to means-ends reasoning, narrowly conceived, the possibility lies open of interpreting his theory of moral deliberation in a different way from the usual.

Deliberation, then, takes the form of working out, in these various ways, what to do in order to achieve given ends. But how far must this process be carried on before a conclusion is reached and action can begin? To answer this question adequately it will

[23] *Aristotle: Nicomachean Ethics Book VI* (Cambridge, Eng., 1909), pp. 46-47.

be necessary to dwell at considerable length on a number of very obscure passages of the sixth book. For although, as I have said earlier, Aristotle might be taken to imply in the third book that no deliberation is ever completed until the agent has hit upon some action that he can perform immediately, careful study of the sixth book shows that this is not Aristotle's view at all. Instead, as I will show, Aristotle only requires that deliberation issue in a decision to perform an action of some definite, specific *type*, and it is a matter of indifference to him whether the time for implementing the decision is the time at which it is made, or somewhat later on. And even in the case where the time for action coincides with the time of decision, deliberation's work is done as soon as an action of a suitable specific type is hit upon as a means of achieving, or beginning to achieve, the end in view. To vary my former example: when some one has a headache and decides to take a couple of aspirin (instead, for example, of some stronger prescription), this decision would normally be the final outcome of whatever deliberation he may have done. He knows where the aspirin is and what it looks like, so he does not need to "bring the starting-point back to himself" by noting that *there* (mentally pointing) is the bathroom or (once standing before the open medicine-chest) that *that* is the aspirin, or that *this* (an act of grabbing) is taking. These further steps by which the decision is implemented do not form part of the deliberation itself, but are instead the content of some acts of perception that he must (normally) perform if he is to carry out successfully the decision he has made.

This, in brief summary, is what I take to be Aristotle's considered view on the question of what terminates a course of deliberation. My interpretation can conveniently be expressed in two propositions: (1) Aristotle requires that deliberation, to be complete, must issue in a decision to perform an act of some suitable specific type (where suitability is determined by a criterion that I shall specify). (2) A "practical syllogism" is not in general any part of the deliberation that leads to the performance of an action. By contrast, the alternative view sketched above makes the practical syllogism itself a necessary part of every complete course of deliberation.

In order to forestall misunderstanding it will be helpful to say something about my use here of that much misused and misunderstood term of art, "practical syllogism." Just what function Aristotle assigns to such syllogisms, and even what the criteria are for the application of the name, have been the subjects of disagreement, and I will not undertake a full-scale discussion of these questions here. But certainly the uncritical use of this expression to refer without restriction to practical thinking in general is very mistaken. Deliberation as Aristotle represents it does not take a form that remotely resembles an Aristotelian syllogism, and Aristotle never says or implies that it does.[24] He does, however, use the technical language of his syllogistic— "term" (*horos*), "premiss" (*protasis*), "conclusion" (*sumperasma*) and even "syllogism" itself (*sullogismos*)—in a small number of passages which deal with some aspect or other of practical thought.[25] It seems quite clear from these passages that Aristotle only suggests a syllogistic structure for at most a very limited part of practical thinking, the final step which actually issues in the performance of an action. His examples show this: "whenever one thinks that every man ought to walk and one is a man, one walks at once" (*De Motu An.* 7 701a14-15); "if one

[24] On this point see Hardie, *Aristotle's Ethical Theory*, chap. XII. To see this, one might try the experiment of casting into syllogistic form the argument presented at *Met.* 1032b18-21, discussed above p. 20. In general, arguments of the form "In order to get C, B is necessary, and in order to get B, A is necessary, so get an A," are evidently not syllogistic in form, nor reducible to anything that is.

[25] *NE* VI 11 1143a35-b5, 9 1142b22-24, VII 3; *De Motu An.* 7 701a6 ff; to these should be added *De An.* III 11 434a16-21, which, though without the technical terminology, links itself by its content to these passages. I omit *NE* VI 12 1144a31-33, since there συλλογισμοί seems to me better taken generally as "reasonings" than as the technical "syllogisms" in particular (see Hardie, *Aristotle's Ethical Theory*, p. 251); the same goes for συλλογισμός at *De An.* 434a11. On 1141b14 ff and 1142a14 ff, see below.

ought to taste everything sweet, and this is sweet . . . necessarily
the man who is able and not prevented does this at that same
time" (*NE* VII 3 1147a29-31).[26] The premisses in these examples
have an obvious syllogistic structure: B belongs to A, *this* (pointing to some individual thing) is A. By an obvious extension of the
rules of inference of Aristotle's syllogistic, this gives the conclusion "B belongs to *this*," or, as Aristotle says (since B stands in
each case for something containing an injunction to act—e.g.,
"ought to be tasted," "must walk"), the enjoined action itself.
Now in all such cases, one premiss, the minor, contains as one of
its terms a reference, by demonstrative or personal pronoun, to
some individual thing (the agent himself or some item in his environment) as what must do, or be the object of, the enjoined
action. So in general one can say that a practical syllogism consists of a major and a minor premiss in which the major specifies
a type of action to be done[27] and the minor records by means of

[26] It is true that in the *De Motu An.* Aristotle gives one example that does
not issue in an act thereupon performed: "I need clothing and a cloak is
clothing, I need a cloak. What I need I must make, I need a cloak, I must
make a cloak. And the conclusion, I must make a cloak, is an action. And
he acts from the beginning. If there is to be a cloak, there must be this first,
and if this, that; and this he does straightaway" (701a18-22). Here the first
sentence is apparently represented as a syllogism (it has a syllogistic form)
but does not issue in an action, but instead in a conclusion which then becomes
a premiss in a further syllogistic argument to a conclusion which, though
it is *said* to be an action is certainly at least not one thereupon immediately
performed, since it is followed by a further piece of reasoning. *This* reasoning
does lead directly to an action, but *it* is not in syllogistic form! This example
is obviously then doubly aberrant, and I take it that Aristotle's
explicit statement in this context (*De Motu An.* 701a11, repeated at
NE VII 3 1147a27-28) that such syllogisms have an immediate action (and/or
the intention *in* such an action: cf. n. 61 below) for their conclusion is meant
seriously; it is borne out by his examples, with the one exception just noted.
Therefore I base my account on Aristotle's explicit claims and set aside this
one inappropriate example.

[27] Commentators (especially Allan and Hardie) constantly speak of the
major premiss, either always or always in a certain type of case, as a *rule*.
Yet not many of Aristotle's examples, though they may be stated so as to
look like rules, are very plausibly so interpreted. See below, pp. 41–46
and n. 74.

demonstratives and personal pronouns the fact that persons or objects of types specified in the major are present; and the performance of the action follows immediately, as the syllogism's outcome.[28]

It should now be clear how the practical syllogism must be intended to function if Aristotle does mean to imply in book III that deliberation continues right up to the point where action is initiated. For since, as we have just seen, it is by means of a practical syllogism that the final link to action is effected, understanding Aristotle in this way will make the practical syllogism itself part of the process of deliberation. It becomes in fact a very last bit of calculation, in which the whole previous course of deliberation must culminate if it is to be effective at all. A specimen completed deliberation would then be somewhat as follows: To see what I'm doing I need light; to get light I can turn on the electric bulb; to turn on the electric bulb I need to turn the switch to "on"; *this* is the switch—whereupon I decide to turn *this* to "on," and do so at once. Thus deliberation when complete yields an action, decided on as the action of turning *this* (pointing), or eating *this*, and so on, an action described in such terms being always calculated as the, or a, way of realizing one's purpose.

This interpretation has some curious consequences. To begin with, it gives a false picture of the considerations actually taken into account when anyone deliberates. When, in deliberating what to do, one decides that to switch on the electric light is a way of realizing one's end, then under the sort of conditions Aristotle's examples seem to envisage there is in fact no need for further deliberation at all. One knows how to switch on the light, and does not need to deliberate about that; nor is it any problem to recognize the switch on sight; there is the switch on the wall before one, so one just reaches out and turns it. To suppose that

[28] The general form of a practical syllogism is given at *De An.* III 11 434a17-19: "The one judgment says that such and such a kind of person ought to do such and such a thing, the other that *this* is such and such a thing and I am of such and such a kind."

in general one must do some further thinking about what to do, after deciding to switch the light on, before actually doing so, seems to be a mistake. That this is the switch is not something I normally take into account in calculating what to do, nor do I have to decide to switch *this*, as a further decision beyond the decision to switch on the light. Having decided that, I simply reach out and switch it on. It is *perception* that is called for at this point and not further reflection.

Now it may be replied that Aristotle himself admits (*De Motu An.* 7 701a25ff) that the minor premiss of a practical syllogism can be so obvious that one does not bother to recite it explicitly to oneself, so that such further reflection as there is, on this interpretation, may be merely implicit in the action finally performed. But there remains that final decision, the decision to switch *this*, which this interpretation represents as a stage of thinking subsequent to the decision to switch on the light. The act of perception by which one recognizes the switch, whether its content is formulated explicitly as a premiss or not, is still being regarded as making a contribution to the process of figuring out what to do. But since, in the type of case Aristotle has in mind, this process is complete already when the practical syllogism is tacked on, my original objection stands. On this interpretation Aristotle will be representing as part of the process of deliberative analysis what is in fact the work of perception by which one brings the conclusion of deliberation to bear on the actual conditions in which one finds oneself.[29]

Did Aristotle himself interpret the practical syllogism in this way? Did he think that deliberation must continue until an individual action is decided upon by means of a practical syllogism? There are two related passages of the sixth book (1141b14-23,

[29] Taking deliberation to represent rather a process of explaining and justifying an action, the objection would be this: if a practical syllogism is part of the process of deliberation, then the action to be explained would be understood as having always the form *doing this* (cf. *De An.* 434a17-19) or (e.g.) *switching this* (cf. *NE* 1147a29-30), instead of *switching on the light*. And that would be a mistake.

1142a11-23) which, as usually translated and interpreted, would support this conclusion. In the second of these passages Aristotle says (1142a20-23): "Further, error in deliberating concerns either the universal (*to katholou*) or the particular (*to kath' hekaston*); for it concerns either the fact that all waters that weigh heavy are bad or the fact that *this* weighs heavy." Here "the particular" is usually taken to refer to some individual object, and then the two sorts of error will be, respectively, not knowing some truth about some type of thing (heavy water, in this case) and not knowing some truth about an individual object (that the particular parcel of water confronting one weighs heavy): that is, ignorance respectively of a major and a minor premiss in a practical syllogism. And because both errors are said to be errors in deliberation, the practical syllogism will be implied to be part of the deliberative process. I think, however, that this interpretation is mistaken. Comparison with what is said in the other passage, to which I shall turn in a moment, will show why; but even without such comparison it can be shown that the interpretation just given is not the only possible one. Everything depends on how one understands the contrast between "universal" and "particular," and how one understands the examples concerning heavy waters. Interpreters far too readily assume that *to kath' hekaston* must refer to an individual object, and hence are led to take it for granted that "this" in "this weighs heavy" refers to an individual. In fact, however, neither Aristotle's use of the expression *to kath' hekaston* nor his use of the demonstrative *todi* ("this") supports any such assurance.

Though often enough when he speaks of *ta kath' hekasta* Aristotle does refer to individuals,[30] this is by no means always the case. Frequently he refers instead to determinate kinds or species, which are "particular" by contrast with the genera to which they

---

[30] This usage is especially prominent in the *Metaphysics*: see, e.g., B 4 999b33 (cf. 27-31): τὸ ἀριθμῷ ἓν ἢ τὸ καθ' ἕκαστον λέγειν διαφέρει οὐδέν; Z 15 1039b28-31; M 9 1086a32-34; Λ 5 1071a27-29. See also *Cat.* 2b3 (but not 2a36), *De Int.* 18a33, *Pr. An.* I 27 43a27, *Post. An.* II 19 100a16-18, *De Gen. An.* IV 3 768a1-2, *NE* III 3 1112b33-1113a2.

belong: man and horse, as opposed to animal.[31] For example, consider the definition he gives in the *Topics* (I 12 105a13-14) of induction (*epagōgē*): "Induction is the progress from particulars (*ta kath' hekasta*) to the universal." Though translators render *ta kath' hekasta* here by "individuals," the example Aristotle immediately supplies (a14-16) shows that they are wrong: "e.g., if the knowledgeable helmsman is best, and likewise the knowledgeable charioteer, then also in general the man who is knowledgeable in any area is best." Induction here proceeds not from individual cases of knowledgeability but from specific types. Sometimes Aristotle seems to reserve the description *kath' hekaston* for the lowest species (the *atomon eidos*) below which no further specific differentiation is possible.[32] But, in any case, a *kath' hekaston* is often merely a determinate *kind* belonging to a more generic class.

As for *todi* in the example "This weighs heavy," it is enough to refer to *Metaphysics* Z 7 1032b18-21, translated and discussed above (p. 20), to show that it can be used to refer not to an individual but to a type of thing.[33]

It is possible, therefore, to interpret our passage from the *Nicomachean Ethics* (1142a20-23) so that it makes no allusion at all to the practical syllogism. The two contrasted types of error may not be ignorance of major and minor premises of a syllogism, but ignorance of some generic fact (e.g., that heavy waters [N.B. the plural] are bad) and ignorance of some fact about a species (e.g., that this, i.e., perhaps, *stagnant water,* weighs heavy).

[31] Especially clear is *Cat.* 15b1-2: ἐστι δὲ ἁπλῶς μὲν κίνησις ἠρεμίᾳ ἐναντίον· ταῖς δὲ καθ᾽ ἕκαστα, γενέσει μὲν φθορά, αὐξήσει δὲ μείωσις. See also *Hist. An.* V 1 539b15, *De Gen. An.* III 11 763b15, *Post. An.* I 13 79a4-6 (where the context makes it clear that detailed empirical facts about types of thing, and not facts about individual occurrences, are in question), and the passages cited in the following note.

[32] See e.g. *Post. An.* II 13 97b28-31, *De Part. An.* I 4 644a28-33, b6-7.

[33] See also ταδί, *NE* 1146b16; and *Pr. An.* I 46 51b5-8: τὸ μὴ εἶναι τοδί ... οἷον τὸ μὴ εἶναι λευκόν.

That this is in fact the correct interpretation is shown by the other passage mentioned above (1141b14-23).[34] Here Aristotle again emphasizes the need to know both universals (*ta katholou*) and particulars (*ta kath' hekasta*): but the example he gives indisputably (though one might not guess this from a reading of the current translations) makes *ta kath'hekasta* not individuals but specific types. He says (b20-21) that one must know not merely the universal principle that light meats are healthful but also the "particular" fact that chicken is light,[35] if one is to have any practical effect on one's own or others' health. In contrasting these two statements as respectively universal and particular Aristotle cannot have in mind the distinction between statements dealing merely with types of persons and things and those

[34] One might be suspicious of my use here of 1141b14-23 to support the interpretation just proposed for 1142a20-23. For whereas the former refers to the need to γνωρίζειν τὰ καθ' ἕκαστα (plural) the latter concerns the possibility of error περὶ τὸ καθ' ἕκαστον (singular); and one might wonder, as T. Irwin has suggested to me, whether this difference is significant—whether τὰ καθ' ἕκαστα in the earlier passage means groups or classes of individuals, more or less as I have insisted, whereas τὸ καθ' ἕκαστον in 1142a22 means the individual itself (rather than the single species of individuals). It is true that one might plausibly find some such contrast in a few passages (e.g., perhaps, *Top.* I 12 105a13), but more often τὰ καθ' ἕκαστα serves simply as plural for τὸ καθ' ἕκαστον and means either "individuals" or "species," depending on what the singular itself means in the context (as e.g. at *Pr. An.* I 27 43a27, 40, which concerns individuals, and *Post. An.* II 13 97b28-29, which concerns species). That these expressions are used in this normal way in these passages is clear on reflection. To begin with, we have τὰ καθ' ἕκαστα being used as simple plural at least once, at 1142a14, where it corresponds to τὸ καθ' ἕκαστον at a22. This latter phrase is, however, immediately replaced by τὸ ἔσχατον (a24), with apparently the same reference (though, as I argue below, a different sense). And the reference of τὸ ἔσχατον is provided first at 1141b28 (to which Aristotle refers back in 1142a24), where it evidently qualifies a decision that is said explicitly to concern τὰ καθ' ἕκαστα (b26); and *here* τὰ καθ' ἕκαστα is plainly used in whatever sense it has in 1141b14-23, which immediately precedes. (On this whole passage see below, pp. 34-36.) So it is clear that τὸ καθ' ἕκαστον in 1142a22 is just the ordinary singular of τὰ καθ' ἕκαστα in 1141b15-16, and it is therefore legitimate to argue, as I do in the text, from the one to the other.

[35] I see no reason to bracket κοῦφα καί in 1141b20. See Gauthier *ad loc.*

containing information about individuals. For both these
statements are equally general; neither contains any singular
terms—"chicken" as used in the statement that chicken is light is
a general term referring to a certain kind of meat, in exactly the
same way as "light meats" in the so-called "universal" principle.[36] The two statements are in this sense both universal in their
scope. In fact, the statement about chicken concerns a particular
in the sense of a species—chicken is a particular type of light
meat. Hence what Aristotle is saying in these two passages is that
it is essential in deliberation that one should get beyond generic
statements about what is to be done or avoided—statements like
"light meats are healthful"—and go on to specify what variety or
varieties, for example, of light and therefore healthful meats are
to be eaten. The reason he gives (1141b15) is that action has
always to do with particulars, that is, with specific types, and not
just genera—for example, there is never an act of eating light
meat that is not one of eating one or another of the species of light
meat. The action to be performed, he implies, will be not just eating a light meat, but eating chicken or pheasant or whatever;
hence, in general, one must continue to deliberate until one has
discovered a specific type of light meat to eat.[37]

Obviously this distinction between the generic and the specific
is highly context-dependent. Compared with the genus light
meat, fowl may well count as specific, though only relatively so,
since it in turn has pheasant, chicken, and so on, as its species.

[36] This is more obvious in the Greek than it is in my English: τὰ ὀρνίθεια,
which I translate "chicken," would more literally be rendered "bird meats";
the literal translation has the merit of bringing out the grammatical identity
of form in τὰ ὀρνίθεια and τὰ κοῦφα.

[37] Hence the difference remarked on in the second of the two passages
(1142a11-23) between practical intelligence and mathematical ability: one
cannot be practically accomplished until one has had enough experience of
life to be familiar with the significantly different types of persons and things
that one must act with and on. Geometry, being abstract, can be mastered
without the kind of practical experience that is essential to ethical life; hence
there are teen-age mathematical wizards, but wisdom comes only with age.

Even chicken itself is not an absolutely specific classification, since there are, after all, different varieties of domestic fowl (Rhode Island red, Leghorn, and so on). Aristotle's insistence that deliberation must extend beyond the genera to the species of things is therefore somewhat vague: it may be that there is no eating of light meat that is not the eating of e.g., chicken, but equally there is no eating of chicken that is not the eating of, e.g., a Rhode Island red. How far must one go in deliberating before something specific enough is reached? A preliminary suggestion, which I shall try to defend later on, is that it all depends on the agent's capacities and circumstances. A description is specific enough if it is one which the agent knows how to apply to things directly, as it were on sight, without having to investigate them carefully first, and if such further specific differences as there may be within the class denoted are not relevant to his purposes. Thus, in the case of the chicken the description "light meat" counts as "universal" because the typical agent does not recognize meat as light or heavy on sight, while "chicken" is specific enough because most people do know chicken when they see it, and for keeping healthy one variety of chicken is about as good to eat as another.

In these passages, then, Aristotle points out the necessity to go beyond very general injunctions which one may not know how, without further ado, to follow, to relatively specific ones that one can put into effect at once, when the time is right, because the terms of the injunction are such that one recognizes the appropriate objects on sight. Aristotle does not, as he seems often to be thought to do, insist here on the necessity for a practical syllogism as the last step in deliberation; instead, he argues for nothing more than a deliberated decision cast in specific enough terms so that the agent recognizes at once when the time for action is come and knows how without calculation to do whatever has been decided on.[38]

---

[38] As usual, I treat deliberation here as a process of working out what to do. If one takes it as a procedure for explaining or justifying an action *ex*

This conclusion is, of course, negative at best: Aristotle might have held that every complete deliberation must contain a practical syllogism while arguing in these passages merely for the additional point just explained. But in a passage that depends on and develops the points made in the passages just considered Aristotle does, I think, maintain that deliberation ceases once such a specific decision is reached, so that the practical syllogism, which is always subsequent to such decisions, cannot be a stage in the process of deliberation. For in this passage Aristotle refers to the specific action thus decided on as "last" or "ultimate," and as I shall try to show, he means by "last" here the last step in the process of deliberation. So Aristotle must be interpreted to hold not just that every complete, effective deliberation must yield a decision to do something belonging to a relevant specific type, but that in general deliberation ceases when this point is reached. The practical syllogism, which has an action referred to as "doing *this* (to *this*)" as its conclusion, is not a required last stage in deliberation.

The passage in question is one of the most difficult in the whole of the *Ethics,* and I will not undertake to discuss at once all the problems it raises; in particular, the explication of what Aristotle means by "perception" here must be put off for the moment.[39] The passage, in literal translation, reads in full:

That practical intelligence is not discursive knowledge (*epistēmē*) is evident. For it concerns what is ultimate (*to eschaton*), as has

post, Aristotle's point will be that in stating what one has done and why one did it, one must bring one's account down to specifics, but need not (normally) go so far as to note by demonstratives and personal pronouns the individual persons and things on or with which one acted. The action that has to be explained will normally already have some specific, but still general, description under which it falls and from which the explanation will take its start: "eating chicken," rather than "eating *this*" or "doing *this* (viz., an instance of chicken-eating)." That what one did falls under this description will not usually be in dispute, and it will therefore not be part of the explanation to argue explicitly that it does so.

[39] See below, pp. 39 ff.

been said: for what is to be realized in action is of this kind. Thus it stands opposed to intuitive intellect (*nous*). For intellect is of the [highest] terms, which are not objects of discursive thought (*logos*), while practical intelligence is concerned with the ultimate, which is the object not of discursive knowledge but of perception—not the perception of the special senses[40] but like that by which we perceive that the ultimate in mathematics is a triangle (*hoti to en tois mathēmatikois eschaton trigōnon*)[41]: for here too one will come to a stop [some place]. But this [viz., perception in the mathematical case] is more truly perception than practical intelligence is,[42] though a different kind (of perception) from the one just mentioned [viz., the perception belonging to the special senses]. (1142a23-30)

Here Aristotle compares something that he calls last, or ultimate, in a practical context, to a triangle, which is said to be last in mathematics. He refers back, at the beginning of the passage (a24), to some statement to the effect that practical intelligence concerns itself with what is ultimate. Ross and the commentators take the reference to be to the passage about light meat which we have just considered.[43] This is probably not right, however, because, as we have seen, though that passage does say that practical intelligence has to do with *ta kath' hekasta,* it says nothing about *eschata,* at least not under that name. But in the passage immediately following the one about light meat (1141b23-29), we do have an occurrence of the expression *to eschaton,* together with the implication that practical intelligence concerns itself with *eschata:* so it is doubtless to this passage that Aristotle is referring.

Now in this passage Aristotle's point is that political wisdom and practical intelligence are the same capacity but, in effect, put

---

[40] Ἡ τῶν ἰδίων (αἰσθητῶν), lit. "that of the special sense-objects."

[41] For a defense of the manuscripts' reading here see Appendix p. 185.

[42] I read ἢ ἡ φρόνησις instead of ἢ φρόνησις in a30, following a suggestion of Burnet, approved by Ross and adopted by Gauthier. There is manuscript evidence in favor of this correction, since some manuscripts give ἢ without ἡ and others ἡ without ἢ; apparently one or the other word has been lost by haplography in each of our manuscripts.

[43] See the note *ad loc.* to Ross's translation.

to use in different relations. Practical intelligence shows itself in the ability to judge well about one's own well-being and how to achieve it; political wisdom is the knowledge of essentially the same thing, viz., human flourishing, but aims at its realization in whole communities. Political wisdom has two branches, corresponding to the distinction between universal and particular knowledge just drawn in the passage about light meat: legislative wisdom concerns universals[44] (i.e., it speaks in very general terms about broad matters of principle, settling by law the constitutional forms and other basic arrangements of the state), while political wisdom, taken now in a narrow sense, deals with particulars (*hōs <peri> ta kath' hekasta*, 1141b26):[45] it concerns itself with day-to-day management of political affairs—for example, getting the people to outfit a fleet, or build a temple, or vote a dis-

---

[44] Cf. *NE* V 10, esp. 1137b13: "every law is universal (καθόλου)"; *Pol.* III 15 1286a10, δοκοῦσι τὸ καθόλου μόνον οἱ νόμοι λέγειν ἀλλ᾽ οὐ πρὸς τὰ προσπίπτοντα ἐπιτάττειν; and *Pol.* IV 5 1292a30-38, where the division between laws as universal and decrees as catering for particular situations is repeated.

[45] Some such addition as that of περί, which I take over from Rackham, seems required. The text as it stands is hardly translatable, as the commentators (Ramsauer, Stewart, Burnet, Gauthier) recognize: Ross's attempt, "that [practical wisdom] which is related to this [viz., legislative wisdom] as particulars to their universal is known by the general name 'political wisdom'," succeeds only by what seems to me an intolerable expansion of ὡς τὰ καθ᾽ ἔκαστα. And in any event the sense that results is not acceptable: it makes this second, "particular" branch of political wisdom a subdepartment of νομοθετική, whereas Aristotle always sharply contrasts decrees and those who make them with laws and lawmakers (see e.g., *NE* V 10 1137b27-32, 7 1134b23-24, *Pol.* IV 4 1292a4-7, 23-25). Gauthier follows Stewart and Burnet in simply deleting τά: this gives the required contrast to νομοθετική, and provides an attractive grammatical parallel with ὡς ἀρχιτεκτονική in the preceding line, but at the cost of introducing a harsh adjectival use of καθ᾽ ἔκαστα on its own (1110b33, to which Gauthier refers as a parallel, has οὐδ᾽ ἡ καθόλου . . . ἀλλ᾽ ἡ καθ᾽ ἔκαστα: the contrast with καθόλου, which makes the adjectival use of καθ᾽ ἔκαστα easier to take here, is lacking in our passage). So, though Stewart's emendation seems possible, I prefer Rackham's. This reading is perhaps supported by the medieval translation, which (as Gauthier reports) reads in its second hand *ut circa singularia*.

tribution of food, and so on. Plainly the notion of particularity
here ought to be what it was in the immediately preceding
passage, on which this one builds. The point, then, is that the
politically wise man, in the narrower sense, knows what specific
political decisions are best, and these are typically rendered, as in
the examples just considered, in terms that do not refer to individuals (and, when they do, it is by name and not by demonstrative
or personal pronoun). Aristotle puts this point when he adds that
"the decree [i.e., executive decision voted by assembly or other
deliberative body] is to be realized in action in the sense of the
ultimate [thing to be done]" (*to gar psēphisma prakton hōs to
eschaton,* b27-28): that is, it is specific, fit for implementation as
it stands, without needing further study or investigation before
the decision is reached what precisely to do.

It should be noticed that here, in its first appearance in book
VI, Aristotle uses the expression *to eschaton* to refer to the action
itself that is finally decided upon—the ultimate outcome of the
process of political deliberation ("Let a temple be built."). Of
course, what enables such a decision to be immediately effective
is, as Aristotle implies, that it contains a reference to a specific
type of thing (a temple, one of the *kath' hekasta*); but it is to the
action itself as a whole, and not to the specific type mentioned in
it, that Aristotle refers here as "ultimate." But given the
connection asserted here between such *kath' hekasta* and the
final decision, it ought to be no surprise to find Aristotle calling
the specific type of thing referred to in the final decision an
"ultimate," according to a related usage: it is in fact the *last
means* discovered by deliberation for realizing the end in view.
Thus the assembly deliberates what to do with certain tribute
monies, decides to use them to build an adornment for the
city, and then settles on a temple as the appropriate form of
adornment. The temple is the last, specific means selected, and
therefore the erection of a temple is the final action the assembly
decides to take (it being left up to the magistrates to oversee the
letting of contracts, and so on).

Now one finds precisely these two uses of *eschaton* in our passage (1142a23-30). Here Aristotle begins by remarking, with a reference back to the passage about political deliberation, that practical intelligence "concerns what is ultimate, as has been said: for what is to be realized in action is of this kind." Here Aristotle is evidently referring to the action finally decided upon, the ultimate outcome of a course of deliberation. A little later in the passage (a26), however, he is clearly referring not to the selected action itself, but to some thing or type of thing mentioned in it, as ultimate: for he compares the ultimate object of practical intelligence with a triangle, which he says is ultimate in some mathematical procedure.[46] There need be no confusion here if, as I have just indicated and shall try to show more fully in a moment, we understand the action ultimately selected as one in which an ultimate, specific means of realizing the end in view is produced, utilized, or whatever.

Now it is essential to consider carefully the point of Aristotle's use of the word "ultimate" in this passage. Ultimate in what order or process?[47] I have just now in discussing political deliberation suggested an answer to this question, but consideration of the mathematical example at the end of the passage will make it clear what Aristotle has in mind. Aristotle says that in mathematics there is perception that the ultimate is a triangle: "for here too one will come to a stop [some place]." It seems very probable that Aristotle is here reverting to his earlier comparison between geometrical analysis and deliberation (III 3): for there we are told that "the ultimate stage (*to eschaton*) in the [geometrical] analysis is the first step in the coming into being" (1112b23-24), and that people deliberate "until they come to

---

[46] Cf. also τῶν ἐσχάτων at 1143a32-33 with the same words at a35-36, where the same ambivalence is found.

[47] It is essential to ask this question; translators often assume without warrant that ἔσχατον in contexts like these means, or at any rate refers to, an individual thing. For a full discussion of Aristotle's usage here, see Appendix, pp. 183–186.

the first cause, which is last (*eschaton*) to be discovered"
(1112b18-20).[48] In mathematics, Aristotle says in the later
passage, the last step (that is, the last step *of the analysis*) is a
triangle; so by referring to particular things, in the sense
explained, as "last" he means that the *last step in deliberation* is
the discovery of a specific thing on which the agent can begin to
act in pursuit of his end. That is to say, the conclusion of the process of deliberation is reached when one has something of the
form of "Eating chicken is a way of achieving my end." And since
the practical syllogism, whatever its function may be, only comes
in after this point is reached, it is therefore no part of the
reasoning that leads to a decision what to do. This decision is already completed before the syllogism can get under way.

[48] One might think of other parallels by which to try to make sense of
this difficult passage. Thus the interpretation adopted by Ross in his translation (and by Grant, Stewart, Greenwood and Dirlmeier) and defended
by Gauthier (but without the excision of ἐν τοῖς μαθηματικοῖς, 1142a28)
implicitly appeals to such passages as *Post. An.*I 71a17-29 and *Pr.
An.*II 21 67a8-25. On this view Aristotle's point will be to compare the
recognition of an individual physical object (a piece of chicken, say) as
belonging to a type about which one has practical knowledge (that it is to
be avoided, for example), with a similar recognition of an individual figure
as belonging to a species (e.g., *triangle*) about which one has geometrical
knowledge (that its members have angles equal to two right angles, for example). The interpretation I adopt in the text is clearly preferable to this, on
the following grounds:
    (1) This interpretation unwarrantedly takes τὸ ἔσχατον throughout the
passage as referring to individual things (or facts), as such; as I show in
the Appendix, it elsewhere has neither this sense nor this reference. By
contrast, my interpretation (following Burnet) provides the only natural
way of understanding Aristotle's references to what is "last" in this context,
by appealing first to 1141b28 and then to 1112b18, 23, where the same expression occurs embedded, as here, in a discussion of practical reasoning,
and where it is given a clear sense.
    (2) On my view the relevance of the mathematical comparison is easily
grasped, since one can take ἐκεῖ in a29 ("here too one will come to a stop")
with its more natural reference, as meaning "there, i.e., in the mathematical
procedure just referred to." For in 1112b20-24 practical reasoning is
explicitly compared in the relevant respects to the analysis of a geometrical
construction: the analysis *does* have to have a definite term (cf. 1112b18-19,

That the final outcome of deliberation, according to Aristotle, is the selection of a specific action and not of an explicitly individual action to perform is for my present purposes the most important result of a study of these passages. But what about Aristotle's claim, here and elsewhere in book VI, that such ultimates are objects of perception, in some sense or other, for the man of practical intelligence? Early in the passage quoted above (p. 33), as I have already mentioned, Aristotle uses the expression *to eschaton* to refer to the specific action itself that is decided upon by deliberation; but in referring to perception at the end of the passage he seems to use the word by a natural extension to refer to the thing that is to be produced or employed in acting. For he says that of *eschata* one must have a kind of perception somewhat like that by which, in analyzing a geometrical figure, one perceives "that the ultimate (step) is a triangle." As I argued above, Aristotle has in mind here a geometer analyzing a problem of construction, and the perception in question seems to be that by which he recognizes that the particular problem he is working

---

ἕως ἂν ἔλθωσιν ἐπὶ τὸ πρῶτον αἴτιον, with reference immediately to deliberation but implicitly also to geometrical analysis), and therefore does have something ἔσχατον. Since for Ross and the others ἐκεῖ understood with reference to mathematical procedures would make no good sense (the process of theorem-proving, alluded to in *Post. An.* 71a17 ff and *Pr. An.* 67a8 ff, either does not "come to a stop" at all, or at any rate does so before the application to individual spatio-temporal figures is made), they must take it as referring back to a25-26: just as there is no discursive justification (but only νοῦς) of the starting points of a theoretical science, so in practical reasoning an intuitive act (the perceptual recognition of an individual) provides the last premiss. But then the point of the reference to mathematics becomes quite mysterious: no doubt we do recognize individual geometrical figures by perception when doing geometry as we also perceive individual persons and things in a practical context, but why drag this in here? It does nothing to help make the main point, or to illuminate it.

(3) As I point out below (p. 40 and n. 50), on the most likely reading of a29-30 (it is both Burnet's and Gauthier's and, in a footnote, Ross's: see n. 42 above), Aristotle says that perception in mathematics is more truly a form of perception than what corresponds in the case of practical reasoning. My interpretation gives a good sense to this contrast, but Ross's does not. (Matters are not improved by reading one of the other, distinctly less probable, alternative texts at a30: see Gauthier *ad loc.*)

on has been solved, once he has found a figure, a triangle, that he already knows how to construct, from which he can, by following the steps of the analysis in reverse, produce the desired figure.[49] So the corresponding perception in the case of deliberation would be the agent's recognition that he has found something he can employ to attain his end without further calculation: the recognition, for example, that chicken is a light meat that he knows empirically and can therefore eat, at the appropriate moment, without further consideration. Aristotle implies that this recognition is closer to genuine perception in the mathematical case than in that of deliberation (1142a29-30), and on this interpretation one can see why.[50] The geometer presumably works

[49] Burnet's account of this passage (see the reference, Appendix, p. 186, below) runs into the difficulty that, as he understands the reference to a triangle here, it should not be by perception that the fact in question is recognized. For according to Burnet it is the general fact, surely one of theory and not especially subject to perception, that the triangle is the simplest plane figure that is being referred to. Burnet's only mistake, as I see it, is to put forward this general truth as what is supposed to be perceived, instead of the recognition *in the context of a particular problem* that a triangle is the first figure to be constructed in building up the figure required.

[50] On the interpretation of Ross (particularly if, like Ross, one follows Bywater in excising ἐν τοῖς μαθηματικοῖς at 1142a28) one cannot, I think, give a satisfactory explanation of the difference between perception in mathematics and in practical affairs which this passage asserts. For on this view practical perception is contrasted simply with the perception "that the particular figure before us is a triangle." But why is it more properly called perception when someone recognizes a triangle by looking at it, than it is when someone recognizes chicken by looking at it? The fact that the former is perception of a κοινόν while in the latter one perceives a κατὰ συμβεβηκὸς αἰσθητόν hardly seems sufficient reason. Hardie meets the difficulty (*Aristotle's Ethical Theory*, p. 234) by supposing that Aristotle here tacitly widens his view of "practical perception" to cover such nonsensory capacities of intuitive judgment as, say, the moral agent's judgment that e.g. the right amount of money for him to give to a charity is $150. But though this sort of thing certainly *is* less like perception, strictly speaking, than recognizing a triangle when you see one, it is also not anything that Aristotle hereabouts even faintly indicates is in his mind. Instead, we have heavy water and chicken and such-like things as the objects of the agent's capacities of recognition, and all of these are perceptible in a straightforward sense.

with a sketch before him, so that he will actually draw the relevant triangle as he analyzes the problem and will be actually looking at it when he recognizes it as the end of the analysis. But in deliberating, one often—even perhaps typically—plans for the future, deciding on a course of action to take not at the moment but somewhat later; and in that case the ultimate means hit upon (say, to eat some chicken) may be recognized as the solution to the "problem," even though no chicken is actually on the scene. So the recognition of something as ultimate in deliberation *is* typically less like ordinary perception than the corresponding thing in the mathematical case.

Now this is certainly a very specialized kind of perception or quasi-perception, and, moreover, it is somewhat awkwardly described. For while, as we have seen, this amounts to the recognition that some step of analysis or deliberation is the last one that is necessary, in referring just before to "perception of the ultimate" (1147a27) Aristotle suggests that he means, more simply, perception, of one kind or another, of the thing or the action itself that is ultimate rather than the perception *that* it is so. And in fact he does comment on this further perceptual capacity in a later passage. Affirming the unity of the virtues of the practical intellect, Aristotle says:

All of these powers [viz., the virtues of good judgment, percep-tiveness, practical intelligence and intuitive understanding] concern ultimates and particulars (*tōn eschatōn eisi kai tōn kath' hekaston*) . . . . Everything that is to be realized in action is something particular and ultimate. Not only must the practically intelligent man know these, but perceptiveness and good judgment have to do with things to be realized in action, and these are ultimates. And intuitive understanding (*nous*) concerns ultimates in both directions: for there is intuitive understanding, and not discursive thought, both of the first terms and of the ul-timates—intuitive understanding in demonstrations having to do with the unchanging and first terms, intuitive understanding in practical arguments having to do with what is ultimate, that is, the means,[51] and the second [i.e., minor] premiss. For these are the starting points for the end in view; for universals come from particulars.[52] Of these, then, one must have perception, and this is intuitive understanding. (1143a28-b5)

It may seem disconcerting to find Aristotle here linking perception of what is ultimate, which, as we have seen, ought to be the specific means to be employed, with the minor premiss of a practical syllogism. For the minor premiss, being of the form "This (pointing) is F," where "F" stands for the ultimate specific means hit upon, introduces as a new term in the chain of argument the demonstrative "this," referring to an individual thing in

---

[51] Ἐνδεχομένου: cf. διὰ τὸ δυνατόν, De Motu 701a25, as a characterization of the minor premiss (cf. NE 1112b27). Understanding ἐνδεχομένου here as parallel to ἐνδεχόμενα at 1139a8, though conceivably correct (it is so understood by Ross and the other translators), seems not nearly so appropriate to the context.

[52] Ross's translation, "for these . . . are the starting-points for the apprehension of the end," seems to me mistaken. Although the Greek (ἀρχαὶ γὰρ τοῦ οὗ ἕνεκα αὗται· ἐκ τῶν καθ᾽ ἕκαστα γὰρ τὸ καθόλου) might in another context be fairly so rendered (see 1139b28-29 and its context), it must be admitted that "apprehension of the end" translates nothing in the Greek, which just speaks of "starting-points of the end in view." That apprehension or understanding of the end is intended would have to be established from a consideration of the context. But I do not see that this idea is relevant at all to what Aristotle is saying here. On the contrary, the passage concerns the necessity, in practical thinking, of knowing how, by way of perception or νοῦς, to apply one's calculations about how an end is to be achieved to the circumstances in which action actually begins. The problem is not how we come to grasp the end, but how we come to achieve a given end by acting for its sake. The point of this sentence is therefore to comment, appropriately, that it is by attaining particulars (such things as chicken) that we achieve the more universal end in view (e.g., to consume light and healthful meats). Thus it is "starting-points for the attainment of ends" that Aristotle is discussing here. Compare De An. III 10 433a16-17, τὸ δ᾽ ἔσχατον ἀρχὴ τῆς πράξεως: since action is for the sake of an end, the Ethics is making this same point in saying ἀρχαὶ τοῦ οὗ ἕνεκα αὗται. (Much is made to hang on this passage for the interpretation of Aristotle's theory of the origins of moral knowledge by J. D. Monan, Moral Knowledge and its Methodology in Aristotle, Oxford: Clarendon Press, 1968, pp. 74-78; if I am right, his discussion is entirely beside the point Aristotle is actually making here.)

the agent's current environment; this new term might seem then to be the last term in deliberation, so that Aristotle would here be referring to "this" and its referent, the perceived individual, as the last stage of deliberation, instead of treating the specific means referred to by the "F" as the last step. The upshot would then be that the practical syllogism is implied here to be itself the last step in the deliberative process.

The passage need not be interpreted in this way, however. Clearly enough, the main point of the passage is to insist that effective agents must have the capacity to recognize on sight the specific means of action selected by deliberation. Aristotle's point is that because the actions to be performed are always specific, and not abstract or general in character, every practical excellence presupposes the capacity to recognize things of all the relevant specific types: there is, as he says, an intuitive understanding of each of these types of things. Now this capacity, though its proper object is the different specific kinds of things,[53] is only exercised on particular instances of these kinds. Thus in our chicken example the agent has the capacity to recognize chicken, a certain specific kind of meat, but of course when he displays this capacity it is by recognizing some particular meat specimen *as* chicken. Hence it is entirely natural for Aristotle to say (1143b2-3) that intelligent agents have an intuitive, perceptual knowledge of various types of things (*nous tou eschatou*) while adding that they know the minor premisses of practical syllogisms: it is in these syllogisms that the actual recognitions in which this capacity is exercised are recorded. One knows chicken intuitively; so one knows that *this* and *this* and *this* is chicken. The mention of the minor premiss here is therefore entirely in place, and does

---

[53] Notice that Aristotle holds, correctly, that the object of perception is never a concrete particular, as such, but always a thing of a certain kind: *Post. An.* I 31 87b29, ἡ αἴσθησις τοῦ τοιοῦδε καὶ μὴ τοῦδέ τινος (and he adds, again correctly, ἀλλ' αἰσθάνεσθαί γε ἀναγκαῖον τόδε τι καὶ ποῦ καὶ νῦν), and II 19 100a17-b1, ἡ δ' αἴσθησις τοῦ καθόλου ἐστίν, οἷον ἀνθρώπου, ἀλλ' οὐ Καλλίου ἀνθρώπου. See also *De An.* II 12 424a21-24.

not have to be taken as indicating that *eschaton* in this passage
refers to something different from what we have found it to refer
to earlier in the sixth book. As I interpret the passage, the practical syllogism is implied to lie outside the process of deliberation
proper: it enters only with the exercise of the perceptual capacity
that Aristotle says agents must have with regard to the specific
types of things ultimately decided on by deliberation as the
appropriate means to their ends.[54]

In this second passage, then, Aristotle brings forward for
comment the ability to recognize in actual practice things and
actions of the types selected for implementation by the
deliberative process. Thus he supplements the earlier passage,
which in the end concerned the recognition, perceptually or
quasi-perceptually, that the deliberative problem is solved, by
attributing to the effective agent the perceptual capacity which
makes this recognition itself possible. For a deliberative problem
is in fact only solved provided that the ultimate means decided
upon *is* something the agent can put into effect, and this entails
his being able to recognize, by perception, the availability of the
means when it is present. To revert to the example of the chicken:
the agent is right to think his problem solved when once he has
decided to eat some chicken only if he can in fact recognize
chicken on sight. Otherwise he will not have selected a means he
can put into effect directly, without further calculation.

The upshot is that Aristotle does shift his focus somewhat in his
references to the perception that intelligent agents must have of
the specific types in which their deliberations terminate; sometimes he has in mind the recognition that a suitable means has

[54] This conclusion might be strengthened by considering further the comparison Aristotle here makes between νοῦς of the πρῶτα in scientific demonstration and νοῦς of the ἔσχατα in practical thinking. For of course νοῦς
in the former case provides some of the premisses *from which* demonstration
sets out (it is not involved in the discursive process of deduction itself); so,
correspondingly, νοῦς of the ἔσχατα takes up the conclusion *in which*
practical "deduction" ends (and is not involved in the discursive process of
deliberation itself).

been hit upon, but at other times the capacity, which makes this recognition possible, to pick out by perception things (or actions) of the relevant kinds. But he does not in the later passage contradict his earlier statements about the scope of deliberation.

There remains to be discussed one passage where Aristotle does apparently commit himself to the inclusion of a practical syllogism within a process of deliberation. At 1142b21-26, in explaining what excellence in deliberation (*euboulia*) is, he says:

> For excellence in deliberation is the kind of correctness in deliberating which achieves a good end. But it is possible to achieve this also by a false syllogism, and to hit upon what one ought to do but not upon the reason why one ought to do it—the middle term can be false. So this, too, by which one hits upon what one ought to do but not the reason why one ought, is not yet excellence in deliberation.

Here the combination of *sullogismos* (which might in another context mean just "reasoning") with *ho mesos horos* ("the middle term") makes it certain that Aristotle is either speaking of a practical syllogism, or else uncharacteristically extending the terminology of his syllogistic to cover ordinary means-ends deliberation. On the former hypothesis, the following sort of case would illustrate his point.[55] A man refuses to drink some water on the ground that it is stagnant and therefore bad. It is false, however, that the water is stagnant—though not that it is bad, since it has arsenic in it. So he achieves a good end, that of not drinking bad water, but not for the right reason; his premisses, "stagnant water is bad; this is stagnant" contain a false middle term "stagnant," which makes the syllogism false even though by its means a good is achieved. If this is the right sort of example, then Aristotle will imply here that a practical syllogism is part of a course of deliberation; in this context (a16-33) he seems clearly concerned to distinguish what are admitted to be cases of deliberation from deliberation that is "excellent."

[55] I follow the interpretation of Hardie, *Aristotle's Ethical Theory*, p. 242.

The point Aristotle makes in this passage is in any case true and important. It might, of course, be as easily illustrated by an error in deliberation, properly speaking, as by a mistaken practical syllogism: for example, the man who, mistakenly thinking alcohol is bad for the heart, decides to stop drinking and thereby unknowingly avoids fatal liver disease. Syllogistic terminology ("the middle term is false") allows Aristotle to make his point succinctly, and that is no doubt why he chooses it here. Hence I do not think it reasonable to dwell on its implications or to insist on making them part of his explicit theory of deliberation and the practical syllogism.

3. Perception and the Practical Syllogism

I conclude, then, that the practical syllogism, at any rate in Aristotle's more cautious moments, is clearly set apart from the process of deliberation and the decision to which it leads. Before leaving this topic, however, it may be useful to comment on the role the practical syllogism does play in Aristotle's system of practical thinking—especially since the main elements of what I think is the correct account have nearly all been touched upon in the preceding discussion. I have already noted that Aristotle never holds that all practical thinking takes a syllogistic form, and that he only speaks of syllogisms, premisses, and so on, in a very special case, namely, where the minor premiss contains as one of its terms a demonstrative or personal pronoun, and where the immediate outcome of the syllogism is an action undertaken at once.[56] But two further points can now be added. First, the practical syllogism does not represent a form of reasoning alternative to deliberation, but is rather the link by which a course of deliberation, yielding a decision to act (e.g., to eat chicken), is enabled to produce an action in furtherance of this decision. Second, perhaps surprisingly, the practical syllogism is not for the most part conceived of as a form of reasoning at all, but is only a way of expressing the content of the intuitive perceptual act

---

[56] Or (part of) the intention with which it is performed: see n. 61 below.

by which the agent recognizes the presence and availability for action of the ultimate means previously decided upon.

I have already noted that D. J. Allan seems to have thought of practical syllogisms that have a rule-instance structure as a distinctive form of thinking totally unconnected with deliberation.[57] This view clashes, however, with much that Aristotle says. Thus, as we have seen, he connects knowing the appropriate minor premisses of practical syllogisms with the perceptual knowledge of *eschata* (1143b3), which in the context are so called because they are the final stage in processes of deliberation. But, more decisively, Allan's view conflicts with the use to which Aristotle puts the practical syllogism in his account of weakness of will.

One standard characterization, often repeated by Aristotle,[58] of weak- and strong-willed persons is that the weak person (the *akratēs*) does not stand by what he has deliberated, but abandons it, whereas the strong man holds to what he has deliberated. That is to say, the weak and the strong do not differ as to *proairesis*,[59]

---

[57] Allan distinguished these syllogisms from others that he thought exhibited a means-ends pattern. But Hardie has argued persuasively (*Aristotle's Ethical Theory* p. 231, cf. 228-229) that it is a mistake to suppose that Aristotle distinguished two classes of syllogisms: the passage on which Allan relies ("The Practical Syllogism," pp. 330-331), namely, *De Motu An.* 7 701a23-25, actually distinguishes the two premisses, major and minor, that any syllogism has, and not two different classes of syllogisms (or two different classes of major premisses). Grant (vol. I, pp. 264-265 of his commentary) seems to have been the source of Allan's mistake.

[58] Thus, in book VII, 1145b10-12, 1150b19-21, 1152a18-19, 27-29; see also I 13 1102b14-18, IX 4 1166b8-10, 8 1168b34-35, *EE* II 7 1223a37-38.

[59] Προαίρεσις is defined in III 1112a15-17, 1113a9-11, as a desire (ὄρεξις) produced by deliberation, which is to say, in effect, that it is a commitment to act, backed by desire, produced by deliberation. (Since this definition is clearly reaffirmed in book VI at 1139a23 and b5-9, I cannot understand Allan's saying in "The Practical Syllogism," p. 338, that the "connection between 'choice' and 'deliberation' . . . is loosened from the sixth book onwards"; he offers no evidence for this remarkable assertion, and it can hardly survive confrontation with the passages just cited, or with the frequent references to deliberation in connection with weak-willed and strong-willed agents, some of which are cited in the preceding note.) Aristotle does not,

the choice of action that they have arrived at by deliberation, but
the one acts against this *proairesis* whereas the other manages to
act as he has decided he should.[60] A weak and a strong man may
agree, for example, that one ought not to filch one's neighbor's
gold, and they will both have reached this conclusion by deliberation (i.e., it is something *proaireton* for them), but when the
moment comes for action the weak man abandons his *proairesis*
while the strong man does not. Now an essential part is played by
practical syllogisms in Aristotle's explanation of how it happens
that the *akratēs* fails to carry through. He gives the following
description of what goes on in such a case:

For one belief (*doxa*) is universal, while the other has to do with
particulars, for which perception is decisive. Whenever a single
conclusion results from these the soul must in the one case [viz.,
that of a theoretical syllogism] affirm the conclusion, while in the
case of practical beliefs one must act it straightaway.[61] For

---

however, count every such deliberated decision as a προαίρεσις, but only
such as are firmly based in a person's fully developed character (cf. 1111b14
with 1142b18-20; 1139a33-35; and G. E. M. Anscombe, "Thought and
Action in Aristotle," *New Studies on Plato and Aristotle*, ed. R. Bambrough,
London: Routledge and Kegan Paul, 1965, pp. 143-158, at pp. 143-147).
But since these decisions of the strong and the weak man *are* basic moral
commitments, however precarious of realization in action, he allows them
this description: see the next note.

[60] See VII 8 1151a5-7, 29-35, 10 1152a15-17.

[61] I follow Gauthier here in taking τὸ συμπερανθέν, 1147a27, with
πράττειν as well as with φάναι (rather than, as Ross and most other translators have it, with φάναι alone). The parallelism of ἔνθα μέν (a27) corresponding to ἐν δὲ ταῖς ποιητικαῖς (a28) strongly suggests this construction.
So taken, as T. Irwin has remarked to me, this passage seems to show that
Aristotle did not hold firmly that an individual action (and not also or
instead some practical judgment) is the conclusion of a practical syllogism:
tasting *this* is said here to be acting the conclusion, so apparently the conclusion itself is some intellectual content other than the individual action.
The truth seems to be that Aristotle thinks of the conclusion as an intention,
e.g. to taste *this*, *with* which an action is done (cf. εὐθύς, a29). So, because
it is not an intention formed antecedently to doing the act, but instead forms
part of the intention with which it is done, there is naturally scope for
Aristotle to say (as at *De Motu An.* 701a11) that the action itself is the
conclusion. For convenience I usually refer in the text to an action as the

example, if one ought to taste everything sweet, and this is sweet,
as one of the particular sweet things, necessarily he who can and
is not prevented, at the same time does this. Now whenever the
universal belief is present forbidding one to taste, but present also
is the belief that every sweet thing is pleasant and this is sweet
(and this belief is active), while it so happens that an appetite [for
sweet things] is present, the one belief says to avoid this, while the
appetite drives one on (for it can put each of the bodily parts in
motion). (1147a25-35)

Aristotle contrasts two cases here. In the first, where there is no
conflict and therefore no call for either weakness or strength of
will, there is the universal premiss, "One ought to taste everything sweet," the appropriate minor, and the action of tasting as
outcome. But in the other case there are two conflicting majors,
one (backed by appetite) announcing that "Everything sweet is
pleasant (and so taste-worthy)" while the other, which is not
stated, forbids one to taste: conceivably Aristotle has in mind the
premiss, "Avoid all sweet things," but more probably the premiss
is something like "Avoid chocolate (sc., because it upsets the
bowels)," which conflicts with the other in the special case where
the tempting sweet is a chocolate.[62] Now it is this premiss which in

conclusion of a practical syllogism, but I do not mean to deny that according
to Aristotle the conclusion is formulable as a judgment; on Aristotle's
theory it hardly matters which way one puts it. (See n. 26 above and my
comments on pp. 56-57.)

[62] So Ross, *Aristotle* (New York: Meridian Books, 1959), p. 217. Joachim
(*Aristotle: Nicomachean Ethics*, Oxford: Clarendon Press, 1951, pp. 223 ff),
Gauthier (pp. 611-613) and, most recently, Hardie (pp. 283-287) take the
other view, that the conflicting majors are "Avoid all sweets" and "Everything sweet is pleasant." On this view, of course, the two syllogisms will
share a common minor premiss, "This is sweet." But though this interpretation may make for a more realistic assessment of actual situations in which
weakness is displayed, it seems not to square very well with what Aristotle
says in giving his solution to the problem of weakness. This solution, stated
just below (1147b9 ff), is that the agent lacks ἡ τελευταία πρότασις, and
it is surely indisputable, despite Hardie's attempts to make the contrary look
plausible (pp. 287-289), that this means the minor premiss and not the
conclusion of the syllogism: (1) Though πρότασις *can* mean "proposition"
and not "premiss" in particular, it surely means "premiss" here, where so

the situation envisaged expresses the judgment that the weak-willed man goes against, so it must be meant as the expression of a deliberated decision (*proairesis*), which, as Aristotle explains the matter, fails to issue in the action of avoidance only because appetite intervenes to prevent the necessary minor premiss ("This is chocolate") from being tacked on: "The last premiss is an opinion about something perceptible and is decisive for action, and this [the agent] either does not have when in a state of passion, or has in the way in which having does not mean knowing but only talking, as was the case with the drunk reciting verses of Empedocles" (1147b9-12). Clearly, then, the deliberated decision to avoid chocolate becomes the major premiss of a practical syllogism which, so long as it is unchallenged by appetite and completed with the appropriate minor premiss, issues at once in action. Avoidance fails only when knowledge of the minor is driven out by appetite. Here the practical syllogism is made to function as the link between deliberation and action—the link which in the case of both strong- and weak-willed persons is subject to attack by appetite, an attack that fails in the one case and succeeds in the other.

Of course, not all practical syllogisms perform this function, since there are also syllogisms of appetite (Everything sweet is pleasant; this is sweet, so this is pleasant), and these serve to link not deliberation but *appetite* to action. But it is quite clear that

---

much is being made of syllogisms, and the terminological distinction between πρότασις for premiss and συμπερανθέν for conclusion is explicitly marked (1147a1, 27). (2) Aristotle says (1147b17) that what is affected by passion is αἰσθητικὴ ἐπιστήμη, and this must mean the knowledge of a minor premiss rather than that of a conclusion, because whereas one does perceive that e.g. something is sweet, one does not, in concluding that it is therefore to be avoided, perceive that it is so. If Aristotle does maintain, then, that the minor premiss of the προαίρεσις-syllogism is absent in attacks of weakness, then Ross's interpretation is plainly the only one proposed so far that is acceptable: on Joachim's view the minor premiss of that syllogism, "This is sweet," must be present, since it is functioning in the syllogism of appetite. (I am grateful to G. E. L. Owen for alerting me to some of the difficulties involved in the views of Joachim and Hardie discussed in this note.)

where deliberation does lead to action it is only by way of such a syllogism. So practical syllogisms are a necessary adjunct to deliberation, rather than being an alternative form of thinking that in certain cases displaces deliberation altogether.[63]

We are now in a position to establish the second point mentioned above, that in fact such syllogisms ought not to be regarded as part of practical reasoning at all. As we have just seen, the major premiss is the conclusion of a piece of deliberation (or expresses the content of some appetite or other current strong desire), and the minor premiss is provided by an act of perception (Aristotle calls the knowledge of the minor premiss "perceptual knowledge," 1147b17). Now it is this connection with perception that makes one doubt whether this so-called syllogism is a syllogism—that is, an *argument*—at all. Does Aristotle suppose that an agent, having decided, say, to eat chicken instead of ham at a buffet, says to himself as he goes to fill his plate, "Ah! Chicken. I'll have some of that"? To be sure there are occasions when one does thus explicitly note to oneself the presence of what one has decided to take or avoid ("Someone else's gold. Hands off!"). But Aristotle affirms the existence of an enormous number of syllogisms in his analysis of *akrasia*, and even more in the *De Motu Animalium*, where he implies that there is such a syllogism *every* time one thinks what to do and does it;[64] and to make these syllogisms always represent practical arguments with actions as conclusions would be very unrealistic. The fact that Aristotle in

---

[63] Notice that in the example discussed in Aristotle's text the syllogism is supposed to represent a piece of *moral* thinking. But it was precisely these syllogisms that Allan thought were to be interpreted as rule-instance reasoning and therefore treated as a different kind of reasoning, to be separated entirely from deliberation. But, as my discussion has shown, these syllogisms do nothing but carry out the conclusion of a previous course of deliberation. Such syllogisms are just as much involved with deliberation as any supposed "means-ends" practical syllogisms would be, and in precisely the same way.

[64] He there (7 701a7 ff) asks "Why is it that reflection sometimes yields an action and sometimes does not?" and answers: when there is a practical syllogism the result is an action, other sorts of reflection do not yield actions.

the passages considered so far emphasizes that it is an act of perception that provides the minor premiss suggests that he need not be interpreted in this way. The claim might instead be that, having decided to eat chicken, the agent approaches the table, sees the chicken and takes some—the act of perception not providing a piece of information which is then, as it were, detached and used in a little argument issuing in the act of eating, but instead itself forming a link in a psychological chain leading from decision through perception to action. On this hypothesis Aristotle speaks as if there were an argument or piece of reasoning here, where really what he means to be describing is a different psychological process in which perception itself, and not some information provided by perception, is the crucial intermediate link. Why he should speak here of argument and inference when actually he has in mind another process would in that case need explaining, and I shall say something about this in a moment.

This second interpretation gains support from what Aristotle says about these syllogisms in the *De Motu Animalium*. After setting out some examples of syllogisms with actions for conclusions he continues,

But just as questioners in dialectical contests[65] sometimes do, so here too thought does not stop and consider at all the second premiss, the obvious one. For example, if walking is good for a man it doesn't spend any time over the fact that one is a man oneself. Hence in actions that we perform without calculation we act quickly. For when one is actually using his power of perception[66] in connection with an end in view, or his "imagination"[67] or intellect, he does at once that which he

[65] So Forster in the Loeb translation, referring to *Pr. An.* 24a24. Cf. also *Top.* VIII 1-3.

[66] Ὅταν ἐνεργήσῃ τῇ αἰσθήσει: cf. *Hist. An.* II 11 503b23 (ἐνεργεῖν τῷ πνεύματι = continue to breathe), *MM* II 6 1201b13 *et seq.* (ἐνεργεῖν τῇ ἐπιστήμῃ = be actually using one's knowledge), *De Mem.* 2 452b24 (ἐνεργεῖν τῇ μνήμῃ).

[67] Φαντασία: i.e., the general capacity to be appeared to, to have it appear to one that so and so . . . (cf. *De An.* III 3, where Aristotle's analysis is

desires: for the active desire[68] takes the place of inquiry or thinking. "I ought to drink," says appetite; "This is a drink," perception or "imagination" or intellect says—he drinks at once. This is how animals are started in motion and action: the last [i.e., immediate] cause of the motion is desire, this desire coming into being either through perception or through "imagination" and thinking. (701a25-36)

The first point to notice about this passage is that Aristotle's words, if taken at face value, imply that the minor premiss is *always* skipped over,[69] but presumably he does not want to say that thought never stops to record a minor premiss explicitly (as happens in the case of the person tempted to theft instanced above), but only that typically the minor premiss, being obvious, is not formulated in the mind. Its obviousness is in fact a simple consequence of its being a matter of perception, in the typical case at any rate. Aristotle actually mentions two other sources here of minor premisses, *phantasia* ("imagination") and *nous*. This is because sometimes what immediately prompts an agent to act is not the perception of a thing of a type already decided on as a means, but the agent's representing it to himself as nearby

---

guided by the attempt to cover all the uses of the verb φαίνεσθαι where an appearance dependent more or less directly on perception is in question). The translation "imagination," though conventional and convenient, as avoiding the otherwise necessary periphrasis, is more misinformative than informative, since it focuses too narrowly on the having of images, and conjures up British empiricist theories of "ideas." My use of it should be clearly understood to be conventional only.

[68] Ἡ τῆς ὀρέξεως ἐνέργεια: cf., among many passages, *Pol.* VII 8 1328a38 (ἐνέργεια ἀρετῆς), *De Gen. An.* II 4 740b28 (ἡ ἐνέργεια τῆς τέχνης), *De An.* III 2 425b26, 3 428b13 (ἐνέργεια τῆς αἰσθήσεως). Forster's "the carrying out of his desire" is a mistranslation.

[69] Farquharson's translation (*The Works of Aristotle*, vol. V, Oxford: Clarendon Press, 1912), "The mind does not stop to consider at all an obvious minor premiss," implying that it is only when the minor is obvious, as perhaps it mostly is not (that I am a man is obvious, anyhow to me, but perhaps not that this is chicken), that it is omitted, is a mistranslation. The Greek is τὴν ἑτέραν πρότασιν τὴν δήλην οὐδ᾽ . . . σκοπεῖ. Forster's translation is correct here.

(perhaps by its appearing to him to be in front of him, or by his remembering that it is just around the corner, or merely imagining that it is there); or again his knowing (*nous*) where the thing is may prompt him to act. In all these cases, according to Aristotle, the agent may act at once, without calculating and without stopping to think the relevant minor premiss and infer that action is in order. The sequence is as follows. First there is a desire (*orexis*), perhaps a *proairesis*, of some specific kind—to have a drink, for example, or to avoid other people's gold. One perceives (or imagines or remembers) a drink, or someone else's gold, or whatever the relevant object may be. When the perception (or "imagination" or memory) occurs while this desire is still present ("when one is actually using his power of perception in connection with an end in view"), it immediately produces the desire (say) to drink the fluid perceived, and this desire generates the action of drinking. In such a case, Aristotle says, the resultant active desire "takes the place of inquiry or thinking" (701a31). That is, no actual, on-the-spot thinking about what to do produces such actions; instead, the desire that is brought into being by perception or "imagination"or *nous*, brings about the action immediately, without thinking taking place at all.

It seems, then, that Aristotle was himself aware that this analysis of the self-movement of animals (all animals, notice, and not just human beings) in terms of practical syllogisms was misleading. Why, then, does he advance such an explanation at all, instead of simply speaking of the role of decision, appetite, perception, "imagination," and so on, avoiding all talk of premisses and arguments and inferences? A partial answer is that this way of speaking develops naturally out of the way an observer will account to himself for another person's or an animal's voluntary motions. "He's hungry for meat; he smells some meat across the clearing, so he goes after it." Here the action is represented as an inference, and it is natural enough to construct an argument leading to that action as conclusion from statements representing the content, as one might say, of his hunger on the one hand and his act of smelling on the other: "Meat would taste good; *there's* some meat." But, secondly, Aristotle seems to have thought that to draw an analogy between such an argument and a syllogism would help to explain fully and in a satisfying way how such things as hunger, taken together with certain acts of perception, could lead to action. For the conclusions of syllogisms follow *necessarily* from their premises, so that if actions can be construed similarly as conclusions of arguments, a similar sort of necessity can be claimed for them;[70] and of course if actions can be shown to be *necessary,* what further explanation of them could be required? To show something to be necessary is to explain why it happens, and by pressing this analogy Aristotle transfers the necessity of a syllogistic conclusion to an animal's actions. Thus the talk of syllogisms here can be seen to have a definite and intelligible point, given Aristotle's intention of explaining how self-motion occurs in animals.[71] And, as we have seen, Aristotle did take some pains to disarm in advance the mistaken impression that he was attributing such arguments to agents (including all animals) when they act voluntarily, although unfortunately his interpreters have not always paid close enough attention to his disclaimers.[72]

[70] Cf. *NE* 1147a26–31, quoted above p. 48, and *De Motu An.* 701a10–12.

[71] It is important to notice that it is only where this object is uppermost in Aristotle's mind that practical syllogisms are ever introduced and discussed at all. This is obviously so for the discussions in *De Motu An.* 7 and *De Anima* III 11, but holds also for *NE* VII 3: the problem in *NE* VII 3 is why the action which, according to this explanation of action, one would expect to be forthcoming does *not* occur. The connection between this concern to explain self-motion and Aristotle's references to the syllogism in *NE* VI is perhaps more tenuous and inexplicit, but it is not totally lacking: see my comments above, pp. 41-46.

[72] D. J. Allan is a rare, but only partial, exception. He holds the view ("The Practical Syllogism," pp. 340 and 336n.) that the reasoning contained in the syllogism is "the thought displayed in action, not that which precedes action," but he leaves this comment unexplained, and in particular does not dwell on the perceptual origin of the minor premiss which is so important in this connection, nor does he refer to the role of perception in *De Motu An.* 701a26 ff as I have done.

Before concluding this discussion of the practical syllogism I would like to add two further points. First, the tendency of some interpreters[73] to speak as if the major premiss of a practical syllogism were always or in general a *rule* is mistaken. As we have seen, the major premiss often represents a *proairesis,* or deliberated decision, and though this may sometimes be a rule ("Don't lie") it obviously will often be instead a particular decision made under given particular circumstances (e.g., not to water one's lawn during a current water shortage); and Aristotle's actual examples of such major premisses are hardly intelligible if taken as rules, though all is in order if they represent particular decisions of this kind.[74] Furthermore, many major premisses are not *proaireseis* at all, but instead are the content of an appetite or some other type of urgent desire, and these are surely not rules of action, but particular preferences on particular occasions for particular kinds of things: Aristotle's examples of such premisses include "I must drink" (*De Motu An.* 701a31). Hence, if the deliberated decision as major premiss is to be at all parallel to such premisses of appetite, it will not typically be a rule—though of course it might sometimes be such.

Secondly, the fact that major premisses express the contents of decisions or occurrent appetites explains why Aristotle insists that

[73] Most notably Hardie (see, e.g., the blank assertion at *Aristotle's Ethical Theory,* p. 240, that the expression "practical syllogism" refers always to a "process in which a rule is applied to a concrete situation"). But it is perhaps Allan who is the original culprit, since he divides practical syllogisms into two types, according as the minor premiss affirms some "instance of a rule" or a concrete "step towards an end" (p. 338). Earlier treatments (e.g. that of Ross, *Aristotle,* p. 209) tend to be more noncommittal (though also much vaguer and less distinctly informative).

[74] They may be stated so as to look like rules; but "One ought to taste everything sweet" (1147a29) or "Every man ought to walk" (701a13), among others, are ludicrous if so interpreted, but are not so strange if tacitly qualified to apply to a particular set of circumstances: maybe in a shortage one would reasonably decide to eat every sweet one was offered, and in some circumstances maybe every man *ought* to walk. It is often overlooked that one of Aristotle's examples in the *De Motu An.* is already so qualified: "No man ought to walk *now*" (701a14) cannot be the statement of a rule, but only a decision, for unexpressed reasons, not to bestir oneself in a given situation.

the conclusion of a practical syllogism is an action immediately performed, and not, as one might have expected if it is anything like a theoretical syllogism, a proposition inferrible with or without any action's actually following. Since it is presupposed that the agent has already determined, whether by making a decision or by adopting an end proposed by appetite, to do a certain thing if given the opportunity, he does of course act when he sees the opportunity. What else should he be expected to do? The tendency of some interpreters[75] of Aristotle to read into his discussions of practical syllogisms a peculiar, not to say mysterious, kind of thinking, the rules for which require that actions and not propositions be inferred from the given premises, is therefore based on a failure to understand properly the presuppositions under which Aristotle's agents are thought of as acting, even in the case where they actually do go through the steps of the syllogistic argument before they act.

In the foregoing account of deliberation and the practical syllogism, I have argued that three impressions readers sometimes get from Aristotle's description of that process in *Nicomachean Ethics* III are mistaken. In fact, Aristotle does not deny that ends can be deliberated about; he does not overlook the possibility that, in deliberating what to do, one may need to take into account the effects of proposed actions on more than one end at a time; and, thirdly, he does not believe that deliberation is brought to an end only when the agent has noted some individual thing, picked out by demonstrative or personal pronouns, as something on which action for the end in view can begin. As I have argued, Aristotle holds instead that if one's deliberations are to lead to action they must terminate (*not* in a reference to a perceived individual thing, but) in something that is particular in the sense of relatively specific and determinate, and also known by experience, that is, ultimately, by perception. In one of Aristotle's examples the agent is deliberating about health; he observes that

[75] See G. E. M. Anscombe, *Intention* (Oxford: Basil Blackwell, 1957), sect. 33-35.

eating light meat is a way of keeping healthy; then he reflects that chicken is a light meat, and thereupon concludes that eating chicken is a way of keeping healthy. Here his deliberation can end (though presumably it *need* not do so, if, for example, obtaining chicken, or eating it, required calculation): he has come upon a way of keeping healthy that he knows empirically and in detail, so that he will be immediately able to act if and when the circumstances are right. Because he knows chicken when he sees it, he does not need to deliberate further as to which of the meats in his vicinity to eat: at the appropriate moment and place he looks, sees the chicken, and eats. Deliberation must continue, Aristotle maintains, until this condition is reached, but once it is reached no further *reflection*—but only *perception*—is needed to set the agent to acting. In particular, there is no need to add that last step (the "practical syllogism") which Aristotle himself sometimes has reason to add: *"This* (pointing) is chicken, so *this* is a healthy thing to eat.'' If regarded as a last step of deliberation, this is in general unnecessary at best; and in the light of what Aristotle says in the passages we have been discussing, it should be regarded not as a step of deliberative reflection at all, but rather as a means of making explicit the contribution of perception to the performance of an action after a deliberated decision has been reached. The conclusion of a process of deliberation does not mention a particular in the sense of an individual picked out by personal or demonstrative pronouns; in the passages of the sixth book which we have examined, no such particular is mentioned, and when, in other passages, they are mentioned they must not be regarded as elements in the process of deliberation at all.[76]

4. Ends, Intuition, and Dialectic

In the preceding sections I have been discussing two parts of Aristotle's treatment of the thought that lies behind action—his

---

[76] That they are not elements in the deliberation is the moral also of what Aristotle says at *EE* II 10 1226a34 ff. Cf. also *NE* 1112b33-1113a2.

theories of deliberation and the practical syllogism. In his theory of deliberation Aristotle deals with the thought by which one connects goals that one wishes to attain (or, more generally, objects to be achieved) with particular decisions leading directly, if not immediately, to action in furtherance of them. And his theory of the practical syllogism sets out the perceptual conditions under which the decisions with which deliberation concludes are acted on. But there is a third part of the theory which we have not yet dealt with, except obliquely. For there is also the question of the objects of pursuit themselves. By what sort of process are these adopted? Aristotle is less explicit in answering this question than he is in the case of the other two parts of his theory, but here, too, patient analysis of what he does say will reveal a definite and interesting theory.

Assuming for the moment that Aristotle thinks the adoption of ends to be a rational activity, something that calls upon some intellectual capacity, it is clear that he cannot in general allow deliberation this role. For although, as I argued above, Aristotle does not deny that *some* ends can be adopted by deliberation, deliberation, on his account, could not exist at all unless for each agent there was *some* end or ends *not* settled upon after deliberation. In fact, Aristotle, for reasons that will be considered in the next chapter, believes that there is, or ought to be, in each person's practical thinking just one such ultimate end—in effect, a grand end which constitutes the agent's conception of what kind of life is best. All other ends are weighed ultimately in the light of this end. Hence this end cannot be settled upon by deliberation. How, then, does he think that one comes to adopt such an ultimate end? If it is not by deliberation, is there any process of reasoning by which a choice could be arrived at, or defended once made? Or does Aristotle perhaps think that each person simply has an intuition, not subject to defense, that some end or other is the one to pursue as ultimate? Aristotle certainly thinks that some people are right and others wrong on this fundamental point; but is he content to say simply that some people are right (their intuition being an instance of intuitive *knowledge, nous*) and others wrong (the victims of misguided intuition), without allowing that those who are right can show why their view is correct?

There are two questions here that need to be kept separate. First, there is the question whether for any agent, and particularly for a practically intelligent man (who, according to Aristotle, has the truth in this, as in other practical matters), the commitment to an ultimate end is based on reasons. Secondly, there is the distinct question whether or not considerations can be advanced which tend to show that a given end (viz., the one pursued by the practically intelligent man) is the best end to treat as ultimate. For Aristotle, these questions must, as we shall see more fully in a moment, be distinct. The first asks for an agent's reasons for pursuing a certain end, but according to Aristotle's theory of practical reasoning, the only reason that can be produced for pursuing an end is the tendency of that end to promote a higher end, and no reason of this kind can, *ex hypothesi,* apply in the case of an *ultimate* end. The second question inquires after, not such reasons for pursuing an end, but, reasons for concurring in a certain (nonpractical) judgment—the judgment that a given end is the best one to pursue.

It seems obvious from what I have just said that Aristotle's answer to our first question must be "No." An agent does not have any *reasons* to pursue whatever end he pursues as ultimate. Werner Jaeger, indeed, held that in the *Eudemian Ethics,* Aristotle's views on this point were more complicated than this. According to Jaeger,[77] Aristotle, when he wrote the *Eudemian Ethics,* held that the theoretical science of theology had as one of its tasks to establish which end is the correct one to pursue as ultimate, so that the man of practical intelligence, since he possesses the scientific knowledge of divinity, would possess in this science reasons in support of his pursuit of his end. These reasons, being derived by demonstration from the basic truths

[77] See W. Jaeger, *Aristotle,* 2nd English ed. (Oxford: Clarendon Press, 1948), pp. 238 ff.

about the divine, would presumably not have the effect of justifying the putatively ultimate end by appeal to an end yet higher; but they would constitute reasons, of some other sort, which the practically intelligent agent himself would have for pursuing that end. Construed in this way, then, the *Eudemian Ethics* would maintain that at least some agents, viz., those who actually know how best to live, would be able to support their pursuit of their ultimate end by reasons—reasons of a theoretical kind, rather than specifically practical reasons, but reasons nonetheless. Whether Jaeger was right in his interpretation of the *Eudemian Ethics* is, however, open to much doubt. In any case, we can conveniently postpone considering this question further until the next section, since there is no doubt that in the *Nicomachean Ethics*, at least, Aristotle regarded the knowledge of ultimate ends, in the sense in which this knowledge is possessed by the practically intelligent man, as a distinct kind of knowledge from any kind of theoretical insight.[78] Hence in what follows I shall put aside the *Eudemian Ethics* and concentrate wholly on the views that Aristotle held in the *Nicomachean Ethics* about the intellectual status of ultimate ends as objects of pursuit.

It is not difficult to understand why Aristotle should have rejected the idea that theoretical speculation could yield knowledge of what end or ends are the right ones to try to attain. Practical knowledge must make, or tend to make,[79] a practical difference in what a person prefers on the whole to do and does do in his life. But it is one's character which determines what one enjoys doing and prefers to do, and character is a function *both* of (developed) desires and (trained) instincts, *and* of rational judgments. No doubt Aristotle is wrong to suggest that the normal, fully developed adult, whether, for example, a brave man or a coward, has desire and judgment in perfect accord; and

[78] Practical thinking (διάνοια πρακτική) is virtually defined (1139a36) as reasoning how to achieve some end, and contrasted as such with theoretical thinking (a23-31).

[79] The qualification is necessary to take account of sufferers of *akrasia*, who know what to do, but fail to do it.

his settled view that such equilibrium is the best state of affairs can certainly be queried. But he is on much firmer ground in holding that, typically, a person shows what he thinks is a good life, at least a good one for himself, by the kind of life he actually leads rather than by giving assent to abstract arguments and conclusions. For in leading that life he is constantly rendering practical judgments whose contents and implications determine such a conception of good living. It is this lived conception which lies at the center of a person's practical thinking, and since it is necessarily connected with conditions of character it cannot be the result of mere theoretical study: success in such study has, as Aristotle rightly thought, no infallible influence on moral character. Hence the practically intelligent man's knowledge of the ultimate end, which determines his conception of good living, must be practical and nontheoretical. And since, as I argued above, this knowledge is not founded on any discursive process of deliberative selection, it must be a kind of intuitive knowledge, not based on reasons of any kind.

Before proceeding, it is perhaps worthwhile to emphasize that by referring here to intuition I mean to refer to the exercise of a certain intellectual capacity, a capacity which in the case of the practically intelligent person issues in the recognition and firm acceptance of a certain true idea, namely, the idea that some particular end is the correct one to pursue as ultimate. The intellectual character of this disposition needs to be insisted on, since there persists a certain confused tendency on the part of some interpreters to claim that for Aristotle it is not by an intellectual power at all that we adopt and pursue ultimate ends. Aristotle's text does to some extent support this view: he does say things in several passages that at first sight seem to reserve to moral virtue, that is, to a condition belonging exclusively to the desires themselves,[80] the setting of ends, restricting the intellect

---

[80] Cf. *NE* I 13 1102b13-1103a7, *EE* II 1 1220a10, 4 1221b30-32. Twentieth-century readers sometimes overlook this fact about the moral virtues as Aristotle conceives them; the correctness of judgment which for us is

to the role of working out how to achieve the ends that desire sets for it.[81] These passages have been referred to and commented on almost endlessly since Julius Walter first adduced them in support of this interpretation.[82] In fact, however, Aristotle holds that moral virtue, which is a certain condition of the desires, and practical intelligence, a condition of the mind, are in every way parallel to, indeed interfused with, one another: one does not have *either* the moral virtues *or* practical intelligence unless (a) one desires a certain ultimate end *and* judges that it is the correct one to pursue; (b) one judges that certain things—states of affairs, actions, and so forth—will serve to achieve this end, *and* desires to produce them; and (c) one recognizes occasions for action as they arise *and* desires to act and, in consequence, does act on those occasions. This is a plausible inference from his insistence that "it is not possible to be a morally good person, in the strict sense, without practical intelligence, nor practically intelligent without moral virtue (1144b31-32)," and there are passages in which he clearly insists, for each of these three stages, that intellectual judgment plays the role just assigned it, and others where he insists equally clearly on the role of desire in each.[83] In particular, in saying that "excellence at deliberation turns out to be correctness as regards what conduces to the end of

---

naturally made a part of goodness of character is handled separately by Aristotle as part of φρόνησις, an excellence of the mind, not of the character. Since he holds (1144b31-32) that the moral virtues are always accompanied by this excellence, his theory does not have some of the paradoxical consequences that at first sight it might seem to.

[81] See, e.g., *NE* VI 12 1144a7-9, ἡ μὲν γὰρ ἀρετὴ τὸν σκοπὸν ποιεῖ ἀγαθόν, ἡ δὲ φρόνησις τὰ πρὸς τοῦτον; also 1144a20-22, 1145a5-6, *EE* II 11 1227b39-1228a2.

[82] See J. Walter, *Die Lehre von der praktischen Vernunft in der griechischen Philosophie*, Jena, 1874.

[83] For (a) see 1142b32-33 (with the footnote next following) and the passages cited in n. 81 above; for (b) see *NE* VI 2 1139a22-26; for (c) see VI 8 1142a23-25, 11 1143a32-34, VII 2 1146a5-9, together with II 6 1106b36-1107a6.

which practical intelligence is the true apprehension (1142b32-33)",[84] Aristotle plainly asserts that at least one job of practical reason is to accept and affirm ends for ultimate pursuit.

In the light of these passages it is clear how to interpret those remarks in which he assigns to moral virtue the provision of the end and to practical intelligence the calculation of means. Given the interdependence between moral and intellectual excellence that we have just seen, Aristotle, understandably enough, attempts to differentiate between them by emphasizing, and playing off against one another, the clearest and most indubitable contribution made by practical thinking (viz., the calculation of means) and the most uncontroversial condition supplied by moral virtue (viz., the desire for the right end). One may regret that he was not always careful to spell out the relations of desire and intellect fully and explicitly, instead of opting sometimes for this easy, but misleading, contrast; but it is only on this interpretation that all the relevant texts can be made plausibly to cohere with one another.

It is, therefore, not open to reasonable doubt that in the *Nicomachean Ethics* Aristotle held that the practically intelligent person knows by some kind of intellectual intuition what the correct ultimate end is. This is something he *knows*, but he does not know it either by having worked it out by deliberation or by having deduced it from the first principles of any theoretical science. This same conclusion can be interestingly supported by

[84] It is quite certain that this is the sense of this passage. Walter, and those who accept his limited view of the intellect on the practical side (including Burnet, Greenwood, and Rackham, but not Ross), attempt to disarm this passage by taking the relative οὗ with the whole phrase τὸ συμφέρον πρὸς τὸ τέλος, thus rendering the passage as "... correctness as regards what conduces to the end, this being what practical intelligence conceives truly." This is grammatically very unnatural, and does not provide an acceptable distinction between εὐβουλία and φρόνησις itself; and in any case the οὗ-clause must be taken with τὸ τέλος, since only so do we get the specification of the end, corresponding to τὸ ἁπλῶς κατορθοῦσα in b30, which is required to mark off εὐβουλία ἁπλῶς from εὐβουλία τις. On this see Gauthier's note *ad loc.*

considerations drawn from Aristotle's theory of scientific reasoning.

Reasoning in science (e.g., geometry) has as its purpose to explain, by demonstration, why things are as they are (why, for example, the sum of the angles of a triangle is 180 degrees). Explanation by demonstration requires undemonstrated, but nonetheless known, first principles, since one cannot be said to have explained a thing unless one has shown that it follows from something which is in turn known to be true; and if what is alleged to explain a certain fact is known by prior demonstration, the same demand can be made of whatever it is that is supposed to explain it. Hence, in the end, if there are to be scientific explanations at all, some first principles must be accepted as known but not demonstrated. Being undemonstrated, Aristotle says that they are known by *nous*, or intuition.[85] Exactly the same argument applies to practical thinking: if one is to justify, and perhaps even if one is to explain adequately, something one is doing, one must be able to show that it follows from something that is itself justified, and the justification ultimately depends upon something that is taken to be justified without being shown to follow from anything else. And since for Aristotle justification consists in showing a thing's relation to some (justified) end, the "undemonstrated" foundation of practical reasoning must be some end (or ends). Having no relation to any further end which might justify them, these ultimate ends would have to be seen to be right immediately and by some kind of intuition. Thus the analogy between theoretical and practical reasoning, which Aristotle is so fond of pressing, supports our conclusion that ultimate ends are known by some kind of intellectual intuition. Now this may seem a most disappointing conclusion to come to. For if, according to Aristotle, the practically intelligent agent only claims to be able to "see" that his conception of how best to live is the correct one, and does not have any reasons in support of his view, and against the alternatives, it might seem that one cannot

[85] See *Post. An.* I 2 71b16-17, 3 72b18-20, II 19 100b5-15.

expect from the practically intelligent, or from Aristotle, any
enlightenment on the fundamental question of morality, why one
ought to live as (it is said) one ought. To this extent Jaeger would
seem justified in his charge that, in his mature moral philosophy,
Aristotle simply rests everything on the unchecked autonomy of
the moral consciousness.[86]

So far, however, we have only considered one side of the picture.
We must revert to the distinction drawn above between the
reasons an agent has for pursuing a certain end and the reasons
that may tell in favor of the nonpractical judgment that a certain
end is the correct one to pursue. For although Aristotle holds that
ultimate ends are not supported by practical reasons, and so are
the object of what one might call a practical intuition, he does not
hold that the nonpractical judgment just cited must be similarly
accepted or rejected on the basis of immediate intuition. To see
this, consider further the analogous case of scientific demonstration. According to Aristotle, the first principles of any
science are not capable of demonstration.[87] He never tires of stig-
matizing as *apaideutoi,* uninstructed, those who look for demonstration of what cannot be demonstrated; and accordingly in the
Physics[88] he dismisses the Eleatics' assertion that there is no
change on the ground that in physics it is a fundamental
presupposition that things do change, so that it would not be
proper for any physicist to argue this question. But it does not in
the least follow that everything which is treated by the sciences,
severally or all together, as indemonstrable is incapable of being

[86] Cf. Jaeger, *Aristotle,* pp. 87-88.

[87] See *Post. An.* I 9 76a16-25. I believe Aristotle means precisely what he
says here: *no* ἀρχή of *any* science is demonstrable at all; the reservations he
makes (see 75b8-17) as to the relations of "subordinate" sciences, such as
optics and harmonics, to those that stand above them do not affect this question. Ross, however, seems to think (see his *Aristotle's Prior and Posterior
Analytics,* Oxford: Clarendon Press, 1949, note to 76a22-24) that in this
special case Aristotle does allow the demonstration of some of the lower
science's starting-points. It does not matter much for present purposes which
of these views is correct.

[88] I 2 185a12-17.

subjected to rational scrutiny, or even to establishment by argument. As G. E. L. Owen has forcefully reminded us,[89] Aristotle has in reserve what he calls dialectic, a method of argument which is not "scientific" and does not pretend to demonstrate the truth, but which he thinks can effectively discuss and even establish the principles of the special sciences: dialectic, he says, is useful for establishing the bases of the sciences, since it is a method of critical examination which provides the way to the first principles of all inquiries (*exetastikē gar ousa pros tas hapasōn tōn methodōn archas hodon echei, Topics* I 2 101b3-4). The details of Aristotle's account of dialectical method can be left to one side; it is enough to observe that dialectic is flexible and informal and takes its start from facts of linguistic usage, or common observation, or simply general agreement.[90] The important point to notice for the present is that Aristotle holds both that the principles of the sciences are known intuitively, by *nous,* and that they can be established by discursive dialectical argument.[91] Aristotle himself, for example, argues at some length in the *Physics* in favor of his own definition of place (*topos*) as the first fixed boundary of a surrounding body (*Phys.* IV 4 212a20-21); yet, as Owen and others have seen, the concept of place is among the first principles of the science of physics, and this

---

[89] "Tithenai ta phainomena," in *Aristote et les problèmes de méthode*, ed. S. Mansion (Louvain: Editions Nauwelaerts, 1961): reprinted in J. M. E. Moravcsik, *Aristotle: A Collection of Critical Essays* (Garden City, New York: Doubleday, 1967). Notice that in the *Physics*, though insisting that no *physicist* has to concern himself with the Eleatic arguments, Aristotle nonetheless does take the trouble to attempt a refutation of them: ἔχει γὰρ φιλοσοφίαν ἡ σκέψις, 185a20.

[90] See Owen, "Tithenai ta phainomena," for discussion of these different sources of dialectical premises.

[91] On the role of νοῦς in grasping the first principles, cf. *Post. An.*II 19: νοῦς at 100b5-15, ἀρχαί at 99b17-19, πρῶτα at 100b4. On the *Post. An.*'s emphasis on sense-perception here, as against dialectical examination, as the preliminary to the grasping of the principles by νοῦς, cf. Owen, "Tithenai ta phainomena" pp. 86-87.

means that it ought to be grasped intuitively. How can Aristotle hold both of these views at once?[92]

It is possible that Aristotle's position on this point is not in the end entirely coherent. That something is grasped by *nous* ought to imply not only that it needs no argument in its defense but also that it rests on none. But, clearly enough, the arguments Aristotle gives on the topic of place are reasons which a physicist can have, and continue to have, for accepting one account of the concept against another; and surely Aristotle thinks there is room for argument, else why does he indulge in it? On the other hand, the inconsistency, if inconsistency it is, is hidden from him by the sharp distinction he draws between dialectic on the one hand and scientific reasoning on the other. The same man who on one occasion engages in scientific reasonings, in which a certain concept of place is presupposed, may on another occasion engage in a dialectical discussion in which rival conceptions of place are pitted against one another and the merits of the prevailing concept are examined. But there is no continuity between the two endeavors; dialectical reasoning is not an extension of scientific, but a different kind of exercise altogether. So it is strictly true that in science the first principles do go unquestioned, and do not rest on argument. The scientist sees immediately that they are correct, and does not produce reasons for them. Yet the dialectician can and does give reasons—*dialectical* reasons—in their defense. The appearance of inconsistency results when one considers the bearing of the dialectical reasons on the scientific intuition. Are they reasons on which the science in general, or its individual practitioners, rest the first principles, or not? Aristotle would seem to be forced to answer no, but he does not say how he would defend this reply.[93] The sharp distinction he draws between

---

[92] The (at least apparent) inconsistency comes out very clearly in a comparison of the *Topics* passage just cited with such passages as *NE* 1142a26, *EE* 1227b23-25 (where the possibility of λόγος is blankly denied).

[93] Perhaps he would say that dialectical discussions merely make explicit certain features of the content of intuitions, or that they are preliminary exercises leading to the acquisition by intuition of the principles in question.

dialectical and scientific thinking prevents him from facing the question squarely.

A similar condition obtains in his moral philosophy. Here too we find Aristotle arguing for a principle which he nonetheless must also hold to be grasped by intuition; and here again behind the apparent inconsistency lies a distinction between dialectical and another, more formal, kind of reasoning. (In the case of the *Ethics* the contrast is not with demonstration but with the method of deliberation.) Burnet was the first to emphasize that Aristotle regarded the method of moral philosophy more or less explicitly as dialectical in character.[94] This character can be seen, for example, in the treatment of *akrasia* in book VII, which is nowadays perhaps generally recognized to be just about the clearest and best example anywhere in the Corpus of what dialectical inquiry meant for Aristotle.[95] But even where the "opinions of the wise," what we all say or think, and the other hallmarks of dialectic are not emphasized in the text, there seems no doubt that Aristotle conceives of his procedure as for the most part dialectical. Particularly is this true of the first book, where the argument concerns "the good for man" and issues in the preliminary statement of what the best life is. The book begins with the statement that every art, inquiry, action, and choice *is thought* (*dokei*) to aim at some good, and in so doing it rests the fundamental axiom of Aristotle's moral theory on the general agreement of reflective persons. And throughout the ensuing discussion Aristotle returns periodically to this dialectical home-base.[96] The dialectical character of even the elaborate and rather formal argument by which Aristotle finally produces his definition of the best life (1097b22-1098a20) is beyond doubt.[97] The connection between

[94] J. Burnet, ed., *The Ethics of Aristotle* (London: Methuen, 1900), Introduction pp. xxxix ff.

[95] See especially the description of his aims and procedures at 1145b2-7.

[96] Cf. 1095a19 λέγουσιν, b23 φαίνεται, b24 δοκεῖ, b31 φαίνεται.

[97] *Pace* Gauthier, who calls this argument "scientific," by contrast with the dialectical treatments which precede and follow. Gauthier seems anxious to insist on this difference (here and elsewhere in the *Ethics*) mainly because

ergon ("function") and good which forms one of the principal premisses of this argument is explicitly (*dokei,* 1097b26-27) claimed to be a matter of general consent, and the other main premiss, that man as such has an *ergon,* is established by a sort of analogical inductive appeal to other, allegedly similar, cases, and induction is said in the *Topics* (105a10-19) to form one of the two kinds of dialectical argument.

Thus Aristotle does undertake in the *Nicomachean Ethics* to argue for his own view of what constitutes the best life for a man to lead, despite the fact that, as we have seen, any such conception must on his theory of practical reasoning be grasped immediately and by intuition, and not be the subject of deliberation. As in the parallel case of the theoretical sciences, so here, the first principle of practical reasoning is established dialectically; and in this case, too, the apparent inconsistency must if possible be explained away by emphasizing sharply the difference between dialectical and practical reasoning. Practical reasoning is deliberation about how to accomplish some end, and according to Aristotle it always has as its first and highest principle a conception of good living, which is treated as the ultimate end in view of which all else is done. The dialectical reasoning by which this end is itself established is not deliberative in form and does not consist in showing that living a certain kind of life is a means to realizing some end assumed or established in some other way. We need not here enquire more closely into the nature of the reasons

---

he has a mistakenly low opinion of dialectic (inherited perhaps from Burnet): see pp. 24-25 of his *Commentaire.* But the resulting conception of an ethical *science* corresponds to nothing in Aristotle's logic. The distinction at 1098b9-11 between considering εὐδαιμονία ἐκ τοῦ συμπεράσματος καὶ ἐξ ὦν ὁ λόγος and considering it ἐκ τῶν λεγομένων περὶ αὐτῆς does not support any such dichotomy. The argument remains dialectical, having as premisses what we say or think about what things have an ἔργον, what an ἀρετή is, and so on; it is contrasted with what we say or think directly about εὐδαιμονία *itself.* For a similar contrast between an argument and the confirmation of its conclusion, see *NE* X 7 1177a12-18, 18-b26.

that might be advanced in the course of this reasoning; it is enough for the present to notice that Aristotle does think himself entitled to give reasons in favor of his own view of the right ultimate end, and that the reasons given will fall into the pattern of dialectical, and not deliberative, argumentation.

Thus, although Aristotle does make the good man's knowledge of how best to live an intuitive and not a discursive knowledge, he does not think that no reasons can be given in support of the intuition on which the good man anchors his deliberations. A virtuous man need not have any reasons to give in defense of his own view of what good living is. But reasons exist, and it is possible to discover them. Aristotle only insists that anyone who does give reasons exercises not his practical intelligence but his powers of philosophical reflection. It is prudent and reasonable, I think, of Aristotle not to insist that ordinary moral agents know, or need to know, how to defend their own view of what kind of life is best: their intuitive conviction is a perfectly adequate foundation for them. But those dialectical and critically alert persons who are moved to deepen their understanding of this foundation can do so by examining, in a dialectical spirit, the deliverances of moral intuition. So Aristotle, insofar as he writes as dialectical philosopher and attempts the latter task, does not simply rest content with the unexamined intuitions of the ordinary moral consciousness.[98]

[98] It is important to notice that despite the dialectical character of moral philosophy in the *NE* (and elsewhere) Aristotle claims (1095a5-6, 1103b27-29, 1179a35-b4; and cf. *MM* I 1 1182a1-6, *EE* I 5 1216b16-25, *Met.* α 1 993b20-21, *De Caelo* III 7 306a16-17) that the point of "political science," to which the *NE* is a contribution, is οὐ γνῶσις ἀλλὰ πρᾶξις—not to learn what to do but to come to do it. He presumably thought (and reasonably so) that dialectic gives one a firmer, clearer and better articulated grasp of what the end actually is and therefore both increases one's commitment to it and makes one better able to act perceptively in its interest. Moral philosophy is a practical study, then, not because the philosopher deliberates about how to live or what to do (as the casuist does) but by providing a comprehensive and critical understanding of the basic structure and goals of the moral life.

5. Intuition and Ends in the *Eudemian Ethics*

I mentioned above that according to Jaeger the *Eudemian Ethics* differs importantly from the *Nicomachean* over the nature of the morally good person's recognition and acceptance of his ultimate end. The *Nicomachean Ethics* distinguishes sharply between theoretical and practical knowledge and implies that knowledge of this end must be both practical and intuitive, but Jaeger contends that the *Eudemian Ethics* draws no sharp distinction between theoretical and practical knowledge and allows the good person's knowledge of his end to form part somehow of his theoretical knowledge of the nature of divinity. Before concluding this discussion I want to address myself briefly to these contentions of Jaeger.

First, a preliminary point which casts doubt on Jaeger's view. The sharp distinction between theoretical and practical knowledge which leads in the *Nicomachean Ethics* to the views we have just been considering is most prominently displayed in book VI. But this book is one of the three *Nicomachean* books (V, VI, VII) which our manuscripts also record as belonging to the *Eudemian* (where they appear as IV, V, and VI). Now there is no good reason to regard them as belonging originally to the *Nicomachean* treatise, and to suppose, with Jaeger, that they were transferred to the *Eudemian* at some undetermined time in the history of our text. For although some scholars think that in their present form they may have been revised somewhat by Aristotle at the time he wrote the *Nicomachean Ethics,* it is extremely probable (and recent scholars mostly agree) that they were first composed for the earlier treatise.[99] But in that case, if Aristotle does somewhere in

---

[99] Jaeger obviously did not consider very closely the question of the provenance of the common books, as he certainly ought to have done, before pronouncing on the *Eudemian* conception of moral knowledge. His only substantial comment on the question of the common books is found in a footnote (p. 258), where he says merely that *NE* VI "cannot belong to the *Eudemian Ethics* because of its view of *phronesis*," which he thinks diverges from that found in the undisputed *Eudemian* books. The evidence for any such "divergence" is very slight indeed: *EE* III 7 1234a29-30 plainly uses

the *Eudemian Ethics* intimate that the theoretical science of theology itself establishes the ends of human action, he will be saying something sharply at variance with the distinction he marks off elsewhere in the treatise (book V) between theoretical and prac-

---

the word in its specifically practical sense, and the close association of φρόνησις and correct action throughout VIII 1-2 hardly tells in favor of Jaeger's thesis of an exclusive *Eudemian* usage of the word to mean "philosophical knowledge." And in fact the same variation in usage can be found within the *NE* itself: at 1096b24 the word quite certainly means "philosophical knowledge" (cf. 1095b17-19 and esp. *EE* I 1 1214a32-33, 4 1215a32-b1). The *Eudemian* origin of the common books (though possibly in a somewhat different form) is accepted by Dirlmeier (commentary to *EE*, pp. 362-363) and by Gauthier (*Éthique à Nicomaque*, ed. 1, pp. 42*-46*). Two very strong reasons in favor of this view have gone unmarked: (1) the casual appearance at 1139a16 of the Academic definition of ἀρετή as ἡ βελτίστη ἕξις, which is fundamental to the *EE* (cf. II 1 1218b38, etc.) but avoided completely in the special *Nicomachean* books; (2) the appearance of χρῆσις (χρῆσθαι) as correlate to ἕξις (ἔχειν) in such phrases as χρῆσις τῆς ἀρετῆς at V 1129b31, 32, 34, 1130a6-8, b20, in place of the *Nicomachean* ἐνέργεια κατ᾽ ἀρετήν, but in accordance with a standard *Eudemian* usage found at II 1 1219a18, b2, etc. (and cf. the corresponding passage of the *MM*, 13-4, 1184b7-1185a1). This use of χρῆσις derives (cf. 1218b37-1219a5) from the way in which the parallel between human ἀρετή and the ἀρετή of an artifact is drawn in the *EE*: the excellence of a cloak shows in its use (its χρῆσις), so Aristotle speaks also of the use (a) of an art that has a product (the housebuilder's, 1219a14-15), (b) a science like mathematics, which contains its end in its very exercise (a17), and finally (c) the soul (a24) and its excellence (1220a33). Here the exercise of one's scientific knowledge or moral virtue is described in a terminology that is strictly appropriate only for objects and capacities whose exercise is instrumentally good, and this is doubtless why even in the *EE* Aristotle tends to prefer ἐνέργεια (1219a33) or χρῆσις καὶ ἐνέργεια (b2-3) to χρῆσις alone when speaking of human excellences. Hence also its avoidance in the special *Nicomachean* books (except for a passing appearance, pointed out to me by M. F. Burnyeat, in X 9 1179b3, where this undesirable implication of the usage is hardly felt). It is noteworthy that the χρῆσις terminology is found also in *Pol.* VII, 1328a38 and 1332a9: this is further evidence that, as I remark below (Chapter II, n. 57), this book dates from roughly the same period as the *EE*. When Aristotle says in the second of these passages (1332a7-9) that, according to his view, εὐδαιμονία is ἐνέργεια καὶ χρῆσις ἀρετῆς τελείας, and refers to the statement of this view ἐν τοῖς Ἠθικοῖς, the reference is to *EE* II 1, and certainly not to anything in the *NE*.

tical knowledge; unless, of course, one simply maintains without further ado that this distinction was absent from the original, *Eudemian* version of the book.

Such an expedient should be contemplated only if in the remaining books of the *Eudemian Ethics* Aristotle does decisively suggest such a "theonomic" moral theory, as Jaeger calls it. I do not believe such a theory is anywhere to be found in the treatise. That the ultimate end is grasped by intuition and not established by any kind of scientific reasoning is at least suggested by the comparison Aristotle draws at one place (II 10 1227a8-9) between the end as starting point for practical thinking with the first principles (*hupotheseis*) of the sciences. As we have seen, this comparison implies that the starting point for practical reason, like the first principles of the sciences, is known by intuition. But, notoriously, Jaeger thought the last page of the last book (VIII 3 1249a22-b5) tells a different story.[100] This is a difficult passage, and I shall have more to say about it in the next chapter.[101] Nor is it entirely clear how Jaeger thought it should be interpreted. Still, it is clear enough that, according to Jaeger, in one way or another Aristotle in this passage maintains that in moral reasoning the fundamental end or ends of action are arrived at by some process of theoretical, scientific thinking. Beyond this, Jaeger leaves us substantially in the dark. The passage concerns philosophical contemplation, which Aristotle here unabashedly glosses as the study of (the cosmic) god who, in his physical system, is the first cause of motion in the universe and so the original cause of the world order we know. The knowledge of the nature and activities of this god is the most exalted kind of knowledge we can attain to: elsewhere, particularly in early writings, Aristotle refers to this science, which he calls "theology" (*theologikē*), as "first philosophy"—first, apparently, because its object is the cause whose effects are most universally felt, and on which no other cause operates. Now in this passage Aristotle is often taken

100 Cf. Jaeger, *Aristotle*, pp. 241-243.
101 See below, Chapter iI, sect. 3, pp. 133 ff.

(though I shall give reasons later on for disputing this view) to be explaining what he thinks the ultimate standard (*horos*) of right action is; and Jaeger, accepting this view, thought that Aristotle was saying that the cosmic god himself is the correct standard. In favor of this interpretation one might cite Aristotle's remark (1249b6-7) that one ought to live "with a view to that which rules" (*pros to archon zēn*), and the fact that a few lines later (b14) he refers to god as the ruler (*ho archōn*). If this interpretation were right, then Aristotle would be making god, the object of a theoretical science, also the highest standard of action; so that by studying this science one would simultaneously be finding out about the ultimate standard of morality. Or perhaps Jaeger has in mind some half-Kantian ideal of regularity or constancy as somehow borne in upon one in the course of the study of the cosmic god.[102]

This interpretation is, however, plainly wrong. Even assuming that the passage does state Aristotle's view as to the ultimate standard of right action, it certainly does not say that *god* is it. Living "with a view to that which rules" means living with a view to the best part of ourselves, viz., our capacity for theoretical thinking (cf. b9-13); and god is mentioned only because he is the object of the highest such capacity. This is made perfectly clear when, just below (b16-19), Aristotle sums up his view by saying: "Whatever choice and acquisition of things that are good by nature will most produce the contemplative study of god . . . is best, and this is the best standard (*horos*)." Not god, but contemplation, is here, if anything is, said to be the ultimate standard of choice: god is only mentioned as the object of this activity. This is decisive against Jaeger's interpretation. For if god and his nature and activities were the standard, then there would perhaps be some plausibility in the claim that by the theoretical study of god one learns not only about god's nature but at the

---

[102] Though, if so, the ultimate standard would not be establishable directly by deductive argument from premises of the science of theology, as Jaeger seems to have wanted to say.

same time establishes and develops the ultimate principle of living. But if instead the activity of contemplating god is the ultimate standard, then it is not true that theology, a theoretical science, has the practical consequences claimed for it by Jaeger. For it studies divine, and not human, nature, and has nothing at all to say about which human activities are better than which others, or which activity is the standard by reference to which to judge right action. Aristotle may declare here that contemplation of god is the best human activity, but he does not derive this view from theological study itself.[103] Aristotle does not, in fact, give any indication at all here as to how he thinks one arrives at the truth in such a matter. But, as I have pointed out, he does elsewhere in the *Eudemian Ethics* seem to imply that it is by some form of intuition; and this view is perfectly compatible with what he says here. So it seems justified to draw the conclusion that the *Eudemian Ethics* agrees with the *Nicomachean* in assigning a crucial role to intuition in fixing the ultimate end of human action.

6. Moral Reasoning

We have now examined Aristotle's theory of practical reasoning in all its varied elements. We have seen that, according to Aristotle, reasoning that leads to action must start from the assumption of some end to be realized in or by acting, and that ultimately for each person such ends must themselves be regarded as means to a single highest end, which in the last analysis all his actions are aimed at achieving. This highest end is fixed by an intuitive act in which the agent "sees" it as good and

---

[103] This result is quite important. For if, as I have argued, Aristotle does not imply a "theonomic" ethical theory in book VIII of the *Eudemian Ethics*, there is no longer any reason to suppose, with Jaeger, that the distinction between theoretical and practical knowledge set out in *NE* VI is foreign to the *EE*. And if it is not, then there is no reason to suppose that that distinction was first introduced into *EE* V as it was being revised for use as *NE* VI. In the nature of the case one cannot, of course, rule out this possibility; but there is no positive reason to entertain it seriously.

accepts it as such. In deciding what to do, the agent seeks to discover ways of achieving whatever end (or ends) may be in question, and weighs the different alternative actions in the light of their effectiveness or availability as means to this end (or these ends). This process of deliberation continues until some specific kind of action is hit upon as a way of beginning to achieve the end, and this act-kind must be one of which the agent has perceptual knowledge: he must be able to recognize by immediate perception the occasion for action when it occurs and he must be able to perform the appropriate action immediately and without need for ancillary calculation. Once this condition obtains he has completed the task of reasoning out what to do, and can be said to have decided on a course of action. Beyond that, it is perception, and not further reasoning, that links his decision to an occasion for action (whether at the very time of decision or later) and thereby produces the action which is the final outcome of the whole process.

Now I remarked at the outset that Aristotle never works out in explicit detail how specifically moral reasoning exhibits this structure, although he clearly thought that moral, like all other practical reasoning, takes this form. But it is now possible to say something about how Aristotle intended his theory of practical reasoning to be applied to this special case.

By moral reasoning I mean the reasoning which lies behind and explains (and presumably justifies) actions of morally good agents in which their reasons for acting are moral ones: that is, actions in which their primary reasons involve the idea that some moral virtue, or virtues, dictate so acting.[104] Aristotle himself sets out a number of necessary conditions for moral action.

[104] It is of course clear that in my use of the expression "moral reasoning" here and elsewhere in explicating Aristotle I diverge widely from the, or at any rate a, standard usage among contemporary philosophers. Many philosophers nowadays regard morality as coextensive with a set of principles, practices, and so forth, which affect (only) the other-related behavior of persons, by requiring due consideration of other persons' interests. Such a narrow idea of morality is, of course, characteristic only of relatively recent times.

The cases of the arts and the virtues are not similar. For things that are produced by the arts have their goodness in themselves: it is enough for them to be produced possessing certain properties. But it is not enough, in order for actions that are in accordance with the virtues to be done justly or temperately, that *they* should have certain properties, but the person who does them must also have certain properties: first, he must act knowingly, next he must choose (*proairoumenos*) the actions, and choose them for themselves, and thirdly he must act from a firm and unalterable character. (1105a26-33)

That is to say, although it may often be clear that a right action has been performed, one cannot say that that action possesses moral value unless in addition the agent has acted knowingly and by choice and out of a firm and settled disposition to choose and to perform actions of that kind for their own sake. Much the same thing is implied by Aristotle's frequent reminder that virtuous persons in acting virtuously act "for the sake of the noble".[105] For the noble is defined in the *Rhetoric* as "whatever, when chosen for its own sake, is praiseworthy; or, whatever is good, and pleasant because it is good."[106] Hence to act for the sake of the noble is to act choosing one's action for its own sake and in the belief that it is praiseworthy. Finally, Aristotle insists in the sixth book that in cases of doing or acting (*praxis*), as distinguished from making or producing something (*poiēsis*), the end in view is good action (*eupraxia*) itself (1139b3-4): "for in making the end is different [from the making itself] but in acting it cannot be so; good action is itself the end" (1140b6-7).[107]

---

[105] Cf. *NE* 1115b11-13, 23-24, 1116a11-12, b2-3, 1117a16-17, 1119b15-18, 1120a23-29, 1122b6-7; *MM* 1190a28; *EE* 1229a1-2, 1230a27-29.

[106] Καλὸν μὲν οὖν ἐστὶν ὃ ἂν δι' αὑτὸ αἱρετὸν ὂν ἐπαινετὸν ᾖ, ἢ ὃ ἂν ἀγαθὸν ὂν ἡδὺ ᾖ, ὅτι ἀγαθόν. Cf. also 1362b8, τῶν δὲ καλῶν τὰ μὲν ἡδέα τὰ δὲ αὐτὰ καθ' ἑαυτὰ αἱρετά ἐστιν (similarly 1364b27). See also *EE* VIII 3 1248b19-20, τούτων δὲ καλά, ὅσα δι' αὑτὰ ὄντα πάντα ἐπαινετά ἐστίν.

[107] Obviously this remark restricts severely (and unnaturally) the concept of an action. For many things we do, that would not normally be regarded as "making" or "producing" something (at least not *artistic* producing), will not by the criterion for "action" here expressed be counted as actions at

These passages, and others of the same tendency, show that at least on occasion Aristotle saw in the virtuous actions of virtuous persons the recognition of an intrinsic, and not merely an instrumental, value in the action itself that is performed. On the other hand, as we have already seen and as the first of the quoted passages implies, he also supposes that such "choices" (*proaireseis*) of action are arrived at by a process of deliberation. Given Aristotle's theory of deliberation as outlined above, our problem is to show how the decision, say, to courageously defend one's property against the threats of marauders, can both be the outcome of deliberative reflection and involve the recognition of moral value inherent in the courageous action itself.

There are in fact two broad possibilities open to Aristotle to resolve this problem. First, he might maintain that in moral action the agent perceives two distinct orders of value, one moral and one not. Take, for example, someone whose ultimate end is to get as much pleasure out of life, over the long run, as possible. Then (leaving aside the difficulties that arise concerning the measurement of pleasures) he would in deliberating what to do always work out, if possible, which action among those available to him would be most likely to result in the greatest total amount of pleasure in his life as a whole. So, if marauders attack his property, he will figure out what to do by considering the likely effect on his pleasures, over the long term, of the various alternatives. He might decide to risk defending himself rather than giving up and moving on, on a combination of grounds: the attackers might be bluffing (so that the risk of harm to himself if he resists is not great anyhow); his possessions are very valuable in providing for his pleasures and are not easily replaceable, so

---

all, but rather as "makings." Thus if I scratch my leg to relieve an itch I do not normally choose to scratch for its own sake, but only for the reason stated. But, though this criterion does not pick out just what would normally be counted as actions, it does characterize an interesting and important subclass of actions; and virtuous actions, which Aristotle has primarily in mind here, in any case, are prominent members of this class.

that the value of what he has is worth risking harm to himself in order to protect it; security of possession, which is essential to enjoyment of property, cannot be obtained unless others think one prepared to defend it, and one cannot expect others to think this unless one resists when challenged. Now it should be observed that in thus calculating that the thing to do is to resist, this man regards his action as at best an instrumental good: he would rather not have to do it, and only does it because it is forced on him by circumstances that require it if he is to achieve the ultimate end he has set for himself. So far, then, he recognizes no moral value in his actions. However, in addition to the chain of reasoning just outlined, and the range of values it encompasses, he might also, having decided to resist, observe[108] that resistance is in any case the courageous thing in the circumstances and that therefore resistance is noble and worth choosing even for its own sake, without regard to its tendency to promote his maximum pleasure over the long term. So in acting he would have two separate ends in view: his ultimate end of maximum pleasure and the additional moral end of nobility. So far as the first end is concerned, his action of resistance is only instrumentally good, but in opting also for nobility of action he sees an inherent value in his action.

Now it should be clear from what has been said already about deliberation that this is at best only a partial solution to our problem. For Aristotle, as we have seen, requires that morally good actions should issue from a firm and unalterable disposition to perform acts of that kind. And our hedonist can presumably not meet this condition. For assuming, as seems reasonable, that often such a hedonist's calculations will lead him away from rather than toward the action that is morally right, he will often

[108] Presumably this observation will be made intuitively: as a result of childhood training he retains the capacity to recognize what counts as a courageous and what as a cowardly act. In any event, for *this* man, it cannot be arrived at by deliberation, since deliberation works out means to achieve ends which themselves stand as means to his ultimate end, and since he is a hedonist the moral end of nobility is presumably not such a means.

find it irrational to pursue the moral end of nobility when it is open to him to do so. He is rationally committed to doing always whatever (he thinks) best promotes his ultimate end, and although sometimes this will also be the virtuous thing to do, often it will not. Hence, although he might on occasion choose virtuous actions partly for their own sakes, he cannot have the settled character that Aristotle requires of a virtuous person and makes a condition of actions that possess full moral value. In order to ensure that this further condition is met, one would have to argue that as a matter of fact the two ends of pleasure and nobility never do diverge as I have been assuming they do.

These considerations suggest, although of course they do not prove, that whenever a person's ultimate end is of such a kind that moral requirements can only be regarded as at best instrumental goods, so far as their relation to this end is concerned, the same failure will be observed. Given their distinctness, the moral end of nobility and the nonmoral ultimate end can be expected to diverge on occasion, and that being so, the commitment to the nonmoral end will override the pursuit of nobility and lead the agent to fail to do something dictated by one of the moral virtues. It is possible, of course, that Aristotle was unclear on this point; conceivably, without being fully aware of the fact, he operates with a theory of the ultimate end that in fact does make it impossible to meet the requirement of constant and steady commitment to virtuous action as such. We cannot settle this question definitively here; to do so will require a full review of the evidence concerning Aristotle's views on the correct ultimate end for human beings to pursue. But in the next chapter I shall consider this possibility at some length and will argue that he does not hold such a view.

In any case, there is another alternative open to Aristotle which does not bring with it these difficulties. For, as we have seen,[109] the conception of "means" to ends with which Aristotle works in developing his theory of deliberation is broad enough to include

[109] Pages 19-22 above.

among "means" not merely things instrumentally related to their ends, but also constituent parts of complex ends and particular actions in which the attainment of some end may be said to consist. Morally virtuous action may then be a "means" to the ultimate end of flourishing, not in the sense that it tends to bring it about, as doing favors for the right people makes a government functionary rich, but in the sense that it is one constituent part of the conception of flourishing which constitutes the virtuous person's ultimate end. On this view there would be no contrast, as there is on the other alternative, between regarding an act of virtue as a means of obtaining one's ultimate end and choosing it for its own sake. For the ultimate end is something desired for its own sake (indeed it is desired for itself *alone*), and if morally virtuous action is one of the constituent parts of this, it—along with the other parts—will thereby also be desired for its own sake.[110] And in performing acts of virtue on particular occasions one will be actually realizing, in the only way it can be realized, that inherent value which one attributes to virtuous action in making it a constituent of the ultimate end. Hence, particular acts of virtue will themselves, in being chosen as "means" to the ultimate end of flourishing, be desired and chosen for their own sakes.

[110] According to G. E. Moore's principle of organic unities (*Principia Ethica*, Cambridge, England: Cambridge University Press, 1903, pp. 27-36), one cannot assume in general that where an organic whole has intrinsic value this value is simply the sum of the intrinsic values of its parts taken separately, or even that every part has any intrinsic value at all. Some of the parts, though necessary to the existence of the whole and to the value inherent in it, may be indifferent, others actually bad (pp. 216 ff). Now, stated thus abstractly this principle certainly seems true. But in the special case I am considering the inference to the intrinsic value of the parts seems justified. For although in any fully articulated conception of flourishing there may be things essentially involved (and not merely as causal conditions of it) that are not intrinsically good, the leading components which determine the conception will certainly be regarded as possessing intrinsic value. And where morally virtuous action is itself such a leading component, the particular forms of virtuous action (courageous, just, temperate action, etc.) will be so regarded.

To make this alternative more concrete and precise it may be helpful to compare such a conception of flourishing with the hedonist conception that appears in my earlier example. These two conceptions of flourishing are not just two different responses to the demand to live one's life according to some coherent overall plan, but responses of fundamentally different types. The hedonist conception is open-ended, in the sense that it bids us maximize in our lives as a whole the amount of a certain good, but without specifying at all what this maximum may be. It leaves it entirely up to us, in principle at any rate, to alter our mode of life in adjustment to changing circumstances and altered capacities for enjoyment as our lives themselves develop. There are no fixed principles of living, though of course there may be a variety of summary rules recording our own or others' experience of the common situations of life and the pleasure or pain that usually issues from various courses of action taken in them. Such rules are only rules of thumb, however, and not fixed principles, because the basic injunction to maximize pleasure may often require that one not follow past ways but strike out on one's own, when one can clearly see that greater pleasure is to be expected from such a departure. Maximization schemes of all types—whether what is to be maximized is one's own pleasure or something else—evidently fail to provide a grounding for any fixed mode of life, structured by settled rules and principles specifying particular actions to perform in definite situations. This is why I remarked above that the hedonist conception and others of the same general type would seem incapable of accommodating Aristotle's insistence that the morally virtuous person must possess a firm and unalterable disposition to elect certain types of action in certain types of situation. The consistent maximizer surely cannot have the kind of permanent and inviolable principles which such a disposition entails.

This feature of life-plans of the maximization type is of course a direct consequence of what seems most attractive about them, their simplicity and adaptability to all manners of persons and every conceivable situation, however unusual or unexpected. For

the more impressed one is with the possibility of wholly new and
different circumstances arising which were not envisaged in the
development of the traditional maxims and conceptions of the
virtues, the more likely one is to be impressed with the rationality
of such a scheme, since it seems to provide the only sensible and
mature way of dealing with life in an uncertain or rapidly
changing world. To have fixed principles is to be irrationally en-
cumbered and to handicap oneself, and perhaps others as well.
On the other hand, if one is impressed rather with the regularity
and stability of human circumstances and human relationships,
then a maximization scheme will inevitably seem inadequate. For
given the assumption of stability one can do much more to plan
one's life than merely aim at the maximization of some good;
rational planning can extend into many relatively concrete details
of life, making definite provision by way of relatively concrete
principles for the sorts of recurrent situations which, on this
perception of permanent human circumstances, form the very
stuff of human life. Naturally, these principles will have to be
fairly flexible since even this more structured conception must allow for a considerable range of variability in human affairs; but
not to adopt principles at all will seem, to one who takes this view
of the conditions of human life, a simple refusal to introduce rational planning into one's life as fully and effectively as one
might.[111]

It would seem to be such an outlook on human life that lies
behind the conception of human flourishing that treats virtuous
action itself as part of the ultimate end. For, according to this
conception, the best life is one structured immediately by the
fixed principles of the virtues. In the next chapter I shall argue

[111] Such a complaint, or a closely related one, seems to lie behind Socrates'
final rejection of Callicles' ideal in the *Gorgias* (503d5-505b12, recapitulated
at 506d5-507c7), and similar ideas can be found in the argument in *Republic* I
where Socrates argues against Thrasymachus that it is justice and not
injustice that is a sign of intelligence in organizing one's life (348b8-350c11).
Definite order, of the kind that is imposed only by fixed principles, is affirmed
to be a necessary feature of any life that exhibits intelligence.

that Aristotle himself accepts this outlook and endorses this conception of flourishing. But although I will not argue the point here, it may be useful in concluding the present discussion to sketch out a specimen piece of moral reasoning on such a view. I will stick to my earlier example in which someone courageously resists the threats of marauders against his property. Such a person's reasons for so acting might be developed as follows:

(1) In order to flourish one must act virtuously (i.e., flourishing consists partly in virtuous action).

(2) To act virtuously one must do what courage bids (i.e., acting courageously is one part of acting virtuously).

(3) Courage consists in not allowing the tendency to feel, or not to feel, fear to influence one's action unduly.

(4) To abandon one's possessions under fear of physical harm, unless the threat is extreme or the possessions are either not worth much or easily replaceable, would be to give in too much to the tendency to feel fear.

(5) To abandon a valuable and built-up homestead in fear of marauders who are neither clearly bent on making a fight of it nor plainly a lot more powerful than oneself would be to abandon one's possessions under fear of physical harm where the threat is not extreme and the possessions are neither worth little nor easily replaceable.

How long deliberation continues will vary with the agent deliberating. It might be concluded at my step (5), issuing in the final decision not to abandon one's built-up homestead in fear of marauders not obviously bent on making good their threat and not obviously a lot more powerful than oneself. Or deliberation might go on somewhat further, bringing forward increasingly detailed specifications of the sort of threat that is to be taken as real and the sort of homestead that is valuable and so worth defending. In any case, as Aristotle insists, there cannot be fully specific principles dictating without question a certain course of action under such circumstances: "It is not easy to determine accurately in what fashion and with whom and on what grounds and for how long one ought to get angry [or feel afraid]... It is not easy to set out in a rule (*tōi logōi*) how much and in what fashion one must diverge [from the mean] to be blameworthy; for the decision rests with the particulars and with perception" (1126a32-b4). And, as we have seen, Aristotle holds that at *some* point one must be able to recognize by perception persons and things of a kind that one's deliberation has led one to single out as relevant to the end one is pursuing. So in our present case the agent might well stop deliberating at the point at which we have broken off. He sees that men actually present are marauders, that their threat is not obviously going to be pressed when resisted, and that they are not obviously a lot more powerful than himself; and he knows his homestead to be built-up and valuable: he has learned by experience to discriminate things having these characteristics more or less immediately, on sight. So, seeing all this, he puts his decision into effect by grabbing the nearest implement and striking out in defense of his home.

In any event, this sample moral deliberation has been carried out far enough to make it possible to identify all the essential features of moral reasoning according to this scheme. (a) The process of deliberation itself, starting from a conception of flourishing as end in view and working down toward a particular action to be performed, leads to the choice of an action for its own sake. (On schemes of the maximization sort, choice of the morally correct action for its *own* sake is not an outcome of deliberation; deliberation selects the action as instrumentally good only.) (b) Principles of virtue appear as steps in the deliberative argument: in the example, (3) provides a definition of courage, (4) and (5) increasingly specific rules or precepts governing action in the sort of context for which the choice is being made. (c) The argument articulates certain details of the virtuous agent's conception of flourishing and of courageous action as a constituent of the flourishing life; it does not attempt to justify the action chosen in nonmoral terms at all. In other words, it is the agent's antecedent understanding of what courageous action is and of its fundamental goodness that allows him to argue as he does; no one not similarly possessed of this understanding could be expected to see the correctness of the steps in the argument or the choice to which they lead. Moral reasoning does not justify particular principles or precepts of the virtues; instead, it simply expresses a particular moral outlook.[112]

Now if I am right in thinking that Aristotle conceives of moral deliberation according to this second pattern, certain important consequences follow. First, his recognition of a value inherent in moral action is not, as Allan and others have thought, something which conflicts with his analysis of deliberation in *Nicomachean Ethics* III and elsewhere. In fact, means-ends deliberation as Aristotle understands it can accommodate this recognition, provided that morally virtuous activity is itself part of the end that is held in view when moral reasoning is being engaged in; and I have suggested that Aristotle avails himself of this opportunity.

Secondly, in the dispute which has raged in moral philosophy since Kant between "teleological" and "deontological" theories of right action, Aristotle does not stand with the teleologists, as is usually assumed,[113] but is in fact in certain respects closer to Kant and the deontologists. For if the distinguishing feature of a teleological theory is that in it "the good is defined independently from the right, and then the right is defined as that which maximizes the good,"[114] then Aristotle's theory of virtuous action

---

[112] This is not to say that Aristotle leaves no place for the justification of the moral life. His argument (*NE* I 7) that being virtuous is part of the ἔργον of man can certainly be construed as an effort in this direction; but, as I have pointed out above (pp. 70–71), this is not a deliberative argument: it does not assume the form of calculating how best to achieve any definite end or ends that human beings have. This argument will therefore not be given by a morally virtuous person in stating his reasons for acting as he does.

[113] Cf. W. D. Ross, *Aristotle* (Meridian Books ed.), p. 184: "Aristotle's ethics is definitely teleological; morality consists in doing certain actions not because we see them to be right in themselves but because we see them to be such as will bring us nearer to the 'good for man'."

[114] John Rawls, *A Theory of Justice* (Cambridge, Mass.: Belknap Press of Harvard University Press, 1971), p. 24, following W. K. Frankena, *Ethics* (Englewood Cliffs, N.J.: Prentice-Hall, 1963), p. 13. On the importance of the first condition, requiring the independent definition of the good, see Rawls, p. 25.

is not a teleological theory. For although he does hold that virtuous action is a means to *eudaimonia*, or human good, *eudaimonia* is itself not specified independently of virtuous action; on the contrary, *eudaimonia* is conceived of as identical with a lifetime of morally virtuous action (together perhaps with other activities as well). It does not follow, of course, that Aristotle must be classed as a deontologist:[115] for although he agrees with Kant in rejecting maximization schemes of all kinds in favor of a definitely structured life, he does not think of moral constraints themselves as imposed on persons without regard for (and even despite) their own good, as Kant (together with most of his modern opponents) tends to do. In Aristotle's theory human good *consists* (partly) in virtuous action, so his theory, while decidedly not teleological in the modern sense, is also not deontological either.

Whether or not it is fair to draw these conclusions will obviously depend on the nature of Aristotle's theory of *eudaimonia*. If he makes morally virtuous activities essential ingredients in the flourishing life, then, clearly enough, his theory of virtuous action is not teleological in the modern sense. But if he does not think of these activities as basic structural elements in the best life, then moral action will turn out to be supported by reasons of a teleological kind exclusively. Although Aristotle's views on the best life for a human being are complex and difficult to interpret, I shall attempt in the next chapter to unravel them. Here I have argued only that his conception of deliberation at least makes room for moral reasoning in which an intrinsic value is assigned to virtuous action. Confirmation that such a theory of moral reasoning is actually Aristotle's must await the conclusions of the next two chapters.

[115] Except by the simple expedient (see Rawls, *A Theory of Justice* p. 30) of *defining* deontological theories as those which are not teleological by the above criterion.

Moral Virtue and Human Flourishing

In the previous chapter I have been almost wholly concerned with the structure and functions, and hardly at all with the content, of moral and, more generally, practical thinking according to Aristotle. In this second chapter, I begin to consider Aristotle's answer to what was for him the most important substantive question of ethical theory: what is the nature of *eudaimonia* or (as I shall, *faute de mieux*, translate it) human flourishing?[1] The notion of human flourishing figures in one way

[1] The traditional English rendering, "happiness," derives from the medieval Latin translation, *felicitas*. But it is not a good choice, since "happiness" tends to be taken as referring exclusively to a subjective psychological state, and indeed one that is often temporary and recurrent. Hence much that Aristotle says about εὐδαιμονία manifestly fails to hold true of happiness as ordinarily understood. Thus (*EE* I 7 1217a24-29, *NE* I 9 1099b32-34, X 8 1178b23-31) only gods and human beings are capable of being εὐδαίμων, and among humans only adults, since it is only acceptable to call a child εὐδαίμων in the expectation that his adult life will be such as to make him later on εὐδαίμων in the full sense (*NE* I 9 1100a1-4, *EE* II 1 1219b5-8). Again, εὐδαιμονία is not the possession of single days (*EE* 1219b5, *NE* I 7 1098a18-20) or short periods of time, but only of the whole adult life of a certain sort of person. These features of εὐδαιμονία, as Aristotle understands it, are to a fair degree captured by the idea of human flourishing: flourishing implies the possession and use of one's mature powers over, at any rate, a considerable period of time, during which, moreover, the future looks bright. It is also fit to bear the weight of Aristotle's treatment of εὐδαιμονία as the fulfillment of the natural capacities of the human species. It can even be said, I think, that this translation comes closer than any other to making comprehensible Aristotle's idea (*NE* I 10 1100a22-30, 1101a22 ff), which he puts forward as a matter of accepted usage, that what happens to children after

or another in every major topic discussed in the *Nicomachean Ethics*, and two books, the first and the last, are largely devoted to developing and expounding it. Yet readers have regularly found the various things Aristotle says on this topic extremely difficult to reconcile with each other. What was apparently meant by its author as a single coherent theory has often seemed to collapse into a set of disconnected remarks—remarks which are suggestive, no doubt, but which seem hardly developed enough to count as a *theory* of anything. In this chapter and the next I present and argue for an interpretation of Aristotle's conception of what it is for a human being to flourish that does, I think, make it a coherent theory and does so without ignoring or doing violence to anything he says which bears on the topic.

I begin in the first section of the present chapter by setting out and examining a natural, and indeed very common, interpretation of Aristotle's conception of *eudaimonia*. This interpretation I call intellectualist because it attributes to him the view that human flourishing consists exclusively in pure intellectual activity of the best kind. I explain the intellectualist thesis and discuss the textual grounds in the *Nicomachean Ethics* for attributing it to Aristotle. I argue that despite a certain initial plausibility such an intellectualist interpretation cannot make coherent sense of Aristotle's theory in the *Nicomachean Ethics* taken as a whole. And I show that certain passages, particularly in the sixth book, suggest that Aristotle's real view of what it is for a human being to flourish includes much more than merely intellectual activity. In the remainder of the chapter, I examine the *Eudemian Ethics,* showing that it explicitly and consistently

---

a parent's demise has an effect on the parent's εὐδαιμονία: for it is plausible to suppose that a man's flourishing partly consists in his having reasonable grounds for a good prognosis for his children's lives, and if after his death he turns out to have been deceived in this regard it does seem natural to say that his life was not so flourishing as it had seemed. (I believe I have adopted this rendering of εὐδαιμονία from G. E. M. Anscombe: see her article, "Modern Moral Philosophy," *Philosophy* 33 [1958], 1-19.)

rejects intellectualism, evincing instead this more inclusive outlook. Finally, in Chapter III, I return to the *Nicomachean Ethics* to consider again those passages, particularly in the tenth book, which do seem to argue for some type of intellectualism. I try to show that what Aristotle says in these places can be, and, everything considered, ought to be, understood not as contradicting the *Eudemian* view, but in fact, though with certain reservations, as actually reaffirming it. An intellectualist thesis remains, but one so hedged about as not to contradict the more inclusive view put forward in the *Eudemian Ethics* and presupposed by the remainder of the *Nicomachean*.

1. Human Flourishing as Ultimate End

It is interesting and important to notice that, despite its virtual omnipresence in the *Nicomachean Ethics*, the concept of *eudaimonia* is not, from the standpoint of logical structure, basic to Aristotle's enquiry in the treatise. *Eudaimonia* is not named until the fourth chapter of book I, where it is introduced as the first preliminary answer to a question formulated already in the first two chapters: "What is at the most extreme limit of all good things achievable in action?" Aristotle implies in chapter 2 that there is "an end of the things that we do, which we desire for itself, desiring all other things on its account,"[2] and it is this end, reappearing as the good that is at the most extreme limit (*to akrotaton*) of good things, that Aristotle identifies in chapter 4 as *eudaimonia.* Hence it is the *conception* of such an end—what I have called an *ultimate end*—and not *eudaimonia* as such that is the logically and structurally basic concept of the *Nicomachean Ethics*. The treatise begins with an effort to make plausible the assumption that there is some such end, and the subsequent development of a theory of human flourishing is explicitly introduced as the identification of the (correct) ultimate end for

---

[2] *NE* I 2 1094a18-19. Cf. *EE* I 2 1214b7-9, where πάσας τὰς πράξεις justifies the "all" of the translation, if justification is needed; cf. also *NE* I 7 1097a22-23, εἴ τι τῶν πρακτῶν ἁπάντων ἐστὶ τέλος.

human beings to aim at. In understanding Aristotle's theory of human flourishing, therefore, it is essential to have firmly in mind both what the function of an ultimate end is supposed to be and why Aristotle thought there is any such thing.

The first of these questions is relatively easy to answer. The passage from chapter 2 just quoted makes it clear that an ultimate end has two properties: first, it is desired for its own sake, and, second, everything else that is desired is desired for the sake of it. On this characterization alone, however, it would be at least logically possible for a person to simultaneously pursue two or more such ends: provided that two ends are desired for the sake of each other, as well as for their own sakes, then if everything else is desired for the sake of one of them, everything will be desired for the sake of the other as well, and both will turn out to be ultimate ends. Aristotle, however, seems not to allow for such plural ultimate ends. We must suppose that he takes for granted that an ultimate end must meet a third condition, in addition to the two already noted: it is not desired for the sake of anything else. (He does in fact affirm at 1097b1—and again at 1176b30-31—that *eudaimonia*, which he identifies as the ultimate end, is never chosen for the sake of anything else; but he connects this feature of *eudaimonia* with its being "most final" or "most end-like" (*teleiotaton*), and does not explicitly make it a defining condition of an ultimate end as such.) In any event, I shall take it that the concept of an ultimate end is to be defined by the three conditions just mentioned. Hence, to hold that someone pursues such an end will be to hold that his desires are so structured that they all come to rest, so to speak, in one and the same object: all his desires can be explained by referring them ultimately to this object, which is desired for itself and for no other reason. Thus, as it might be, he desires to secure a job as an industrial manager in order to become rich, and desires to become rich for the sake of something else that is desired for itself and for nothing else; and *all* his desires are similarly dependent on this leading desire.

Now the notion that human desires thus converge on a single

object of pursuit certainly does not immediately recommend itself. One might rather have thought that human beings have a variety of fundamental desires, none dependent on any of the others. What then makes Aristotle think that anyone's desires do exhibit such a bizarre structure? In the *Nicomachean Ethics* he has sometimes been thought to argue that everyone's desires must follow this pattern, since otherwise one could not avoid having desires that are "empty and vain"; that is, presumably he means to say, altogether ungrounded.[3] What he says is this: "If, then, there is an end of the things that we do, which we desire for itself, desiring all other things on its account, and we do not choose everything on account of something else (for on this basis one will go on infinitely, so that desire is empty and vain), clearly this would be the good, that is, the best thing there is" (1094a18-22). The conditional form of his assertion here suggests not so much an argument to the conclusion that there is such an "end of the things that we do," as an inference from the supposition (not argued for in this sentence) that there is one:[4] if there *is* such an end, then desire is assuredly not empty and vain, and this end (if we could only be clear exactly what it is!) will constitute human good. Still, this leaves one wanting to know what reason there is to believe that any person does pursue such an end.

---

[3] Thus G. E. M. Anscombe, *An Introduction to Wittgenstein's Tractatus* (London: Hutchinson, 1959), pp. 15-16, and *Intention* §21. Construed thus the passage is an obvious fallacy turning on a failure to observe the difference between $(x)(\exists y)(xRy)$ and $(\exists y)(x)(xRy)$.

[4] So it is taken by B. A. O. Williams, "Aristotle on the Good: A Formal Sketch" (*Philosophical Quarterly* 12 [1962], 289-296) and W. F. R. Hardie, *Aristotle's Ethical Theory*, pp. 16-17. Williams agrees with Miss Anscombe that Aristotle thought there must be for each person some such end; he attempts (but without success) to put together a valid argument to this conclusion using as premises other remarks of Aristotle in the first book of the *NE*. See also further developments in C. Kirwan, "Logic and the Good in Aristotle" (*Philosophical Quarterly* 17 [1967], 97-114). I do not think these reconstructions, ingenious as they are, do anything to bring out the reasons Aristotle may be supposed to have had for accepting, in whatever way he did accept, the existence of an ultimate end.

In fact, Aristotle's words tend to imply that we all have such an end. But in the *Eudemian Ethics* he holds not that everyone does have his desires organized on this pattern, but that everyone ought to. There (*EE* I 2 1214b6-14) he says that "everyone who is able to live according to his own choosing sets up[5] some goal (*tina skopon*) for the good life—honor, or reputation, or riches, or intellectual cultivation—by looking to which he will perform all his actions (since not to organize one's life with a view to some end is a sign of great stupidity). Hence, we must above all first determine for ourselves, neither precipitately nor frivolously, in which of the things that belong to us good living consists, and what are the conditions for human beings' coming to possess this." If this is his view, then one can understand why he might in the *Nicomachean Ethics* have suggested that "we" all do have desires structured in this way. As he explains there, lectures on ethical theory are directed only to mature listeners who, since they can be presumed not to be totally foolish, can on this principle from the *Eudemian Ethics* be taken to have erected for themselves such an ultimate end: the "we" means "we sensible adults."

But why must it be a sign of stupidity not to have such a single "goal for the good life"? Aristotle does not say, but given his views about practical reasoning, as I have developed them in the previous chapter, I think one can see why he should have thought so. Consider first an obvious objection to what Aristotle seems to be insisting on here. Surely, it might be said, it would be very irrational to plan one's life in the way Aristotle seems to suggest; the variety and complexity of normal human capacities, needs, and interests are such that any rationally planned life must identify a great variety of different ends, and not just one. Ends that it would seem rational for most people to adopt would include the development and exercise of the sexual capacities, the

<hr/>

[5] Or: "ought to set up." The manuscripts differ here; but the difference in sense is not substantial, since in any case the parenthesis makes it clear that Aristotle's intention is to recommend the setting up of such a goal.

cultivation of the mind, and the nurturing and engagement of the instinct for sociability. Of course, beyond identifying a set of ends, a rational plan must also assign priorities: how far to develop the various capacities, how much time to devote to their exercise, what to do when the pursuit of one end will require slighting another, and so on. And it seems natural to suppose that two different types of considerations would come up as one used such a plan to decide on courses of action in particular circumstances. Some of the time one would simply be deciding how best to achieve some one of the ends identified in the plan. On the other hand a different sort of reasoning would be called for in deciding which end to pursue in a situation in which one might devote oneself to any one of several, or in deciding among means for the pursuit of a given end where one's choice also affects the achievement of some other end. The former sort of reasoning would be of the means-ends variety, while the latter, in which the priority principles are invoked, would not have that form at all: to apply such principles is not the same thing as to hit upon a means of achieving some end.

Now Aristotle is notorious for having presented a view of the practical intellect according to which the only discursive function it discharges is that of calculating means to ends. But then it is not open to him to allow for a rational life-plan of the kind sketched in the preceding paragraph, with its distinction between means-ends reasoning and the application of ordering principles to the ends themselves. His conception of practical reasoning makes no provision for principles of choice and preference other than appeal to ends. It follows that in Aristotle's conception of practical reasoning a person must abandon the attempt to introduce rational order into his life at the point where he determines how best to achieve some end he has adopted, unless he selects some one end as the single, *ultimate* object of pursuit in his life. For if he does not have such an ultimate end he can have no means of deciding rationally what to do on those numerous occasions in his life when his ends come into partial or total conflict; the only means of resolution he can envisage is to regard the conflicting ends as alternative means to some further end and then opt for the course of action that is the most eligible means to this end. It thus follows directly from Aristotle's insistence on the means-ends structure of all practical reasoning that rational order can be adequately introduced into a person's life only if he does "set up some goal for the good life, by looking to which he will do all his actions." It seems plausible, then, to regard this conception of practical reasoning as responsible for Aristotle's commitment to the rationality of having a system of desire and pursuit which has at its apex a single end lying ultimately behind every desire and pursuit, of whatever kind.

But to explain why Aristotle was driven to hold this thesis is not to condone or to justify it. One might well take the view that if this is what Aristotle's analysis of practical reasoning commits him to, then, upon reaching this conclusion he ought simply to have abandoned that analysis: there must be additional functions for practical reasoning to perform besides seeking means to ends. This is, I think, essentially correct. But one ought not simply to condemn Aristotle on this score, since in doing so one would fail to appreciate the mitigating subtlety with which he interprets and applies his conclusion. For, as I noted above, his first preliminary attempt to identify the ultimate end for us is simply to say that it is *eudaimonia*, or human flourishing. This means, in effect, that according to Aristotle it is a person's conception of what it is to flourish that he is, if he is fully in control of his life, putting into effect in all his actions: he acts always with a view to living a certain kind of life, which kind of life he regards as a flourishing one. Now, put this way, having a single ultimate object of pursuit does not seem such a bizarre idea. For flourishing as an end clearly belongs to a different order from any of the concrete ends one might plausibly adopt in one's life—ends like the exercise of one's sexual, intellectual, and social capacities, mentioned above. To aim at having a flourishing life is to pursue a second-order end—that is, to attempt to put into effect an orderly scheme for the attainment of these, or other such, first-order ends.[6] Thus, in the first instance, Aristotle's insistence on the rationality of having an ultimate end as the single and constant object of ultimate pursuit in one's life is simply the expression, in the only way allowable within his theory of practical reasoning, of the reasonable demand for an overall plan of life.

Furthermore, in Aristotle's scheme, such a plan might well coincide substantially, though not structurally, with the life-plan sketched earlier. For it might consist of a list of different first-order ends taken together with ordering principles or an assignment of weights to these ends: a plan of this kind would establish a conception of human flourishing which would allow for the independent value of a number of different activities and interests, each in its own time and place and each pursued with the vigor appropriate to it. This conception would differ from the life-plan previously sketched only in this: that whereas in the latter plan means-ends reasoning is sharply distinguished from the application of priority principles to ends, in the Aristotelian scheme the scope of means-ends reasoning would be extended so as to encompass the application of priority principles as well. In effect, the life defined by such a plan—ends together with weights or other ordering principles—would be regarded as a single comprehensive end which one has constantly in view and which one is seeking to realize in each and every decision one makes.

Such an ultimate end would be an *inclusive* second-order end, because it includes as fundamental values a variety of independent activities and interests.[7] On the other hand this is not the only

[6] The terminology of first- and second-order ends, in application to conceptions of "happiness" like Aristotle's, I owe to John Rawls. In working out my interpretation of Aristotle's theory of human good I have been influenced by Rawls's own theory of good, for which see now *A Theory of Justice*, chap. VII.

[7] The distinction between inclusive and exclusive (or dominant-end) conceptions of human good I derive from W. F. R. Hardie's excellent article, "The Final Good in Aristotle's *Ethics*" (*Philosophy* 40 [1965] 277-295; reprinted in J. M. E. Moravcsik, ed., *Aristotle: A Collection of Critical*

possible such plan. The passage quoted above from the *Eudemian Ethics* suggests a different structure, in which a single first-order end ("honor or reputation or riches or intellectual cultivation") is made (as W. F. R. Hardie puts it) dominant over all others. In such a scheme a flourishing life is conceived of as one in which a maximum of some one concrete good is achieved, and everything else that is pursued is pursued as a means to attaining this dominant end. Some one might, for example, have a conception of flourishing which makes the accumulation of money a dominant end. He might have other ends and interests in life, but he would have to see them as contributing to the pursuit of money, and could only pursue them so far as they are not in conflict with it. Thus he might enjoy family life, and genuinely like playing with his children, and might even make the maintenance of a good family life an important end in his life. But he can do this only if (he thinks) it is at the same time among the most effective ways of achieving his goal of accumulating money—for example, if his parents-in-law are rich, and are attached to his wife and children. As soon as keeping up his family ties ceases to be an effective means of making money, he must simply abandon them: the interest which he takes in his family has no independent weight, however small, that could be balanced against his dominant aim.

Thus it is easy to see that in principle Aristotle's insistence that each person should articulate a conception of flourishing, pursuing it as the ultimate end in his life, does not necessarily imply that everyone should have any one *dominant* end. Still, he sometimes gives the impression that this is his view. So, as we have seen, when introducing the conception of an ultimate end in the *Eudemian Ethics* he illustrates only conceptions of flourishing that posit a dominant end—honor, wealth, and so on. But it is not difficult to understand why he should do this: it is natural and

---

Essays). In much of what I say here and elsewhere about Aristotle's theory of εὐδαιμονία I am developing and filling out ideas of Hardie's; see also his *Aristotle's Ethical Theory*, chaps. 2 and 15.

easy to explain the idea of an ultimate end by giving examples of dominant-end conceptions of flourishing, rather than the more cumbersome inclusive conception, according to which one cannot identify any single end, beyond the conception of flourishing itself, as the end to be pursued. And, in any case, the impression that Aristotle recognizes only dominant-end conceptions of *eudaimonia* is a false one. For, as has recently been pointed out,[8] in one passage of the *Nicomachean Ethics* (1097b16-20) Aristotle explicitly recognizes that flourishing must be conceived of as including a number of good things rather than as dominated by a single end, on the ground that flourishing must be the consummately best thing, whereas any quantity of a concrete good thing can be bettered by the addition to it of some quantity, however small, of another good thing, however slight. And, as I shall argue at length below, Aristotle's own account of flourishing in the *Eudemian Ethics* clearly conforms to the inclusive, rather than to the dominant pattern.

But although these considerations do at least leave open the possibility that in Aristotle's considered view human flourishing should be conceived of according to the inclusive scheme, the *Nicomachean Ethics* is standardly interpreted as espousing a conception of flourishing which makes dominant a single end, the development and exercise of one's capacity for theoretical activity. Textual evidence can be brought forward in favor of this interpretation. Thus in book I chapter 7, where he first states his own summary account of what flourishing is, Aristotle characterizes it as "excellent spiritual or mental activity, or, if there are several forms of excellence, spiritual activity expressing the best and most final excellence" (1098a16-18). Now we hear very soon (I 13) of various forms of excellence, falling into two main types, excellences of mind and excellences of character, and in the tenth book the implied ordering among them is explained.[9] There

[8] By Hardie, in the article cited in n. 7 (Moravcsik reprint, p. 300), and in his *Aristotle's Ethical Theory*, pp. 22-23.

[9] Cf. also VI 1143b33-35, 1141a20-22.

(1177a12-18) we are told that the best excellence is that of the best thing in us; and though Aristotle is unwilling straight off to commit himself on what this best thing may be, he is clear that its activity is theoretical. Hence to be flourishing is to be theorizing excellently: or, as he later specifies, to possess and use the excellence of theoretical wisdom (*sophia*). So it seems not unreasonable to conclude that in his first book account Aristotle is paving the way for the theory of the tenth book: "activity expressing the best and most final excellence" in the earlier passage seems to be a reference to the exercise of theoretical wisdom.[10]

[10] One might be tempted to resist my explication of 1098a16-18 by appeal to the book X theory. Thus, for example, one might instead take ἡ ἀρίστη καὶ τελειοτάτη ἀρετή to mean (as T. Irwin has suggested to me) all the human excellences, moral and intellectual, taken together as a whole: this ἀρετή, i.e. ἀρετή as a whole, could be called best and most final (or most complete). One might attempt to support this interpretation by pointing to *EE* 1219a39 (on which see below pp. 116–117), where ἐνέργεια κατ' ἀρετὴν τελείαν clearly does mean the exercise of human excellence as a whole. However, (1) the context of these words in the *EE* is crucial for the establishment of this sense there (cf. a37), and in the *NE* the contrast between πλείους αἱ ἀρεταί and τὴν ἀρίστην καὶ τελειοτάτην surely does strongly invite one to take the "best and most final excellence" as one among the several particular excellences. (2) In any case, there is a large difference between ἡ τελεία ἀρετή and ἡ τελειοτάτη ἀρετή: the former could easily, even without the explicit indications in the *EE* context, be taken to mean excellence as a whole (cf. *Phys.* III 6 207a13-14), but the superlative, being by its very nature exclusionary, could only do so in a very special context. (3) Furthermore, it seems likely that the sense of τελειοτάτη here is in any case a special one, introduced earlier in the chapter (1097a25-b6) where τελειότατον is explained (a34-b1) as meaning (something like) "most having the character of an end" (i.e., being chosen for its own sake more, and for the sake of another thing less, than others). (Hence my preference for the translation "most final" instead of "most complete.") And the excellences do differ with respect to this feature, as Aristotle grants, since (leaving aside εὐδαιμονία itself) morally virtuous action does bring with it other desired goods, while σοφία does not (1177b2-4); so σοφία is the "most final" because it, more than the other excellences, has its value entirely within itself.

But while it is clear on reflection that σοφία is the ἀρίστη καὶ τελειοτάτη ἀρετή referred to here, it is important to notice that Aristotle does not say so explicitly, and even leaves it an open question whether in the end εὐδαιμονία is to be fully specified only by drawing distinctions among the excellences. For if my interpretation (see below, pp. 110 ff) of the theory of

It is hard to deny that taken together these passages, which are extremely explicit, commit Aristotle to the view that the correct ultimate end for a human being to aim at in life is the active exercise of theoretical wisdom. Given what the notion of an ultimate end involves, this must mean that we ought in everything we do to be realizing, or working for the realization of, this end, and to abandon all others ends to the extent that they cannot be subordinated to this one. Hence, since the *phronimos*, or practically intelligent person, is someone who knows what the correct end of human life is,[11] it follows that the *phronimos*, accepting these views of Aristotle's, will organize his life and make all his practical decisions accordingly. But inasmuch as *phronēsis* is, *inter alia*, the intellectual excellence corresponding to and supporting the excellences of character, which in turn consist in the disposition to behave morally, it follows that in deciding what the moral thing to do is, and doing it, the practically intelligent man is concerned ultimately only with the furtherance of his own intellectual life. It follows, therefore, that if Aristotle holds singlemindedly to the intellectualist view he must hold also that moral values are to be seen as effective means to the enhancement of one's intellectual life, and that the *phronimos*, who is a moral person par excellence, so views them.

These inferences about practical intelligence and moral reasoning might be thought to find at least some support from the sixth book itself. For the book opens with the apparent promise to give us an account of the practically intelligent man's criterion in adopting the rules defining the moral virtues, and it is plausible to believe that the criterion envisaged is the furtherance of the agent's own intellectual life. The book begins:

Since, as it happens, we have said earlier that one ought to choose the mean, not the excess or the deficiency, and the mean is

---

moral virtue and φρόνησις given in the torso of the work is correct, he must give us here an account of εὐδαιμονία broad enough to accommodate the moral agent's end while at the same time permitting the intellectualist development found in book X.

[11] See VI 1140a28, 1142b33.

as right reason says, let us examine this.[12] For in all the states of character we have mentioned, as also in the others, there is a target (*skopos*) to which the man who possesses reason looks, as he applies and relaxes pressure, and there is a principle of definition (*horos*) for the mean states, which we say are between excess and deficiency, being in accordance with right reason. But to speak thus is, though correct, not at all clear . . . If a man knew only this he would not be a wise man: for example, he would not know what remedies to apply to the body, if someone should say, "Those that medicine prescribes and as the man of medicine bids." Hence it is necessary also in the case of the states of the soul not merely that this true statement be made, but that it be determined what is right reason and what is its defining principle. (1138b18-34)

It does certainly appear that Aristotle here encourages his reader to believe that the man of practical intelligence has an independent criterion by which he determines which states of character are intermediate and so the right ones to have. Aristotle also encourages the expectation that he is going to provide, in the sixth book, at least a sketch of what this independent criterion is. Furthermore, by referring to it at one place as a *skopos*, or target, he gives a very important clue to its nature: for in setting out the doctrine of the ultimate end in book I, Aristotle had said that if

---

[12] Cf., for example, II 6 1106b36-1107a6, where Aristotle states in summary form his theory that virtue lies in a mean: "So virtue is a disposition to choose, which lies in a mean relative to ourselves and defined by a rule, i.e. the rule by which the practically intelligent person would define it. It is a mean between two vices, one of excess and the other of defect—a mean, furthermore, in that some of these vices are deficient with respect to, and others exceed, what is right both in feelings and in actions, while the virtue both finds and chooses what is intermediate." It should be noted that Aristotle here refers to the state of character itself as a mean (μεσότης) between two vices, on the ground that the actions and feelings that are characteristic of it are typically intermediate (τὸ μέσον) between actions and feelings that lie on either side, according to some scale of measurement, and such that those to one side are typical of one vice, while those to the other side are typical of the other vice. Hence, the criterion for moral virtue apparently promised in our passage of the sixth book will presumably specify the intermediate states of character that are the virtues by specifying which feelings and actions

one has a grasp of the correct ultimate end he will, like an archer, have a target (*skopos*) to shoot at in life and therefore be all the more likely to act as he ought (1094a23-24).[13] The suggested criterion for the rightness of states of character is therefore conduciveness to the ultimate end.

But what ultimate end does Aristotle have in mind? Here the apparent independence of the suggested criterion becomes decisive. For let us suppose for the sake of argument that Aristotle has in mind an ultimate end consisting at least in part of morally virtuous activity itself. Conceivably, he might describe the practically intelligent man as looking to this end as at a kind of target in determining which states of character are moral virtues, and he might even refer to it as a defining principle of moral virtue. But in this case the process of looking to the end would not provide an independent criterion of moral virtue, since the notion of moral virtue would, at least to some extent, be already presupposed as given in the conception of the end itself. The process of consulting the end in order to derive rules would then become something like the process of trying to make explicit what was previously only vaguely grasped: that is, rules would be proposed and then tested against a strong but unarticulated intuition of what morality involves, and the derivation of rules would really be the progressive articulation of the end. In this case the end would be, in a manner of speaking, the *horos,* or defining principle, of

are intermediate in the required sense.

The Aristotelian doctrine of the mean raises many interesting and difficult questions, but most of these lie outside the scope of this book. It is most illuminatingly considered, I think, in connection with Aristotle's views on moral training. Moral training, as Aristotle conceives it, is a matter of tempering and molding those primitive feelings and emotions which we are endowed with at birth that affect what we do (or are inclined to do), rather than (as a Kantian might hold) building up as a counterweight to natural inclination a further, and specifically moral, impulse to action: on this see Hardie, *Aristotle's Ethical Theory*, chap. VII, who rightly emphasizes the difference between the psychological structures belonging to the (Aristotelian) virtuous person and those characteristic of the various forms of "continence" (ἐγκράτεια).

[13] Cf. also σκοπός, VI 12 1144a8, to the same effect.

moral virtue, but it would clearly not provide an *independent* criterion of the kind Aristotle might seem to be promising in the sixth book.

But if the end must be conceived independently of the rules to be derived from it, there seems no other choice, among the candidates to be found in the *Ethics*, than pure intellectual activity. And although Aristotle certainly never explicitly fulfills his promise to tell us about this *skopos* in the sixth book, one passage can at any rate be interpreted so as to accord with the intellectualist interpretation.

At the very end of the book Aristotle says (1145a6-11):

But nor does it (viz., practical intelligence) exercise authority over theoretical wisdom (*sophia*) or over the superior part of the mind—no more so than medicine does over health. For it (viz., medicine, or practical intelligence, or perhaps both) does not make use of it (viz., health, or theoretical wisdom, or both), but sees to it that it comes into being. So it gives orders for the sake of the other, but not *to* it. Further, to say it does exercise authority is like saying that political knowledge rules the gods, because it gives orders concerning everything in the city [religion included].

This passage does not say that *all* the directives of practical intelligence are ultimately aimed at the production of *sophia* and its free exercise; strictly, it says only that at least some part of its activity has this aim. But the stronger thesis, though not stated explicitly, could easily be seen lying behind Aristotle's remarks here, if there were good reason to think he held it.

A *prima facie* case can therefore be made for the intellectualist interpretation, drawing on explicit texts in the first and tenth books, supported by not implausible inferences drawn from passages of the sixth book as well. Nonetheless, I think it must be rejected. To begin with, this interpretation, besides forcing on Aristotle an objectionable theory of moral reasoning, is difficult to reconcile with other equally clear statements Aristotle makes about practical intelligence; indeed, it is, I think, hardly compatible with much that is most characteristic of Aristotle's theory of moral reasoning.

Two groups of passages constitute the main source of difficulty for the intellectualist thesis. First, there are all those places where Aristotle says that anyone who is morally virtuous acts *dia to kalon* or *tou kalou heneka* ("on account of the noble," "for the sake of the noble") and makes *to kalon* ("nobility of action") his end.[14] And, secondly, in the sixth book itself Aristotle twice maintains (1140b7, 1139b3-4) that the end aimed at by the practically intelligent man is *autē hē eupraxia* ("goodness of action itself"). It is obvious that both these sets of passages emphasize a *style* in or of action—that is to say, something inherent in actions themselves rather than some further aim to be achieved or promoted by the actions one chooses to perform. And by making this style the characteristic concern of the morally virtuous and practically intelligent man, Aristotle introduces an element that is at least foreign to the main intellectualist scheme as outlined so far.

It is important, however, not to exaggerate the degree to which concern for goodness of the action itself is foreign to concern for an ulterior intellectualist end. For there is, in itself, nothing inconsistent in the thesis that pure thinking is the ultimate end recognized by the practically intelligent man, while he still recognizes and pursues other ends as well, among them *to kalon* or *autē hē eupraxia*. For the notion of an ultimate end of all that we do is defined by Aristotle as that which we desire for itself alone, desiring all other things for its sake; there is no bar against some of these other things also being ends—that is, desired for their own sake—and Aristotle himself makes this clear (1097b2-5).[15] If intellectual activity is pursued as ultimate end, then three conditions must be fulfilled: intellectual activity must be desired (1) for its own sake and (2) not for the sake of anything

---

[14] *NE* III 1115b12-13, 22-24, 1119b16, IV 1122b6-7, and the other passages cited above, Chapter I, n. 105.

[15] And cf. X 6 1176b3-10, with b27-1177a1: play that is pleasant is, like virtuous activity, chosen for its own sake (τῶν δι᾽ αὑτὰ αἱρετῶν, 1176b8-9); yet it is also chosen by sensible people as a respite from more serious endeavors and so for its effects on these.

else; while (3) anything else that is desired must be desired as a
means to this end. This does not imply, however, that other things
can be desired for this reason alone. So morally virtuous action
might be desired for its own sake while also pursued as a means to
the realization of purely intellectual values.

A price must be paid, however, for rendering Aristotle's account of practical intelligence consistent in this way. Consider
again the case of the man who makes the accumulation of money
his Aristotelian ultimate end.[16] He may, as I remarked, have
other ends and interests in life besides money-making, but he
must see them as contributing to the pursuit of money, and can
only pursue them so far as they are not in conflict with it. As soon
as maintaining a good family life, for example, ceases to be an effective means of making money, he must simply abandon it: the
interest which he takes in his family has no independent weight,
however small, that could be balanced against his dominant aim.
At the first sign of conflict, the subordinate end must simply be
dropped. Now, to be sure, money-making is a peculiarly unprom-
ising candidate for an ultimate end. Nonetheless, the logical
features which partly make it so carry over to the case of the
moral agent bent on the realization of intellectual values. Moral
virtue can make no claims on him except insofar as the
performance of virtuous actions, or the maintenance of the kind
of character from which such actions issue, is made rational as a
means to the realization of intellectual values. A contradiction in
Aristotle's account of practical intelligence immediately comes to
light once it is allowed that for some persons or in some
circumstances intellectual values might best be pursued by doing
something that goes against the principles of some virtue. For if
that can ever happen, the two ends, which on this theory the
practically intelligent man will pursue, will conflict; and then,
given the dominance of intellectual values, he must abandon
goodness as an end. So it will *not* be true, as Aristotle says it is,
that you cannot be practically intelligent without being morally

---

[16] See above p. 98.

virtuous (1144a36 f); indeed, in the situation envisaged, one will only show practical intelligence by not acting morally. If the intellectualist interpretation is to be maintained at all, plainly one must also hold that Aristotle thought it could not happen that the two ends should conflict.

There would seem to be two ways in which Aristotle might have defended this extraordinary proposition. One would be to hold that when pursuit of intellectual values leads one to go against what are accepted as the principles of some moral virtue, say those of justice, the principles in question are not in fact correct. The vulgar may *think* that justice requires repaying debts, but in fact this rule is correct only if qualified in favor of the free pursuit of intellectual interests when occasion arises. Thus Aristotle might adopt a revisionist attitude to commonly accepted moral rules and maintain that the cases of conflict between these and the pursuit of the intellectualist ultimate end merely indicate ways in which the moral virtues, as conceived by the practically intelligent man, differ from the same virtues vulgarly conceived. If Burnet's interpretation[17] of Aristotle's use of dialectic in the *Ethics* were correct, there might be some plausibility in attributing this line of defense to Aristotle. But it is all too plain that Aristotle's principles will not permit him to make wholesale revisions in the moral judgments of ordinary people.[18] Hence, this defense would seem to be closed to him.

Alternatively, leaving the principles of the moral virtues substantially unrevised, one might argue that the possession and exercise of moral virtue, so defined, is a necessary condition for the maximum realization of intellectual values. A natural way of arguing in favor of this thesis would be to hold that the actual conditions of human nature and human life make it necessary to

---

[17] Cf. *The Ethics of Aristotle*, pp. 142, 153, 179, and passim, where Burnet too easily allows that the dialectical "analysis" of ἔνδοξα in ethics is divorced from the search for truth. His official account of dialectic in moral philosophy is better (ibid., pp. xxxix-xliii).

[18] Cf. 1172b35-1173a2.

acquire some definite settled character; and that, given the
natural limitations on the types of character that can actually be
acquired, the moral virtues taken in sum constitute the best available type of character to have from the point of view of the
maximum realization of intellectual values. To make good this
claim would require a very minute examination of the elements of
human nature and the conditions of human life and their inter-
relations. Aristotle never attempts such an examination, nor
indeed does he give any hint of how it would proceed. In fact, he
never comes close to explicitly claiming that a virtuous character
is necessary for this purpose. One might expect, however, that in
his delineation of the moral virtues some signs of this thesis would
occasionally be visible, if he in fact accepted it. But such indications as there are, one way or the other, seem to tell against the
hypothesis that Aristotle thought a morally virtuous character
necessary for the fullest possible realization of intellectual values.

Consider, for example, Aristotle's accounts of temperance
(*sōphrosunē*), liberality (*eleutheriotēs*), and magnificence (*mega-
loprepeia*). In accordance with his general scheme, each of these
is opposed to a vice of deficiency as well as to a vice of excess.
Thus the temperate man avoids not only taking an excessive
interest in the bodily pleasures of food and sex, but also avoids
being less interested in these things than he ought to. Likewise,
the liberal man must concern himself with the maintenance of his
material substance and its disbursement to the right persons and
on suitable projects; and similarly, but with a difference of scale,
for magnificence. Aristotle's theory requires, therefore, that one
take *more* interest in the pleasures of food and sex and in the
spending of money than one might; to take less interest in these
things is to become a kind of inferior person. This poses an
obvious difficulty for the intellectualist interpretation. For one
might think that the more entangled one was in the proper
management of one's money, and the social interests and
obligations that accompany it, the less time one would have to
develop and exercise one's intellectual powers. And similarly one

might think the proper rule with regard to the pleasures of food
and sex should, on intellectualist presuppositions, be an ascetic
one: reduce one's dependence on these allurements to the
minimum, so as to have as much time as possible for thinking.[19]
Yet, clearly enough, Aristotle rejects an ascetic ideal: the
temperate man, according to him, indulges not only in those
pleasures which conduce to health and good condition, but also in
such additional pleasures as do not actually interfere with his
health (1119a16-18). The actual maintenance of health and its
attendant pleasures could obviously be justified on intellectualist
grounds. Conceivably, even indulgence in the further innocent
pleasures just alluded to could be justified, despite the fact that
enjoying them would necessitate taking time off from intellectual
work. They might, for example, be needed for recreational purposes, or in some other way serve to enhance the total sum of the
intellectual values realized in a person's lifetime as a whole.
Aristotle does not, however, mention any such ground; in fact he
pretty clearly implies that the justification for indulging in the
surplus bodily pleasures is just that they are pleasant. And this is
one reason that an intellectualist conception of the ultimate end
will not permit. For it assigns to these pleasures a value of their
own, albeit a small one, and treats them as worth giving up some
amount of thinking in order to enjoy.[20] And, similarly, Aristotle's
account of liberality quite clearly implies that there are values in
social life that are supported according to their true worth by the
moderate kind of expenditure implied by liberality. These
features of social life seem to be implicitly accorded an independent value of their own, and the reference to the leading role of
intellectual values, which would be required on the intellectualist
interpretation in order to forestall this natural inference, is

[19] Cf. VII 1152b16-18: no one could keep his mind on geometry while
enjoying sex.

[20] It is important to notice that Aristotle says about the ἀκόλαστος that
he loves the bodily pleasures *more* than they are worth (μᾶλλον τῆς ἀξίας,
1119a19-20): clearly, the ἀναίσθητος loves them *less* than they are worth.

nowhere to be found. In general, I think it can be said that the accounts of the particular moral virtues given in books III-V are constructed on the assumption that there is a plurality of independent values which it is the function of the moral virtues to support, each at its appropriate level. The alternative intellectualist view—that there is only one basic good, which is most effectively realized by the exercise of the moral virtues—seems not to lie behind Aristotle's account of the virtues.

There is, then, no direct evidence for, and some evidence against, the hypothesis that Aristotle thought a morally virtuous character necessary for the fullest possible realization of intellectual values. If he did not think it necessary, then on his view the pursuit of moral virtue can, and presumably will, conflict with the single-minded pursuit of purely intellectual values. At the least we can conclude that he nowhere shows any concern even to affirm, much less argue for, the thesis that the pursuit of intellectual values never comes into conflict with moral values. Yet it is a sufficiently counter-intuitive proposition that one would certainly expect Aristotle to argue for it if he held it. That he does not is fair reason to doubt that he ever accepted it. But if these ends can conflict, then Aristotle's theory of practical intelligence is inconsistent, if he holds that the ultimate end adopted by the practically intelligent man is exclusively intellectual: for, given the conflict of ends, he cannot maintain that the practically intelligent man constantly pursues both "nobility of action" and pure intellectual values as ends.

I think, then, that the attempt to impose the intellectualist conception of *eudaimonia,* drawn from the passages of the first and tenth books which I have cited, upon the moral theory of the middle books of the *Nicomachean Ethics* is in error. The attempt was only encouraged by initially plausible inferences from things Aristotle says in the sixth book, and we have now seen some of the difficulties the theory encounters when followed to its logical conclusion and confronted with a number of other passages. There are, moreover, three passages of the sixth book which, taken together, seem to deny explicitly the intellectualist conception. In chapter 5 Aristotle begins his consideration of *phronēsis* by

pointing out that usage tends to support the view that *phronimoi*
are people who know how to deliberate well about the things that
are good for themselves, not (just) in some restricted context,
such as matters of health, but with regard to life as a whole—*pros
to eu zēn holōs*. Since *to eu zēn* is a synonym of *eudaimonia*[21] and
eudaimonia has been identified as the ultimate end, this amounts
to saying that the *phronimos* knows what the correct ultimate end
is and how to achieve it. Now reading this with one eye on the
tenth book, one might naturally suppose, as we have seen, that
the end in question is *theōria*. But there is no need to go so far
afield to find out what end is intended. For Aristotle immediately
proceeds to tell us what object the *phronimos* pursues as ultimate.
The deliberation, he says, at which the *phronimos* excels is
practical deliberation, or deliberation issuing in action, and not,
as it were, technical deliberation, or deliberation issuing in artistic production. That is to say, he adds, it is deliberation which
does not aim at some end beyond the action to be done, as technical thinking does, but takes goodness of action itself (*autē hē
eupraxia*) as its end. Having just said that the *phronimos* excels at
deliberation concerning *to eu zēn holōs,* i. e., concerning how to
realize the correct ultimate end, Aristotle is plainly saying here
that goodness of action itself *is* the ultimate end.

What, however, does Aristotle mean by "goodness of action?"
The association a page earlier (1139a34) between *eupraxia* and
moral virtue makes it clear that he is referring at least to action
expressing the moral virtues. Question arises only with regard to
the exercise of the theoretical excellences. Do these also possess
"goodness of action?" Are they included here as activities whose
inherent goodness the *phronimos* pursues as part of his ultimate
end?[22] On balance, it seems best to interpret the passage so; at

---

[21] See 1095a19, 1098b21.

[22] One might suppose that the word εὐπραξία could not be used to refer
to the nonpractical uses of the intellect that Aristotle refers to collectively as
θεωρία. But in *Pol.* VII 3 1325b16-21 he insists that αἱ αὐτῶν ἕνεκεν θεωρίαι
καὶ διανοήσεις are πρακτικαί, and maintains that with them too ἡ γὰρ
εὐπραξία τέλος, ὥστε καὶ πρᾶξίς τις.

any rate, two other passages of the sixth book imply that morally virtuous activity does not by itself constitute the practically intelligent person's ultimate end. In these passages Aristotle makes the ultimate end something complex, consisting of more than one type of activity; and he explicitly mentions (the exercise of) theoretical wisdom as one (but only one) of the activities in which *eudaimonia* consists.[23] When these passages are taken into account, Aristotle's conception of the ultimate end in the sixth book turns out not to be exclusively "moralist"; the moral agent on his view pursues a bipartite end, consisting jointly of morally virtuous activity and excellent theorizing. (Further discussion and

[23] See 1144a5-6: "For, being a part of virtue as a whole it (viz., theoretical wisdom) causes a man to flourish [merely] by being possessed and exercised." Here the exercise of wisdom is made *part* of the end, alongside the exercise of the other "parts of virtue as a whole"—an expression paralleled and explained by *EE* 1219a37, 1220a2-4, where it is clear that the other main constituent of virtue as a whole is moral virtue (see below, pp. 117 ff). Hence, it is clear that Aristotle here makes εὐδαιμονία consist of the exercise of moral *and* intellectual excellences, and not the intellectual alone.

Gauthier, in his note on the passage, ignores these striking parallels from the *EE* and fancifully appeals to a passage of the *Protrepticus* (frg. 6 Ross = B 59-70 Düring) to show that Aristotle can speak of wisdom as "part of virtue" where he means "immanent in virtue and human flourishing," without implying that there are other immanent parts as well. Relying on this "parallel," he attempts to interpret our passage as saying that wisdom produces εὐδαιμονία not as something further to which it serves as means, but by being that in which (alone) flourishing consists. Thus he construes the passage as meaning: being something immanent in virtue, i.e., human flourishing, wisdom causes a man to flourish merely by being exercised. To achieve this end, however, Gauthier must, without a semblance of textual warrant, import into his interpretation points made in the *Protrepticus* context but not so much as hinted at in the *NE* passage; and he also overlooks one crucial difference in the language of. the two passages. (1) The alleged parallel comes in an extended passage whose point is to explain what the ἔργον of wisdom is: in particular, the author is anxious to argue that wisdom is not one of those capacities, like house-building, whose job it is to make some *end-product*. House-building, he says (B68), makes a house, but is not itself *part* of the house, μέρος τῆς οἰκίας: the house is a separate thing. Having said this, he can go on, as he immediately does, to contrast wisdom by saying that it *is* part of what it produces, μόριον τῆς ἀρετῆς (i.e., excellent activity) καὶ τῆς εὐδαιμονίας. That μόριον *here* does not

explication of this inclusive end itself can be left to the next section.)

We must conclude, then, that the theory of the two ends, which, as we have seen, the intellectualist interpretation is forced to adopt, is untenable. The moral end of nobility or goodness of action is not an end subordinate to the realization of intellectual values: it is itself a coordinate part of the ultimate end pursued in the morally virtuous man's activity. The thesis of intellectualism cannot be made to square with what Aristotle says about practical intelligence.

This result once achieved, it still remains to give an alternative account of the relation between this partly moral conception of the ultimate end and the purely intellectualist end apparently defended in the tenth book and adumbrated in the first. Does Aristotle simply assert, in one part of the treatise, that the best

---

imply that there is some whole of which wisdom is one part among others, but has the reduced sense of "something immanent in," is entirely a function of what is said in the preceding context. And, secondly, it is made clear that μόριον τῆς ἀρετῆς does not mean, in effect, "one excellence among others," by the addition of the epexegetical καὶ τῆς εὐδαιμονίας. In the *NE* passage, where we have neither the necessary context nor this explanatory addition, one could not be expected to understand μέρος τῆς ἀρετῆς as meaning "immanent in virtue, i.e., human flourishing". (2) But in any case the *NE* does not merely say that wisdom is μέρος τῆς ἀρετῆς; it says μέρος τῆς ὅλης ἀρετῆς, where the crucial addition of ὅλης makes it quite certain that σοφία is being thought of as *one* part of a complex whole. (Even in the *Protrepticus* passage, in B 68 = 6 Ross, p. 36, when the author says ἅπασα . . . ἀρετή, he clearly means to imply that there are several constituent virtues; nor does Gauthier deny this.) There can really be no doubt that μέρος γὰρ οὖσα τῆς ὅλης ἀρετῆς means "being one among the virtues which constitute human excellence as a whole": and consequently the next clause, which implies that the exercise of σοφία is a constituent part of εὐδαιμονία, implies the same thing for the other "parts of human excellence."

The second passage, 1145a6-11, has been quoted and discussed above (p. 104). I would just reinforce what I said there, that if φρόνησις is here made the servant of σοφία it is not implied that it pursues no other end than the flowering of the pure intellect. In fact, the second comparison (with statesmanship and its relation to religion) implies that it does have other purposes: the statesman's activity is hardly limited to arranging everything so that religious observances can go off without hindrance; this is just one of his responsibilities.

ultimate end is a life of moral *and* intellectual virtue, and in another part that the best such end is a life devoted exclusively to theorizing? On its face that would be a contradiction a good deal more blatant than the one I have uncovered in the intellectualist interpretation of Aristotle's theory of moral reasoning. I will return to this question in the next chapter; but first we must turn to the *Eudemian Ethics,* in order to further develop and evaluate the bipartite conception of *eudaimonia.*

Before turning to the *Eudemian Ethics,* however, it is important to notice one consequence of the interpretation I have given of the sixth book. I said earlier that in the first chapter of the book Aristotle might seem to give his reader to understand that the practically intelligent person has a definite criterion for determining which states of character are virtuous, and that this criterion is their conduciveness to the realization of the ultimate end. This encouraged us to identify the ultimate end as (a lifetime of) pure intellectual activity, since this end seemed to possess the definiteness and independence required if it was to serve as a criterion. On the other hand, as I pointed out, Aristotle never in the sixth book fulfills the promise that would be made in this passage, so interpreted, to state what this independent criterion is. And we have now seen that in the sixth book the ultimate end said to be pursued by the practically intelligent man is goodness of action itself. Hence this way of understanding the first chapter must be mistaken. Certainly the practically intelligent man can be said to determine which states of character are virtuous by considering them in the light of the ultimate end; but since the end is itself specified partly as morally good action, or better, a life of such action, it cannot provide a *criterion* of moral virtue. The process of deriving rules for the virtues by looking to the end now becomes, as I put it above, a progressive articulation of the end itself. Thus the process of deliberation, as it is exhibited in moral reasoning, follows the second of the two patterns distinguished at the end of the last chapter.

But if the practically intelligent man cannot, by looking to his ultimate end, obtain a criterion for the determination of the virtues, are we to infer that he *has* no criterion? This question will occupy our attention briefly in the next section. But appeal to a distinction made in Chapter I (pp. 60-61) may help to put the question at issue into proper perspective. *Prima facie*, at least, there would seem to be a distinction between the procedure which a practically intelligent man actually follows in making his practical decisions and other practical judgments, and the question of what proof, if any, there may be that the judgments he makes are correct. Even if in ordinary life practical reasoning, and more especially moral reasoning, does not arrive at rules by applying a defining criterion, there might nonetheless be a criterion, discoverable perhaps by philosophical reflection on moral experience, by which the results of ordinary moral reasoning could, at least to some extent, be defended. So, as I argued in Chapter I, Aristotle may be best interpreted as maintaining a theory of moral reasoning, and so of practical intelligence, which makes the *phronimos* operate without an independent criterion of virtue, while at the same time being prepared, in his capacity as philosopher, to put forward some such criterion. In the next section I shall offer an hypothesis as to what this criterion might be.

2. The *Eudemian Ethics* on Moral Virtue and Flourishing

Unlike the *Nicomachean Ethics*, the *Eudemian Ethics* does not formally make the concept of the ultimate end its central topic. Instead, Aristotle begins by taking issue with a Delian inscription which made three different things supreme respectively in beauty (*kalliston*), goodness, and pleasure. In fact, he says, *eudaimonia* is at once the best and most beautiful and also the pleasantest of all things. He then goes on (1214a14-15) to pose two questions about *eudaimonia*, around which the succeeding discussion is to revolve: namely, what it consists in and how those who have it come to get it. It is only in the second chapter (1214b6-14) that the notion of an ultimate end to be pursued in all one's actions is alluded to; so it is *eudaimonia* itself and not the notion of an ultimate end which occupies the center of the stage. Nonetheless, in the *Eudemian* as in the *Nicomachean Ethics*, Aristotle makes it clear that different conceptions of *eudaimonia* are in effect differences in the ultimate ends pursued by the persons who have those conceptions. And once the identification of *eudaimonia* as the ultimate end has been made, this aspect of *eudaimonia* dominates the ensuing attempt to say what it *is*.[24] As in the *Nicomachean Ethics*, it is *eudaimonia* as *telos tōn praktōn* ("end of what we do," *NE* 1097b21), as *to hōs telos agathon anthrōpōi kai to ariston tōn praktōn* ("the good for man, in the sense of an end, and the best of things realizable in action," *EE* 1218b25-26), that the *Eudemian Ethics'* account of human flourishing is meant to define.

The formal definitions of *eudaimonia* given in the two works are, however, clearly not the same. In the *Nicomachean Ethics*, as we have seen, the definition is incomplete; it makes flourishing consist in excellent spiritual activity of some kind, but without specifying the precise kind. Detailed specification depends upon further considerations to be advanced later on, in the tenth book. The *Eudemian* definition, however, makes no such reservations. It reads simply: "Flourishing is the activity of a complete life in accordance with complete excellence" (*zōēs teleias energeia kat' aretēn teleian*, II 1 1219a38-39). The meaning of "complete excellence" here is explained immediately before. Aristotle has said that *eudaimonia*, being something *teleon* (complete, fully developed), must be the exercise of something similarly *teleon*. But there are particular excellences as well as excellence taken as a whole (*hē men gar holē, hē de morion*, 1219a37)—literally, excellence the whole and excellence the part. So when he says that to flourish is to be active "with complete excellence" he means "with

[24] Particularly beginning in I 7, where Aristotle abandons the comparative examination of common opinions for a philosophical argument leading to his own definition. The ἄριστον τῶν ἀνθρώπῳ πρακτῶν (1217a39-40) is the same as the ultimate end (cf. 1218b9-14). But before chapter 7 the same point of view is to be found at 1215b17-18, τί τῶν ἐν τῷ ζῆν αἱρετόν, καὶ λαβὼν ἄν τις ἔχοι πλήρη τὴν ἐπιθυμίαν.

all the (soul's) excellences, taken together as making up a whole."
A little later he explains that in fact not all the soul's excellences
form part of this whole: excellence at digestion, for example,
which is a life-function and so something the soul performs, is
nonetheless not a part of *hē holē aretē*, excellence as a whole
(1219b10-11). One might have expected Aristotle to defend this
exclusion by drawing on, and further explaining, his earlier
distinction between what is actually a constituent part of
flourishing and what is merely a necessary condition of it (*hōn
aneu ouch hoion te eudaimonein,* 1214b36); as examples of the
latter he had mentioned breathing and being awake
(1214b19-20). In fact, however, the only reason he gives
(1219b37-39) is that these excellences are not, strictly speaking,
human excellences. They belong to us insofar as we are merely
alive, and not insofar as we are alive in a distinctively human way.

What excellences, then, are the parts of which *hē holē aretē*
consists? The answer is not made as obvious as it might be. To be
sure, Aristotle identifies the relevant parts of the soul as two in
number, *ta logou metechonta* (the rational parts, 1219b29), and
further specifies these as (the part responsible for) *logismos*
(reasoning) and that containing *orexis* (desire) and *pathēmata*
(passions) (1220a1-2). There is no doubt that at least the moral
virtues are included: they are the excellences of the "desiring
element" which, Aristotle explains here as in the *Nicomachean
Ethics,* "shares in *logos*" in the sense that it can be brought to
obey reason (1219b30). The doubt arises concerning the other
part. For in distinguishing the reasoning part from the
desires Aristotle actually alludes only to practical, and not
theoretical, uses of the mind. Thus he says that this part "shares
in *logos*" by giving orders (*tōi epitattein,* 1219b30), which is
plainly a function of the practical intellect.[25] And the *logismos*
which he says is distinctive of men is said to *archein . . . orexeōs
kai pathēmatōn* ("rule over desire and the passions," 1220a1-2).
This would seem to suggest that the distinctively human

[25] Cf. *NE* VI = *EE* V 1143a8, 1145a9.

excellences are the moral virtues, on the one hand, and the virtues of the *practical* intellect on the other. Nonetheless, it is clear from what Aristotle says elsewhere in this same book that the theoretical excellences, *sophia* and the rest, are meant to be included. For when he comes to name the two types of excellences corresponding to the two parts of the soul, he uses the generic names *ēthikē* ("pertaining to the character") and *dianoētikē* ("pertaining to the mind"), and to illustrate the latter he refers to *hoi sophoi* ("the wise," 1220a6, 12). And in chapter 4, in summarizing what he has said here, he refers to the *dianoētikai* (*aretai*), *hōn ergon alētheia, ē peri tou pōs echei ē peri geneseōs* ("intellectual excellences, whose function is truth, either as regards how things are or concerning coming into being" 1221b29-30), which is clearly a reference to the two classes of intellectual excellences distinguished in *NE* VI, the theoretical and the practical.[26] So the "complete virtue" in whose exercise *eudaimonia* consists, according to Aristotle in the *Eudemian Ethics*, is a whole made up of all the moral and intellectual excellences.[27] Thus in his definition of *eudaimonia* Aristotle in effect gives his answer to the question raised in the first book (1216a39-40), whether moral virtue and philosophical wisdom, or the actions expressing them, are *parts* of the good life or human flourishing; his answer on both counts is affirmative.

It is important to recognize that this account of human flourishing is in no way retracted or altered anywhere in the treatise. Admittedly, the concluding passage of the work, at least such of it as has come down to us, and in the arrangement in which it has been transmitted, has been thought by some to argue in favor of a

----

[26] Cf. *NE* VI = *EE* V 1139b8 περὶ τοῦ ἐσομένου with *De Part. An.* 640a3 τὸ ἐσόμενον and *Post. An.* 100a9.

[27] Thus, as noted above (n. 10), τελεία ἀρετή in the *EE*'s formula means something quite different from τελειοτάτη in the *NE*'s (1098a18). It has a different meaning also from τελεία ἀρετή in 1249a16, where the reference is to complete *moral* virtue (as also at *NE* = *EE* 1129b26, where it is applied to justice). Cf. also 1232a37-38, where πάσας τὰς ἀρετάς means "all the moral virtues," and not all the human excellences *simpliciter*.

wholly contemplative ideal. I will consider this passage fully in the next section, but I can say now in anticipation that the kind of precedence given there to intellectual values does not amount to a redefinition of *eudaimonia* in terms of theoretical excellence alone, nor (therefore) does it support the view that at the end of the *Eudemian Ethics*, as, apparently, in the tenth book of the *Nicomachean,* Aristotle comes out in favor of an intellectualist view of the best ultimate end for a human being to adopt.

There is no doubt that the *Eudemian* conception of human flourishing is more plausible, because more inclusive, than the intellectualist view. At the least, it makes the use of the mind in reasoning and acting morally a fundamental good, coordinate with the intellectual values realized in excellent theorizing. And a life organized round the pursuit of these two ends (or, more exactly, round the single end consisting of them both) would seem to be more reasonably structured than one organized round either end alone. For, assuming that there is a distinctive value in directing one's behavior in accordance with the rules of morality, this value would seem to be important enough so that one ought not to make its realization a mere by-product of the pursuit of intellectual values. To do this would be to suppose (absurdly) that no degree or amount of moral good is important enough to justify foregoing the attainment of the very slightest intellectual good, if it should turn out to be impossible to have both. The same could, I suppose, be said for intellectual values. So, even if one of the pair is more important than the other, each is important enough to deserve protection of the kind that can only be assured by making them both constituent parts of the ultimate end.

But though the *Eudemian* definition of human flourishing is more plausible than the intellectualist one, it is not on the face of it obvious why one should accept even it as the correct, or the best, definition. For, after all, on this definition only two values are taken as fundamental. Is it any more reasonable to be prepared to sacrifice all other actual or potential objects of desire to these two, than it would be to sacrifice the moral to the intellectual, or vice versa? Ought one not to grant a similarly

independent value to lots of other things, in addition to the values
of exercising moral control and using one's mind in speculation?
To take some partly un-Greek examples: there are values in work,
art, and personal relations which one might think should be
allowed an independent place, greater or smaller, in any reasonable conception of human flourishing. Yet it might seem that no
room is made for these or other such goods in Aristotle's scheme.
Would it really be reasonable to concentrate exclusively on moral
control and pure thinking, foregoing the realization of all other
possible goods except insofar as they make possible the dominant
pair?

I think this objection to Aristotle's view can to a considerable
extent be answered, once one understands what moral control
means for him. In effect, exercising moral control entails the realization of values of many other kinds besides moral value itself.
So even though these other values are not constituents of the
ultimate end, their claims are not neglected in Aristotle's scheme.
This point is worth developing at length.

To begin with, it is important to notice that in each of the
ethical treatises Aristotle shows himself aware of the fact that a
reasonable conception of human flourishing must make room for
a variety of different kinds of values, and not merely for one or
two. First of all, there is Aristotle's remark in the *Eudemian
Ethics* that in asking what *eudaimonia* consists in one is asking
what would fully satisfy one's desires if one had it ([*ti*] *labōn an tis
echoi plērē tēn epithumian*).[28] Now of course what would satisfy
someone's desires depends on what his desires are; so that the attainment of an ultimate end consisting of only a single activity,
like contemplation, or some few activities, would satisfy the
desires of someone who desired nothing else. But Aristotle's
remark would be trivial if he were not taking it for granted that
any human being's desires are to some extent and in some ways
fixed and not up to him or anyone else to alter beyond a certain

---

[28] I 5 1215b18. Note that τί τῶν ἐν τῷ ζῆν αἱρετόν, b17, = τί τὸ εὖ καὶ τί
τὸ ἀγαθὸν τὸ ἐν τῷ ζῆν, 1216a10.

point. Obviously, Aristotle is supposing here that the desires a person has are partly at least given at birth or acquired in the course of the natural process of maturation, so that no one can avoid having desires of a number of different kinds. Plainly if in attaining *eudaimonia* one's desires are fully satisfied, and if one inescapably has a variety of different desires, no conception of *eudaimonia* can be satisfactory unless it provides fairly explicitly for a number of different good things answering to the different desires.

There are other passages of a similar tendency in the ethical writings. The most noteworthy of these is in the *Magna Moralia*.[29] The author is explaining the sense in which *eudaimonia* is the best thing there is. He has said (1184a8-12) that *eudaimonia* is a *teleion,* or complete good, in the sense that it is something such that if we have it we need nothing further.

"Suppose," he says, "someone should say that philosophic wisdom (*phronēsis*) is the best of all good things, compared singly. But perhaps the best good [in the sense in which *eudaimonia* is the best good] is not to be sought for by this method. For we are seeking the *teleion,* or complete good, and wisdom by itself is not complete [that is, after one has it one still needs other things as well]. So this is not the best thing which we

---

[29] The general consensus that the *MM* is a late compendium of Peripatetic moral theory, which has prevailed among scholars at least until the publication of F. Dirlmeier's German translation and commentary (1958), seems to me not sufficiently supported by careful and sensitive reading of the treatise. See my article, "The *Magna Moralia* and Aristotle's Moral Philosophy," *American Journal of Philology* 94 (1973), 327-349. But whatever may be the truth about the origin of the work as a whole, it is quite clear that *MM* 11-3, in which the passage cited is found, consists of material not drawn from either *NE* or *EE* or any other extant Aristotelian writing, and the references in chap. 2 to διαιρέσεις have very plausibly been argued by Dirlmeier (*Magna Moralia*, p. 186) to signal the use there, whether by Aristotle or by some later compiler, of the Διαιρέσεις mentioned in ancient lists of Aristotle's writings. So even if the *MM* were as a whole composed by someone else from Aristotelian materials, we have in this section Aristotelian materials not available to us elsewhere. I do not think there is any serious danger of being misled by treating the passage cited as containing genuine Aristotelian doctrine.

are seeking, nor is what is best in this way [best in the way *we* mean.]" (1184a34-38)

This passage of the *Magna Moralia* is also the key to the obscure remark in the *Nicomachean Ethics* (1097b16-17), alluded to earlier, that *eudaimonia* is most choiceworthy of all things without being added in (*pantōn hairetōtatēn mē sunarith-moumenēn*). The point being made in both passages is the same: in *eudaimonia* one attains a number of different good objects, which together meet all one's needs and desires. This is plainly to treat *eudaimonia* as what I have been calling an "inclusive end," or more fully, as an inclusive second-order end.

Now the simplest way to conceive of *eudaimonia* as an inclusive second-order end is to view it as a whole of which all the various desired good things, or types of good things, are the parts: that is, to view it as made up of the various first-order goods. The *Magna Moralia* seems to take this line in a passage just before the one quoted. "*Eudaimonia*," it says, "is composed of certain good things . . . it is nothing else besides these, it *is* these" (1184a26-29). The goods in question are not named, but the "parts of *eudaimonia*" listed in the *Rhetoric* (1360b19 ff) are examples of the kind of thing that is apparently envisaged. This list begins: good birth, plenty of friends, good friends, wealth, good children; and it contains also health, beauty, strength, fame, and virtue. Now this is a mixed group, including, as Aristotle himself remarks, both "external" and "internal" goods,[30] and it is one of the most important theses of the ethical treatises that the possession and mere use of the external and most of what are here called internal goods cannot be what

[30] Here (1360b25-28) Aristotle counts as external only things that are external to the person, so that health and beauty count as internal. More usually, however (as, e.g., at *NE* 1099a31 ff and *EE* 1248b27-30, where 1249a15 shows φύσει ἀγαθά = ἐκτὸς ἀγαθά), the goods of the body, which count by the *Rhet.*'s criterion as internal, are reckoned as external. "External" usually seems to mean "external to the soul"; cf. *EE* 1218b32 πάντα δὴ τὰ ἀγαθὰ ἢ ἐκτὸς ἢ ἐν ψυχῇ and other similar passages. To avoid confusion I shall follow this latter usage.

eudaimonia consists in. To think the contrary is to confuse those things which one must have if one is to flourish with the condition of flourishing itself.[31] *Why* Aristotle thinks it would be an instance of this confusion to equate flourishing with the possession (or even the use) of all these good things is another question, to which I shall turn in a moment. The fact that he does think this, however, is beyond dispute; and this means that he cannot treat *eudaimonia* as a second-order end in the straight-forward way suggested by the *Magna Moralia* passage just examined—that is, as simply composed of these various first-order goods.[32]

Aristotle's reason for rejecting this way of thinking is quite simple, though its significance, curiously enough, is usually over-looked. Aristotle points out that the actual attainment of external goods is in large measure the result of sheer good fortune; but *eudaimonia* must be something which is attained, if at all, by a person's own efforts. The theory that moral character and the actions to which it gives rise (partly) constitute *eudaimonia* accords with this requirement, because everyone is responsible for his own character and its manifestations. But the view that the possession or the use of external goods constitutes *eudaimonia* conflicts with it. This point is argued at several places in the Corpus, including passages in both of the *Ethics*. Perhaps the clearest statement is found in *Politics* VII. There Aristotle says his own view of *eudaimonia* is supported by the facts about god,

who is *eudaimōn* and blessed, but not on account of any external goods but on account of himself and because he is by nature of a certain sort — which shows that being fortunate must be different from flourishing. For the goods external to the soul come of themselves and by chance, but no one is just or temperate by or through chance (1323b24-29).

[31] See *EE* 1214b12-14, 24-27; *NE* 1099a31-b8.

[32] I conjecture that this is why Aristotle does not make more, in the two *Ethics*, of the fact that on his view εὐδαιμονία is an inclusive second-order end. To do so would run the risk of suggesting, as we have seen the *MM* suggests, that εὐδαιμονία is just a collection of various concrete good things.

124 Reason and Human Good in Aristotle

The two *Ethics* are making the same point about the external goods when they maintain that it is a mistake to make *eudaimonia* consist in anything which is the gift of chance (*EE* 1215a12-19, *NE* 1099b18-25): for in saying this they are, of course, presupposing that it is external goods which people come to possess as a result of chance.[33]

The importance of this is evident. First of all, it shows that Aristotle goes out of his way to avoid the error which some allege is endemic to Greek moral thinking, namely, the glorification of success, however attained. For Aristotle, *eudaimonia* is necessarily the result of a person's own efforts; success, of whatever kind, could only count as *eudaimonia* if due to one's own efforts. But, secondly, and more importantly from our present point of view, these passages suggest an interpretation of what moral virtue is that will allow Aristotle's theory of human flourishing to satisfy his own requirement that a variety of different independent values be provided for.

Aristotle, as we have seen, rejects the view that human flourishing can consist in the possession of the classic external goods of health, wealth, and friends and other good things for the distribution of which fortune is responsible, on the ground that on that view a person could be said to be flourishing even though

---

[33] The relationship between τὰ ἐκτὸς ἀγαθά and τὰ ἀπὸ τύχης, and their connection with εὐδαιμονία, is not made perfectly clear and consistent in the *Ethics*. Often τὰ ἐκτός seem to be limited to certain broadly useful instrumental goods like wealth, strength, health, political influence, and friends (regarded not as partners in social life but as instruments to be used in one's private projects): thus *NE* 1099a31 ff, 1178a23-24. On the other hand, in passages like *EE* VIII 3 1248b8–1249a16 (on καλοκἀγαθία), to be discussed in a moment, τὰ φύσει (or ἁπλῶς) ἀγαθά, which are apparently identified with τὰ ἐκτός (1249a15), are a much wider group: included, I think, are all kinds of goods other than the excellences themselves, goods such as sexual intercourse, the goods of social fellowship, food, drink, and so on. Similarly, the goods of fortune seem sometimes to be simply equated with τὰ ἐκτός of the classic restricted list, as e.g. at *NE* 1099b8 (and cf. *NE* = *EE* 1153b18 τῶν ἐκτὸς καὶ τῆς τύχης: καί epexegetical); sometimes εὐτυχίαι are counted as one *among* τὰ ἐκτός (see e.g. *EE* 1248b29); but yet again in the chapter on εὐτυχία in the *EE* (VIII 2) a much broader view is assumed. There, a

he had not applied his mind to working out and securing his own well-being. But it is repugnant, Aristotle correctly thinks, to our idea of what it is for a human being to flourish, to allow that anyone is flourishing except insofar as he has taken charge of his own life. It is rather in the taking charge that flourishing consists. Now according to Aristotle, to take intelligent and effective charge of one's life is in the first instance to come to possess, and exercise, the virtues of character. It is tempting to suggest that Aristotle regards as moral virtues those states of character which one ought to acquire if one is to be in the best position (so far as this is determined by oneself) to secure the basic, first-order goods, including prominently the goods distributed by fortune.[34] This suggestion can, I think, be best explained and developed in the course of an examination of the main passages in Aristotle that tend to support it.

On the view I am suggesting, to flourish is not actually to possess a full portion of all the basic good things, but rather to be living in accordance with principles which are rationally calculated to secure them. The correct ultimate end to pursue is not the collection of first-order goods themselves but the maintenance of the pattern of control designed to bring about their attainment. The value that Aristotle makes fundamental is the

---

good actually attained by fortune is any object one wanted to achieve or bring about, and which one might have tried to achieve by taking thought and planning, but which one got, unexpectedly, without making any intelligent effort to achieve it. Aristotle mentions here the effect of luck on the successful outcome of even planned endeavors, such as those of the intelligent general or helmsman (1247a6). Now when he has in mind only the classic instrumental goods, like health and wealth, Aristotle thinks of them as needed by the person who flourishes as instruments for the performance of his proper activities: money needed for acts of beneficence, strength for the larger acts of courage, and so on. But when the broader usage of τὰ ἐκτός and τὰ ἀπὸ τύχης is in his mind, he can hardly think of the goods in question as merely in this way instrumental (see n. 46 below). In what follows I concentrate on the broader class of goods and try to show how in the EE Aristotle thought of their relation to εὐδαιμονία.

[34] Cf. *Rhet.* I 9 1366a36-8: ἀρετὴ δ' ἐστι μὲν δύναμις . . . ποριστικὴ ἀγαθῶν καὶ φυλακτική.

value of rational design in the pursuit of these goods, rather than
the value of the goods themselves.[35] Strictly, this should mean
that a person has achieved his ultimate end if he is living that
kind of life, whether or not the expected basic goods are actually
forthcoming—so that if two persons have the same good
character, but one is thwarted and disappointed at every turn by
blows of fate, while the other's life is one dazzling success after
another, they would have to be said to flourish in precisely the
same degree. Sensibly enough, Aristotle shies away from this
paradox when, for example, he remarks against Socrates that

those who say that the man who is tortured on the rack or beset by
great blows of ill-fortune is flourishing, provided he is a good
man, are talking nonsense, whether they mean to or not (*NE* VII
= *EE* VI 1153b19-21).[36]

But it is not easy to see exactly how he thought his own theory of
eudaimonia could accommodate this insight; and elsewhere
(1100b30-33) he emphasizes the morally virtuous man's indifference to even large-scale ill-fortune. This his theory allows him to
do, because, of course, the overriding concern of a virtuous
person's life is with, as we might put it, the fitness to achieve success rather than success itself, and he retains the knowledge, even

[35] To see the importance of this distinction, consider the difference between
the value of the food a person eats and the value of his feeding it to himself.
It is a value of this latter family that Aristotle makes fundamental. See
Thomas Nagel's interesting discussion of these values in *The Possibility of
Altruism* (Oxford: Clarendon Press, 1970), pp. 92 ff.

[36] This is nonsense because though he is living virtuously he does not have
the expected successes. One might interpret the paradox otherwise: being
on the rack, it might be said, a person is prevented from exercising his
virtuous capacities, and flourishing consists in the exercise, not just in the
possession, of virtue—so that a virtuous person on the rack does not after
all flourish. But on Aristotle's theory εὐδαιμονία requires only a lifetime of
regular, not one of *continuous*, virtuous activity. And being prevented while
on the rack from acting virtuously need not disrupt one's whole life or any
considerable part of it. Likewise, not every blow of misfortune affects one's
capacity to engage in regular virtuous activity. So I prefer the interpretation
in the text. See also 1099a31 ff, 1100a8-9.

in near-disastrous misfortune, that he has attained this end. Compared with *this* success his disappointments are of small moment. He has no ground to regret his choice of life; if it has nonetheless turned out badly, that is the fault of the inescapable vagaries of chance, and he has the considerable satisfaction of knowing that he has done all that any human being could reasonably do. Though one may well think that Aristotle here exaggerates the importance of mere fitness to obtain the various basic goods, there can be no doubt that he is right to emphasize it as an important part of our idea of human flourishing.

But although these first-order goods themselves do not form part of the fundamental value in Aristotle's scheme, their claims do not go unattended to. For the states of character whose realization and maintenance do partly constitute the ultimate end themselves entail a comparative evaluation of the worth of various kinds of good things, and the consequent tendency to try to obtain those good things in accordance with that evaluation of their worth. Under ordinary circumstances the virtuous person can expect to attain them, as well. I have already alluded in passing to this fact about the moral virtues, but I must now show that Aristotle's theory of virtue is really founded on it.

In several places in the ethical treatises Aristotle distinguishes between things which are good *haplōs* (absolutely, without qualification) or *phusei* (by nature), and those which are good merely *tini* (for some particular person, or from some particular person's point of view).[37] In some of the same contexts, as well as others, he also draws the related contrast between *to agathon* and *to phainomenon agathon*, the good and the apparent good.[38] In drawing both distinctions Aristotle makes the morally virtuous person's experience decisive: what appears good to him *is* good, what is good for him or from his point of view is good without qualification and by nature. The connection Aristotle makes in

[37] *EE* 1235b30 ff, 1236b32 ff, 1238a3 ff, 1228b18 ff, 1248b26 ff; *NE = EE* 1152b26, 1129b3-5. Cf. also 1176b24-27.

[38] *EE* 1236a10, 1227a22, 1235b26 ff; *NE* 1113a16, 1114a32.

several passages[39] between apparent good and pleasure suggests
the following way of distinguishing *phainomenon agathon* and
agathon tini: what *appears good* to a person is what he actually
enjoys doing and wants to do, whereas what is good *for him* is
what, given the totality of desires, interests, and so on, that he actually has, promotes his good.[40] Thus something could *appear
good* to someone, because he enjoys it, while yet it would not be
good for him, much less good absolutely and without
qualification. And vice versa. Thus the effect of making the
morally virtuous person the measure of what is really good and
good without qualification is twofold. What he enjoys is really
and not merely apparently good; and what promotes his good, as
this is determined by the interests, desires, and so on, which he
actually has, is absolutely and unqualifiedly good. Now this is to
treat the desires and interests of the morally virtuous person as
providing a norm for others, even though they do not have the
desires that he has: just as what appears bitter to a normal
healthy palate *is* bitter, so (Aristotle says at *NE* 1113a26-31) what
appears good to the virtuous man and what is good for him is
good, period.

That this principle is meant to provide a practical norm is
clear, because Aristotle is prepared to draw practical consequences from it. Thus in discussing the question whether one
should regard as one's friend the person who is unqualifiedly,
i.e., morally, good, or the person who is good for oneself, i.e.,
satisfies needs and interests one happens to have, Aristotle has
the following to say:

The two [viz., the unqualified good and the good for oneself]
must be made to come together. For what is not unqualifiedly

[39] *De Motu An.* 700b29, *EE* 1235b26-27.

[40] This applies, I believe, even to akratic and enkratic persons: for though
they may know full well that what they have done (or been strongly tempted
to do) and will want to do again is bad, it will nonetheless, at least inter-
mittently, continue to appear good to them. Cf. *De An.* III 3 428b2-4: you
can know that something is bad even while, because you want it, it appears
good to you.

good but may chance to be bad[41] is to be avoided; and although what is not good for a given man is no concern of his, still what is sought for is that unqualified goods should be good in just this way. For the unqualified good is the [unqualified] object of choice, but the choice for oneself is what is good for oneself: and these ought to agree. This is produced by moral virtue; and the job of the political art is to see to it that this agreement occurs in those in whom it does not yet exist (*EE* 1236b36-1237a3).[42]

This amounts to saying that we ought to come to have the desires and interests of the morally good person, so that in the long run it is the unqualified good which we should try to obtain, and not the good which suits the desires we may happen to have. In particular, we ought to bring it about that those we choose as friends are not merely good from our own particular point of view, as every genuine friend must be, but also unqualifiedly and morally good as well. We must become the sort of person who is benefited by and enjoys association with the virtuous. But what ground does Aristotle have for saying this?

The first point to notice is that the unqualified goods, which are good for the morally virtuous person or from his point of view, form a large and varied class of desirable things. In two separate passages of the *Eudemian Ethics* (IV = *NE* V 1129b1-6 and VIII 1248b26-1249a2) Aristotle identifies these as the goods which fortune has a hand in distributing, including the classic external goods of honor, wealth, the bodily excellences, friends, and power and influence. The goods of fortune, as I remarked above, despite the limited list of examples, certainly include most of the ordinary and not so ordinary things people have reason to want, given normal human desires and needs: luck affects the attainment of all of these. The only goods Aristotle clearly excepts from this rule are the moral and intellectual excellences themselves. The first exception is plainly made in favor of the

---

[41] Reading ἄν πως for the second ἁπλῶς of the manuscripts in 1236b37 (with Jackson and recent editors).

[42] Cf. 1238a3-8 with *NE* = *EE* 1129b4-6; also *Met.* Z 3 1029b6-7.

intuition, which he attempts to defend elsewhere, that to be an independent adult agent entails that one accept as one's own the character one has got, however in fact it may have been formed. The second exception is a concession to the Platonic idea, which Aristotle makes his own, that the expression of the intellectual powers is a free act of the intellectual personality. But with these two exceptions, I believe the unqualified goods (*agatha haplōs* or *phusei agatha*), which are subject to intervention by fortune, include the objects of all the normal human desires and interests.[43]

According to Aristotle, then, these things will be good from the point of view of the virtuous man, but perhaps not good for less than virtuous persons, as they are actually constituted. The reason why they are not always good for the nonvirtuous is, Aristotle says, that such people are apt to do themselves harm as a result of getting them (1248b30-34). An intemperate man, he suggests, would not profit from the uses to which he might put a quantity of money: presumably because, though he will be enabled thereby to satisfy more of his many carnal desires than he otherwise could, the consequent loss of other goods, such as bodily and perhaps also mental vigor, more than outweighs the increase in quantity of sensual pleasure. Thus he would be better off without the money, even considering the deprivation he would have to undergo as a result.

There are two ways in which one might begin to develop this point, and correspondingly two ways in which the virtuous person might be said to be in a superior position. First, taking the intemperate man's good to consist simply in the objects of the interests and desires he actually has, it could be said that there is a gross internal conflict between his carnal desires and other interests he

---

[43] See n. 33 above. These goods are also, I think, the good things which Aristotle several times in *NE = EE* V calls τὰ ἀνθρώπινα ἀγαθά, the human goods (not to be confused with τὸ ἀνθρώπινον ἀγαθόν), which he says the φρόνιμος is expert in evaluating: cf. 1140b21, 1141b8. Cf. also τὰ ἀνθρώπῳ ἀγαθά, 1140b5 (cf. a26) and similar expressions.

has: he cannot help but be, on balance, relatively badly off, because to satisfy his voracious appetites entails the imposition of actual suffering and dissatisfaction later on, whereas in order to prevent the later dissatisfaction extreme deprivation must be borne earlier.[44] By contrast, then, the virtuous person's desires and interests would constitute a coherent whole: the amount of carnal desire he feels can be satisfied without injury to health or the production of lethargy, and, on the other side, the interest he takes in other pursuits does not require that his carnal desires be frustrated. All the different types of desires and interests he has can be harmoniously satisfied. So, the intemperate person will be no better off, and perhaps somewhat worse off, if he does have the means to satisfy his desires.

But, secondly, a further point might also be intended. The intemperate man might by his self-indulgence be said to be preventing the full development in himself of certain desires and interests of a kind which, if he had them, instead of the ones he actually continues to have, he would be better off. What it means to say, on this ground, that he would be better off is different from what it meant on the other: there it meant a greater fulfillment, on balance, of the desires and interests he actually has, but here his desires and interests are regarded as subject to development and change, and the claim is made that he is worse off to settle, as it were, for the satisfaction, so far as this is at all possible, of his actual desires, rather than their alteration. The ground of preference here is certainly not immediately obvious, but the fundamental idea would be that on some absolute scale the total amount of satisfaction in the intemperate life, even at its best, is less than that in another kind of life, also originally available to the intemperate man: the total quantity of goods achieved by the one kind of man is greater than that achieved by the other.[45] By contrast with the nonvirtuous, then, the virtuous

[44] Cf. *NE* 1166b7-25 on the μεταμέλεια of οἱ φαῦλοι.

[45] I have deliberately avoided discussing the controversial question how this quantity of good is to be measured. I think Aristotle relies on simple

person would have the character which provides him with the best possible set of desires and interests, in the sense that the good things he will (or can expect to) achieve in life constitute the greatest sum of good possible for a human being.[46]

I think that Aristotle had in mind both of these ways in which a morally virtuous person might be said to be better off than any nonvirtuous person. The set of interests and desires which is given to him in the character he has attained is both a consistent and harmonious whole, and also the best such set a human being can acquire. For present purposes, however, what matters is that on either view the virtuous person's character does give him an interest in a variety of different good things—the classic external goods, as well as all the other goods of fortune—which, as he goes through life, he chooses each in its turn and each to the right quantity and degree. It is therefore clear that, in making the exercise of the moral virtues a constituent part of the ultimate end, Aristotle also allows for the full realization, in the best life as defined by that end, of many different interests and many different kinds of good things. Having a virtuous character entails placing a value on each of these different good things, in some

---

intuitive ideas like the following: the cultivation of taste in music and art repays the effort involved in learning to appreciate them; whereas the active cultivation of the pleasures of couch and palate do not, or not as much. Naturally this ultimately amounts to claiming that any one who makes himself virtuous *will* find the "higher pleasures" more important than the "lower." But this fact might itself be based on general truths about human psychology which would support the claim of maximality. Rawls, in chap. VII of *A Theory of Justice*, develops this possibility. How far Aristotle had any concrete theory in mind here I would rather not venture to say.

[46] I believe this thought lies behind what Aristotle says about the πολιτική ἕξις which characterized the Spartans (*EE* VIII 3 1248b37-1249a16). These were people who cultivated the moral virtues, but as a means of getting the φύσει ἀγαθά, and not for their own sakes. They were, in other words, people who concentrated only on the first-order goods, making it their ultimate aim to achieve the greatest total quantity of these, and judging that to be virtuous is the best means to this end. By contrast, the truly virtuous person concentrates on the state of character first and the goods it enables one to get second. Plainly the φύσει ἀγαθά here include very much more than the classic instrumental external goods.

cases greater and in others less; and living according to virtue entails pursuing these objects according to that evaluation of their comparative worth. The conception of the ultimate end as partly consisting in a life of morally virtuous action, therefore, is in effect a conception of *eudaimonia* as a comprehensively inclusive second-order end.

3. The *Eudemian Ethics* on Intellectual Values

So far I have been considering the moral virtues and the consequences of making them constituents of the ultimate end. But, as already noted, Aristotle makes the intellectual excellences, and particularly the excellences of pure theoretical thinking, equally part of the ultimate end. This feature of his theory also calls for comment.

It can seem surprising, if the matter is regarded from the point of view of the theory developed in the preceding section, that Aristotle should make the exercise of the theoretical excellences part of the ultimate end at all. For this activity would seem to be just one of the first-order goods, though perhaps the most important of them, as the *Magna Moralia* claims, and therefore it might seem that it should enter the scheme in the same indirect way that the external goods and the other goods of fortune do, and not stand alongside moral virtue as a coordinate constituent of *eudaimonia*. But there is a good reason, already alluded to, why nonetheless the exercise of these excellences cannot simply be treated as parallel to the other first-order goods. Succinctly put, it is that on Aristotle's view *sophia* is not a good of fortune, as the other first-order goods are. Where goods of fortune are concerned, all one need do is to become morally virtuous and live accordingly: provided that fortune does not maliciously interfere, these goods will be forthcoming. But it is not so with the highest intellectual values. One must subject oneself to further training in order to realize these; the achievement of the theoretical excellences is a further task, in addition to the attainment of a morally virtuous character, which one must undertake if one is to have even a chance for the greatest sum of good possible for a human

being. Hence it is entirely in order for Aristotle to make the
activity of excellent theoretical thinking part of the ultimate end,
and not merely an object pursued indirectly through the exercise
of the moral virtues.

On the *Eudemian* theory, then, the person who flourishes
actively displays an excellent developed moral personality and an
excellent developed intellectual personality. *Qua* morally virtuous, he is implicitly committed to a relative evaluation of the
importance of the basic goods of all the various types: the bodily
pleasures, the goods of social intercourse, material possessions,
instrumental goods like wealth, and finally, intellectual values.
His moral character consists in the disposition to make all his
choices in such a way that this scheme of goods can expectably be
realized. For the acquisition of the intellectual goods, however,
moral character is not enough; so in addition to pursuing intellectual values, along with the others, by maintaining a good moral
character, the man who flourishes will pursue them directly by
maintaining and exercising a well-developed theoretical intellect.

I have already noted in passing that Aristotle does not attempt
to spell out precisely what the principles are according to which
the morally virtuous person assesses the relative value of these
various good things. For the most part he seems content to hold
that one learns such things by experience, and he emphasizes in
two often-quoted passages of the *Nicomachean Ethics* the impos-
sibility of articulating *detailed* principles in any case:

It is not easy to determine how one ought to become angered, with
whom and on what sort of grounds and for how long, or up to
what point one acts rightly or goes wrong . . . It is not easy to
declare in a rule (*tōi logōi*) by how much or what manner of
variance a person becomes blameworthy. For the decision
depends upon the particular facts and upon perception.[47]

But he fails even to state the broader principles which he implies
might be helpfully formulated. And, as I have already remarked,

[47] *NE* IV 5 1126a32-b4. See also II 9 1109b14-23. It is noteworthy that
similar sentiments are nowhere voiced in the *Eudemian Ethics*.

he does not explain what criterion is to be used in deciding upon these broad principles, or in defending them once adopted. I have conjectured that he means to appeal to the notion that the principles of the moral virtues are such as will, under normal conditions and for normal persons, lead to the achievement of the maximum combination of first-order goods. But this idea is only suggested by things that he says, and not stated by him; nor does he give any indication how the claim of maximality might be made out. It is, in short, a conviction Aristotle has about moral virtue rather than a developed *theory* of virtue.

On the other hand, as we have seen from the *Magna Moralia* and elsewhere, Aristotle does hold that among the first-order goods intellectual attainments come first. The nature of this priority is only explained in any detail in a single passage of the *Eudemian Ethics*, and nowhere in the *Nicomachean*. To understand what Aristotle is saying in this *Eudemian* passage will require more careful reading than the text has usually been given. For on the passage in question, which concludes the treatise (in the form in which it has come down to us),[48] Jaeger based his

---

[48] In all our manuscripts the treatise concludes with the three chapters which together make up book VIII. They have no apparent connection with what immediately precedes (if one brackets φίλῳ, 1246a26, as a particularly inept attempt of some scribe to provide the missing connection), nor do the opening words (ἀπορήσειε δ᾽ἄν τις) suggest the introduction of a new topic of discussion; and the book concludes so abruptly that many have suspected that a continuation of the passage has somehow been lost. It is interesting that in the Middle Ages (so far as has yet been discovered) the only part of the *EE* to be translated into Latin was VIII 2 and 3 (VIII 2 with the first sentence of 3, to 1248b11, forming the Greek original of the second part of the little book *De Bona Fortuna*, while three medieval manuscripts contain a translation of the whole of VIII 3, either by itself or together with VIII 2: cf. Dirlmeier, *Eudemische Ethik*, 119-120). This fact, together with the fragmentary appearance of the book as a whole, suggests that possibly what we know as book VIII early became detached from the rest of the treatise and in that form had an independent history. The further reflection that in the *MM* the corresponding passage comes not at the end, after the discussion of friendship, but rather immediately before (II 7 1206a36–II 10), has led Dirlmeier (*EE*, 366-367) to revive the view of Spengel (*Uber die unter dem Namen des A. erhaltenen ethischen Schriften*, 499-503) and von Arnim

treatment of the *Eudemian Ethics* as containing what he called a
"theonomic ethics" in which god was regarded as a "highest
good" from the knowledge of which a rule of life might be
deduced.[49] Such an overblown interpretation cannot, however,
withstand confrontation with the text itself.

The passage reads as follows:

> Since even the doctor has a principle of determination by refer-
> ring to which he decides what is healthy for a body and what is
> not, and how far each thing ought to be done and is good for
> health, while if done less or more it is no longer so; so also the
> morally good person must in doing and choosing things that are
> naturally good but not praiseworthy have a principle for
> determining his possession and choice and avoidance both in
> quantity, great or small, of money and in things distributed by
> fortune. In the preceding we said [this principle of determination]
> is "as reason [*logos*] directs." But this is just as if some one with
> regard to food should say "As medicine and its principles (*ho
> logos tautēs*) direct." For this is true, but obscure.—Well, one
> must as in other matters live with reference to that which rules [*to
> archon*], that is, with reference to the condition which accords

(*Sitzungsberichte d. Wien. Akad.* 202(2), 96; *Rhein. Mus.* 76 [1927] 114-115),
that the fragment has been wrongly placed in our manuscripts of the *EE*,
and that originally its position was at the end of *EE* VI (which he takes to
have been an earlier version of what is now *NE* VII). This would give the
EE the same order of topics and general construction as the *MM*, so that it
would conclude with an account of friendship and not, as it does in our
manuscripts, with the references to contemplation which some have wanted
to see as a counterpart of *NE* X6-9, with its intellectualist definition of
εὐδαιμονία. Dirlmeier's motive for wanting to make this adjustment is
apparently to underscore the truth that *EE* VIII 3 is not to be interpreted in
parallel to *NE* X6-9. This motive I applaud; though the truth in question is
not made doubtful by leaving these chapters where they stand. But, so
far as I can see, these chapters cannot have preceded book VII, since at
VIII 3 1249a17-18 Aristotle unmistakably refers *back* to the argument of
VII 2 1235b30 ff—an argument, indeed, found nowhere else in the Corpus.
Dirlmeier's invention (*EE*, 497-498) of a passage for *EE* VI in which the same
thing was said is best left undiscussed. So, whatever may be the correct
explanation of the fragmentary character of these three chapters, it does not
seem possible for them to have originally stood in book VI, or indeed anywhere before the end of VII.

[49] W. Jaeger, *Aristotle*, 238-246.

with the activity of that which rules, as a slave lives with reference to that of his master, and each thing with reference to its appropriate ruling authority. But since a human being is naturally constituted of a ruling part and a ruled, and each person ought to live according to their own [sic] ruling authority—and this has two senses: for medicine is authoritative in one way and health in another; the former exists for the sake of the latter.[50] And this holds for the contemplative faculty. For god is not a ruler in the sense of issuing commands, but he is that for the sake of which practical intelligence issues commands (that for the sake of which has two senses; they have been distinguished elsewhere), since *he* has no need for anything. So whatever choice and possession of things good by nature will most produce the contemplation of god—whether goods of the body, or money or friends or the other goods—this is best, and this is the finest principle of determination. But whatever choice hinders the service of god by contemplation, whether by being deficient or by being excessive, this is bad. (*EE* VIII 3 1249a21-b23)

Now taken out of context, as it has often been read, this passage might plausibly be interpreted together with the opening lines of *NE* VI=*EE* V, quoted and discussed above (pp. 101 ff). Each passage raises the question of what *horos*, or principle of

[50] Text and interpretation in this sentence are uncertain. The "since"-clause lacks an apodosis (καί 10 to ζῆν 11 not being correctly so taken: cf. W. J. Verdenius, "Human Reason and God in the *Eudemian Ethics*," *Untersuchungen zur Eudemischen Ethik*, ed. P. Moraux and D. Harlfinger, Berlin: de Gruyter, 1971, p. 287), and ἑαυτῶν 11 jars badly with ἕκαστον. Verdenius thinks that ἕκαστον here means "each of the two parts" just said to constitute the human being, so that the thought Aristotle means to express is this: since the human being consists of two parts, and each of these parts ought to live according to its authority (but authority has two senses), the lower part should live according to the authority (in sense 1) of the higher and the higher should live according to the authority (in sense 2) of god, the object of its contemplation. Perhaps this is right; although ἕκαστον, instead of ἑκάτερον, remains awkward, despite Verdenius' disclaimer, and to speak of the parts of the soul as *living* according to this or that seems an odd and uncharacteristic extravagance. The detail here fortunately does not much matter for my purposes; on any reasonable interpretation of these lines, Aristotle is declaring that the contemplation of god is an end that ought to determine certain choices, and my interest is in understanding what choices these are, not in the details of god's mode of rulership. (On the reference of "god" in this passage see below n. 56.)

determination, the morally good man uses in making certain decisions, and each insists on the necessity of there being such a principle by comparing the good man's situation to the doctor's.[51] But the *Eudemian* context shows clearly that the passages are not concerned with the *same* decisions of the good person. For in the sixth-book passage the question is how to determine which dispositions are intermediate and morally good (*tis estin horos tōn mesotētōn*, 1138b23); that is, this passage concerns the reasoning engaged in by the good person in deciding what is the morally virtuous thing to do. But the *Eudemian* passage professes to answer only the question what principle for determining his choice of *naturally good but not praiseworthy* things the morally good person possesses. And, as becomes clear from the context, these choices are not identical with choices made because required by the virtues themselves. For a little earlier in the chapter (1248b18-25) Aristotle distinguishes between those good things that are also noble (and hence praiseworthy) and those that are good but not praiseworthy; and in the former class he

---

[51] See also *MM* II 10 1208a5-30, which "corresponds" to *EE* VIII 3 1249a21–b25 both in the sense that it too follows immediately on an account of καλοκἀγαθία, and, in a rough way, in its content. The differences between the two passages are, however, more important than their similarities. *MM* II 10 does not refer to any ὅρος, either for determining what is virtuous or for anything else; nor does it raise directly the question what standard the virtuous person (or the doctor) uses in reaching his conclusions. The *MM*'s question concerns rather whether, and how far, an explicit and informative account can be given of what morally virtuous action consists in (which is not formally equivalent to the question what criterion, if any, the morally virtuous person uses). Furthermore, the answer given is emphatically not: "to act virtuously is to promote so far as possible excellent contemplation," although, hastily read, it might be so misinterpreted (see ἔστιν οὖν κατὰ τὸν ὀρθὸν λόγον πράττειν, ὅταν τὸ ἄλογον μέρος τῆς ψυχῆς μὴ κωλύῃ τὸ λογιστικὸν ἐνεργεῖν τῆν αὐτοῦ ἐνέργειαν, 1208a9-11; ὅταν οὖν τὰ πάθη μὴ κωλύωσι τὸν νοῦν τὸ αὐτοῦ ἔργον ἐνεργεῖν, τότ' ἔσται τὸ κατὰ τὸν ὀρθὸν λόγον γινόμενον, 1208a19-20). The Platonic expression τὸ λογιστικόν, together with the reference to νοῦς doing its own job (τὸ αὐτοῦ ἔργον), shows the error of reading the reference to the activity of νοῦς as an appeal to contemplation as the end and standard of morally virtuous activity. The argument of the passage hardly differs at all from things that Plato says in the *Republic*: to act virtuously is to be following reason rather

mentions "things which are the source of praised actions and are themselves praised, such as justice itself and just actions, and temperate actions;[52] for temperance too is praised." Hence it follows at once that Aristotle is not here discussing principles governing the choice of certain actions as morally good: such acts are noble and praiseworthy, and so excluded from the scope of his remarks here.[53] Aristotle indicates which goods are in question when he adds: "but *health* is not praised" and goes on to mention also "the goods that are contended for and regarded as important—honor and wealth and bodily excellences and blessings of fortune and power" (b23, 27-29). The choices in question are therefore choices of the external goods and, in general, the goods of fortune.

If this were all, however, this passage would not be raising a question so very different from that broached in the passage from *NE VI=EE* V. For if his question concerns the principle to be employed *in general* by the morally good person in deciding how much to care about various ordinary first-order goods, then the *Eudemian* passage will only be pressing a refinement on the

----

than the passions, since in that case reason will be doing its job of leading and deciding (ἄρχειν, *Rep.* 441e3, βουλευόμενον, 442b6). Plainly, here in the *MM*, as in Plato, it is not the theoretical use of the mind but, if the distinction is to be insisted on at all, rather the practical which the passions are called upon not to interfere with. The fact that this leaves entirely up in the air what principles the mind will appeal to, if not interfered with, in making its practical decisions, is in effect admitted in the *MM*. The author grants (1208a22-30) that he has said nothing concrete about the condition the passions must be in if they are not to interfere, but rejects the request for further information, instead appealing to perception (a theme not found in *EE* VIII 3). It would, of course, not be at all natural to appeal to perception at this point if the criterion being argued for were the promotion of contemplation: doubtless a variety of relatively concrete things could be said about what one's emotional state should be if one is to do effective pure thinking. This passage of the *MM*, in short, implies no independent standard by which to determine what condition of soul and mode of action is virtuous; *a fortiori* it does not imply an intellectualist standard.

[52] Reading αἱ for οἱ in b22, with Solomon.

[53] I have to some extent been anticipated in this judgment by J. D. Monan (*Moral Knowledge and its Methodology in Aristotle*, p. 129). See also P. Defourny, quoted in Gauthier-Jolif, p. 563.

question raised in the other passage, and not making a distinct point. For if the account I have given of moral virtues is right, a good moral character consists largely in the correct relative evaluation of precisely those first-order goods for which Aristotle will then be claiming to tell us the correct principle of evaluation. So he will, after all, be in effect giving us the defining principle of good moral character, but without calling it that: since the specifically moral features of moral character and moral action, their nobility and praiseworthiness, are excluded from consideration, Aristotle is careful here, as he is not in the sixth book, to say he is not giving the principle by which moral character and moral choice *as such* are determined. But the difference, though important, would be of little significance from the present point of view.

But in fact the passage is not concerned at all with the principles to be employed by virtuous persons in any and every circumstance in deciding what ordinary first-order goods to choose. Aristotle does not here tell us how a generous man decides how much money to acquire or spend, or a temperate man how much sex to have or how much food to eat. For, according to what Aristotle says earlier in this chapter, when a good man opts for one of the things that, considered by itself, is merely naturally good (but not praiseworthy)—say, money or sex—with the idea that it is virtuous and noble to get this money or have this sex (that is, when his end in making the choice is nobility of action),[54] then not only is his action noble and praiseworthy, but the money or the sex itself acquires these properties as well.[55] This point is obviously important to Aristotle: he repeats it four times in the space of ten lines. But it follows from this that the choices being discussed later in the chapter do not include *any* choice made by a virtuous person in which his aim in making the choice is to attain the peculiarly moral value of nobility. Goods like money and

[54] I read διό for διότι in 1249a7 (with Solomon).

[55] 1249a2-5. The point comes out most clearly if one reads, with Dirlmeier, οὐ γὰρ ὑπάρχει αὐτοῖς τὰ καλὰ δι᾽ αὐτά. ὅσοις δὲ ὑπάρχει δι᾽ αὐτά, καὶ προαιροῦνται καλὰ κἀγαθά. καὶ οὐ μόνον ταῦτα κτλ. (reconstructed from a newly appreciated Latin manuscript containing a translation of this passage); but there is no doubt as to the general sense.

power and so on when chosen by such a man with such an aim become noble and so praiseworthy, whereas what are being discussed are choices of goods that are not praiseworthy.

What choices, then, does Aristotle have in mind here? It is clear from what I have said already that they must be choices of ordinary first-order goods by morally good persons, but choices in which they are not pursuing the specifically moral value of nobility. This suggests two closely connected possibilities. First, in many situations in which one must either take or forego some good thing, no principle of moral virtue declares either for or against either option. One is neither morally required nor forbidden, most of the time, to spend an evening at the movies or acquire a rose bush for one's garden. Some things are forbidden and some are required, but much of the time the choices that present themselves do not include either. Such choices would be choices (or avoidances) of good (or bad) things where, *ex hypothesi*, no moral value is an object of pursuit. Secondly, even where moral considerations do arise in deciding what to do, they often do not determine a specific course of action. Thus, when someone is in need of assistance, friendship will bring his friends to his aid, but often it will not be clear exactly what, or how much, they must do to help. Certainly, niggardliness is ruled out, but how much must one abandon one's other concerns, and for how long? Within certain limits, any decision one makes will conform to what friendship requires. If one does employ some principle here to select a specific course of action within these limits, one will not in choosing that action, instead of an alternative, be aiming to achieve specifically moral values; any choice within the range specified by moral considerations will be morally good, and other considerations, such as one's own convenience, must motivate the particular choice one makes.

If Aristotle has choices of these two kinds in mind (and it is hard to see what else he can mean), then he will be saying that for such choices the correct principle is to do whatever will most advance one's own attainment of the highest intellectual values: in such circumstances "whatever choice and possession of things good by nature will most produce the contemplation of god[56]—whether goods of the body, or money, or friends, or the other goods—this is best." That is to say, Aristotle recommends the unrestrained pursuit of intellectual goods within a certain definitely limited context: moral values are in no case sacrificed to, or made dependent on, intellectual values, but where moral requirements are already fully met, or do not apply, then theoretical activity is to be promoted, if necessary, to the exclusion of all else. The superiority of intellectual goods to all other goods thus consists, according to the *Eudemian* theory, in this: such goods are to be pursued single-mindedly, and preferred to any amount of other goods, once the requirements of the moral virtues are met. A person who lived a flourishing life, according to this *Eudemian* conception, would, like more ordinary folk, live his life in the midst of social and family connections, and would, like them, place a definite value on such connections and the good things they bring. But within the frame of this social and moral life he would devote himself specially to the cultivation and exercise of his highest intellectual powers. Whereas another person might engage himself more deeply than the virtues require in the routine of social and family life, this man would make as much room as he could, compatibly with not failing in any re-quirement of virtue, for intellectual concerns.

The upshot is that in the *Eudemian Ethics* Aristotle consistently holds to a conception of human flourishing that

---

[56] I take τὴν τοῦ θεοῦ θεωρίαν, 1249b17, in the most natural way, with θεοῦ objective genitive. Dirlmeier's reading (*ad loc.*) of θεοῦ as subjective genitive (thus making it refer to νοῦς itself, which Aristotle would therefore here call a god) seems to me most improbable—first, because it requires an unlikely mental juxtaposition of this passage with 1248a25 ff, where on Dirlmeier's interpretation Aristotle refers to human νοῦς as not merely θεῖον but even a θεός; secondly, because I do not think Aristotle does, in the earlier passage, refer to human νοῦς as a θεός. There is no cause for alarm if Aristotle does speak here as if god were the sole object of the highest kind of thinking: passages where he implies the same thing are sufficiently numerous. See now W. J. Verdenius, "Human Reason and God in the *EE*," (above, n. 50), pp. 288-291, who takes the passage the way I do.

makes provision for two fundamental ends—morally virtuous
activity and intellectual activity of the highest kind. Neither of
these is subordinated to the other; moral virtue comes first, in the
sense that it must be provided for first, but once moral virtue is
securely entrenched, then intellectual goods are allowed to pre-
dominate. This same conception seems to lie behind Aristotle's
discussion of the moral virtues through the main body of the
Nicomachean Ethics. The *Nicomachean* treatment is complicated, however, as we have seen, by the appearance in the first
and tenth books of statements apparently in conflict with it.
There are indications there of an alternative view of flourishing
according to which intellectual values would be made not merely
first, in the way we have just seen the *Eudemian Ethics* makes
them, but dominant over all other values in all contexts. We have
found this intellectualist view nowhere stated or even hinted at in
the *Eudemian Ethics*;[57] its role in the *Nicomachean Ethics* will be
the subject of the next chapter.

[57] This interpretation of the *EE* is strongly corroborated by the fact that
Politics VII-VIII seems to adopt in its account of εὐδαιμονία the *Eudemian*,
inclusive end, and not the intellectualist one: for, given the very substantial
coincidence of terminology, which Bendixen first pointed out (*Philologus* 11
(1856), 578-581: cf. Dirlmeier, *EE* p. 132-133) and which suggests a chron-
ological affinity between the two works, one would expect the basic outlook
to be the same. Cf. *Pol.* VII 1 1323b1-3, τὸ ζῆν εὐδαιμόνως ... μᾶλλον
ὑπάρχει τοῖς τὸ ἦθος μὲν καὶ τὴν διάνοιαν κεκοσμημένοις εἰς ὑπερβολήν;
b21-23, ὅτι μὲν οὖν ἑκάστῳ τῆς εὐδαιμονίας ἐπιβάλλει τοσοῦτον ὅσον
περ ἀρετῆς καὶ φρονήσεως καὶ τοῦ πράττειν κατὰ ταύτας, ἔστω
συνωμολογημένον ἡμῖν. This view is accepted as fundamental throughout
the ensuing discussion. For example, Aristotle argues (1325b16-21) that the
way in which the life of a practical politician who is constantly studying the
effects of this or that political decision is "practical" is not the only way a
life can be "practical"; and he goes on to insist that intellectual work that is
not "practical" in this sense is nonetheless (and in a higher degree) practical
in the sense in which flourishing is identified with a "practical life." But it
does not follow from this that a life completely devoted to such studies is
the best: the point is rather that the part of one's life that remains when the
ordinary citizenly and social duties have been allowed for, is better devoted
to intellectual work than to practical politics. That is, morally virtuous
activity plus intellectual work makes a better life than morally virtuous
activity plus immersion in practical politics.

III

Intellectualism in the *Nicomachean Ethics*

1. Introduction

In the *Eudemian Ethics* Aristotle expounds and articulates what I have called a bipartite conception of human flourishing. On this conception the values of social and family life, which are organized by the moral virtues of justice, courage, temperance, and the rest, are given a place alongside the value provided in the development and exercise of the intellectual virtue of philosophic wisdom. The two fundamental ends of morally excellent action and pure speculative thinking are thus the two coordinate parts of the single ultimate end, which is to live a flourishing human life. In the constitution of this life the theoretical side is given a special weight since, within the fixed frame provided by the moral virtues, intellectual values will be pursued and promoted to the maximum degree possible. Moral action is thus assigned a definite, but limited, value whereas pure thought is made the object of unrestricted pursuit once moral requirements are fully met. Such a life would be identical with none of the three types of life distinguished by Aristotle in book I chapter 4, the investigation of which has sometimes been thought the central concern of the *Eudemian Ethics*.[1] It is neither a "political life" one-sidedly

---

[1] So W. Jaeger, *Aristotle*, pp. 235-238, according to whom the three basic goods on which these lives are founded (moral virtue, pleasure, wisdom) are studied *seriatim* in the *Eudemian Ethics*, then finally synthesized at the end in an ultimate conception of εὐδαιμονία. This crude picture is derived from the brief programmatic remark at 1216a36-40, rather than any sustained reading of the treatise. In fact, however, Aristotle sets out his account of

devoted to moral virtue, nor an equally one-sided "philosophical life," nor yet a crass "life of pleasure." It is a carefully articulated "mixed" life, combining elements drawn from each. It would not be unreasonable, in view of the special place assigned in it to theoretical pursuits, to call it a "philosophical" or "contemplative" life; but it is the life of a philosopher fully engaged in social, political, and family activities.

The chief argument Aristotle gives in favor of this view is disappointingly abstract, even scholastic in character. It derives quite directly from the argument at the end of *Republic* I by which Plato shows (it having earlier been agreed that justice is an excellence of the soul) that justice is a necessary condition of a good and flourishing life. Both arguments turn explicitly on the assertions (1) that a thing's excellence is the essential condition of its performing well its *ergon*, or definitive work, and (2) that the soul's work is the production of life, from which it is inferred that the exercise of the soul's excellence will produce a good life.[2] To

---

εὐδαιμονία already at the beginning of book II, and does not develop it out of a study of the three basic goods, or present it as a synthesis of the three one-sided lives. The study of the three lives no more provides the structure of the *Eudemian Ethics* than it does that of the *Nicomachean*; Jaeger was grasping at straws here with which to prop up his theory of Aristotle's development. See also the further researches of R. Joly into the development of the different life-ideals discussed by Greek philosophers in *Le thème philosophique des genres de vie dans l'antiquité classique* (Brussels: Académie Royale de Belgique, Mémoires, vol. 51 fasc. 3, 1956).

[2] The closeness of the *EE*'s argument to the *Republic*'s is all the more striking when it is compared with the corresponding passage of the *NE* (1097b24 ff): there Aristotle discusses directly the human being, not the human soul, asking what the ἔργον of a *man* is and arguing from that to the nature of human excellence and human flourishing. Aristotle's later argument brings an improvement over the earlier in at least one important respect: it avoids the at least apparent fallacy, which has long troubled readers of Plato, of inferring, as the *Republic* and the *EE* do, from the fact that the exercise of the soul's excellence makes its work good (that is, that its excellence causes the soul to do a good job of making the person whose soul it is alive) that the soul's excellence makes its possessor's life good, i.e. happy. The biological function of the soul, which is alone appealed to in the premises of the *EE*'s argument, seems much too weak a basis on which to establish a

this Aristotle adds that since such a life is thought to be a complete and finished one (*teleon ti*), it must involve the exercise of all the soul's excellences and not just some of them—which leads to the final statement that "flourishing is the activity of a complete life in accordance with complete excellence."

Now what is disappointing about this argument (aside from the fact that it talks about the soul's work and its excellences, instead of the person's whose life is in question) is that it is too abstract to be informative. It tells us at most only that the excellences, whatever these may turn out to be, are the essential condition of a flourishing life, but if one is in doubt, or in need of confirmation, as to precisely what states of mind and character are excellences, then the abstract statement in Aristotle's conclusion is not very interesting or helpful.[3] And even if one accepts, as Aristotle seems to do without argument, that justice, temperance, and so on, as conventionally conceived, plus theoretical wisdom and practical intelligence as he analyzes them, are the excellences in question, we still cannot derive from this argument any significant information as to how it is that these qualities contribute to a flourishing life. For the basis brought forward in the argument for believing that they do is just that the possession of excellence by a cloak, or a boat, or a house, and so generally for all things with excellences, makes their work good. And even if we accept the analogy between these other things' excellences and the soul's, all we have to go on is the bald and unanalyzed fact that excellence means goodness of work; in each of these cases the contribution made by

conception of human flourishing. For just as a knife's excellence guarantees only efficient cutting, and does not control whether the product it helps to produce will be good or not, so (on Aristotle's analogy here) the soul's excellence ought only to ensure abundant vitality and ought not to determine the goodness or badness (satisfactoriness or the opposite) of what is made of this vitality. These differences between the *EE* argument and that of the *NE* are very powerful confirmation of an early date for the *EE* (see below, n. 5).

[3] It should be observed that Plato's argument in the *Republic* is not open to this criticism. In the *Republic* context it has already been argued, and accepted by all participants in the discussion (348c2-352b), that justice is an excellence of the soul.

an excellence is obviously quite different, and reflection on how a
well-made cloak keeps you warm, or a well-made boat gets you
speedily and safely across the sea, is unlikely to throw any light on
how a virtuous existence will make you happy.

On the other hand it is clear that, in asking and answering the
question what life is best for a human being, Aristotle is guided
by a certain conception of what sort of creature a human being
is—what his fundamental capacities and needs are, how far these
are subject to alteration, development, manipulation, and so on.
This broad, indeed commonsense, conception emerges clearly in
the same chapter as the abstract argument just considered, where
Aristotle says that "the excellences of the faculty of nutrition and
growth are not even *human* excellences; for insofar as one is a
human being there must be present reasoning as a governing
element and action, and reasoning governs not reasoning but
desire and passions, whence it is necessary that one have these
parts" (II 1 1219b37-1220a2). A human being necessarily possesses a mind and also desires, so that he is necessarily at once an
emotional and an intellectual being. Having both intellectual
and emotional needs, and the possibility of both intellectual and
emotional satisfaction, a human being needs both intellectual
and moral virtues in order to achieve all the good things attaching
to the two parts of his nature. Thus what determines the
conception of flourishing in the *Eudemian Ethics* is the conception, to which Aristotle holds in that work, of a human being
as jointly and indissolubly both an intellectual and an emotional
creature.

The same bipartite conception of human flourishing is also
found in the *Nicomachean Ethics*, implicit in the treatment of the
moral virtues throughout the central books and occasionally
explicit in the sixth book.[4] On the other hand, as we saw in the
last chapter, in his formal discussions of the topic of flourishing,
in the first and tenth books, Aristotle does not, or does not
unambiguously, defend this conception. In the definition of

[4] See above, pp. 105–110.

flourishing in the first book, instead of saying, as he does in the
Eudemian Ethics, that a flourishing life is one lived according
to all the specifically human excellences, Aristotle hedges:
flourishing is "excellent spiritual or mental activity, or, if there
are several forms of excellence, spiritual activity expressing the
best and most final excellence." That is, the ultimate end is not
the exercise of several excellences, but rather that of one among
them. And in the tenth book (1178a6-9) the intellectual life (*ho
kata ton noun bios*) is pronounced "most flourishing," while the
moral life is relegated to the rank of "flourishing in the second
degree"—which, whatever precisely it means, seems clearly to
deny that morally virtuous activity is a constituent of the most
desirable conception of flourishing.[5]

[5] I assume here and throughout that the special *Nicomachean* books were
all composed after the *Eudemian Ethics,* and therefore that the arguments of
NE I and X which I consider in this section are late developments in
Aristotle's theory. It would hardly be necessary to say this, were it not for
J. D. Monan's recent book *Moral Knowledge and Its Methodology in Aristotle*
(see esp. pp. 108-111, 133-134, 151-152). Monan, impressed with the difficulty
of making the tenth book's intellectualism cohere with the moral theory of
the two *Ethics,* argues that the intellectualistic passages are fragments of an
early, heavily Platonic, Aristotelian moral philosophy. He finds traces of this
view in the remains of the *Protrepticus,* and thinks it has somehow found
its way into the *NE,* even though Aristotle had by the time he composed the
NE got well beyond it. It is, however, certainly not true that the passages
in question in the *NE* were written, as Monan claims, before the *EE* and before
the main body of the *NE.* The "function" argument as it appears in
NE I 7 (1097b22-1098a20), which is an integral part of the chief intellectualist
passage in book I, is in fundamental respects a distinct improvement on the
corresponding argument of the *EE* (II 1 1218b31-1219a39): as I argued above
(this chapter, n. 2), where *EE* follows Plato (*Rep.* I 353d–354a) in inquiring
into the ἔργον of the *soul* (1219a24) and concluding by what looks like
Plato's questionable inference (the soul's job is to produce life, so a good
soul produces a good life, i.e. εὐδαιμονία, 1219a23-28) that excellence of the
soul is the condition of flourishing, the *NE* argument speaks of *man*'s ἔργον
and *man*'s excellences, and avoids altogether Plato's quick, but suspicious,
path to the conclusion. The shift from the soul's excellence to the man's is
entirely in accord with Aristotle's strictures in the *De Anima* (I 4 408a11-15)
against treating the soul, instead of the man, as agent, subject of experiences,
etc. Clearly the function argument of the *NE* is an improvement on the
EE's and shows affinities to Aristotle's mature psychological theory. So the

What to make of this intellectualist strain in the *Nicomachean Ethics* and how to integrate it with the moral theory found in the rest of the treatise has always been a major problem for Aristotle's interpreters. Nor is there as yet any secure general agreement on the matter among scholars. In the present chapter I shall examine afresh the whole question of Aristotle's intellectualism.

2. Three Inadequate Interpretations

Most commentators appear to rest content with an unadorned interpretation of Aristotle's argument in the tenth book. They seem to take Aristotle's assertion that flourishing, or the ultimate end, is to be identified with theoretical activity carried on throughout a lifetime as implying directly that, in a life that truly flourishes, other activities—for example, morally virtuous activities—will be engaged in only so often and in such a way as to contribute to the flowering of the intellect. One might imagine that anyone who actually lived his life by this scheme would show himself on numerous occasions somewhat less than morally upright. He might indeed find it useful to have a façade of virtue, in view of his need for at least the forbearance of others; and he might find a certain advantage for his dominant purpose in the disciplining of his inclinations and emotions which moral virtue brings. But being ultimately concerned only with his own intellectual accomplishments, he would, it would seem, surely on

---

passage in which it occurs is late rather than early, and in particular it must be later than the *EE*.

It is also not true that the *NE*'s intellectualism is a throwback to the views of the *Protrepticus*: the *Protrepticus* draws no fundamental distinction between theoretical and practical uses of the mind (cf. frag. 13 Ross, esp. the passages printed as B 47 and B 51 in Düring's edition), so that it cannot, in arguing the identity of a man with his νοῦς, mean what the *NE* means by what is verbally the same recommendation. (See further pp. 168 ff and n. 22 below). If the *NE*'s intellectualism is in a certain sense Platonic in spirit, this represents a late *rapprochement* between Aristotle and Plato, and not a return on Aristotle's part to his earliest psychological and ethical theories. As I argue below, the links between *NE* X and the mature psychology of the *De Anima* make it clear that the intellectualistic strain in the *NE* is altogether a late development in Aristotle's moral theory.

occasion find it rational at least to neglect to do some positive act
of virtue, if not actually to do something immoral, as a means to
the furtherance of his consuming interest. He would in fact live a
retiring, contemplative life, with no special concern for the
supposed values of social, political, and family life. Some,
however, who interpret Aristotle along these general lines, finding
such an ideal unpalatable, deny in Aristotle's name that concen-
tration on intellectual goods would lead one to such a pass.
Somehow, they suppose, Aristotle must have held that moral
virtue and the flowering of the intellect are so intimately related
that the committed intellectualist will never find it rational to
neglect his mundane duties. Virtuous action in Aristotle's view
must be not just an occasionally, but a constantly, necessary
means to a flourishing life of contemplation, so that the
successful contemplative will also be morally virtuous, with all
that that entails. On either view, however, Aristotle will be
recommending the pursuit of contemplative activity as a
dominant end.[6]

[6] It is not easy to find scholars who are self-consciously committed to
either version of this traditional view; they mostly do not formulate the issue
clearly enough to make a decision seem necessary. But Ross (*Aristotle*,
Meridian Books ed., p. 226) takes the contemplative life recommended in
the tenth book as in principle, at any rate, quite free from moral or social
concerns. For although he finds hints that according to Aristotle moral
virtue would play *some* role in the life of any actual person who undertook
to live a contemplative life, he thinks he leaves largely undetermined what
this role would be. And in any case Ross sees the ideal, whether fully realizable
or not by any actual mortal, as one that places the flourishing person beyond
morality. Many other writers speak at least occasionally as if this were their
view (thus most notably G. Rodier, in the introduction to his edition of *NE* X,
reprinted in his *Etudes de philosophie grecque* [Paris: Vrin, 1926]). But if
this is correct (as I believe it is) one must also note, as none of these interpreters does, that φρόνησις, which Aristotle defines as "a disposition to act,
involving the truth, together with the power of reasoning, concerning human
goods" (1140b20-21), is then apparently misdefined. For the φρόνιμος is a
devotee of moral virtue and lives a virtuous life; but in that case he cannot
really know the truth about human good, since the truth, according to
Aristotle, is that another life than his is better.
This consequence of Ross's view may seem to encourage the other version,

Now I have already pointed out that this conception of flourishing and this attitude to moral virtue do not play a role in the central books of the *Nicomachean Ethics*. The morally virtuous person described in these books is clearly not such an intellectualist; for he regards morally virtuous action as not merely an end in itself but even one of the constituent ends in the conception of flourishing which it is his ultimate aim to realize in his life. On the other hand there is no guarantee that Aristotle should have continued to hold this conception of flourishing and its attitude to moral virtue in the tenth book itself. Conceivably, in the middle books he describes the attitudes of morally good people of a conventionally worthy sort, while in the tenth book he sets out his own higher ideal, which conflicts with, because it goes beyond, this more ordinary conception. Perhaps the view outlined above (see p. 147 f) is Aristotle's considered opinion, expressed in book X, even though it is not the view he advances while giving his account of moral virtue in the earlier books.

Such an interpretation has obvious drawbacks, however. It makes the *Ethics* an untidy and somewhat incoherent book, and tends to give Aristotle a much less elevated view of moral values than most interpreters have themselves been anxious to concede. So certain French scholars have put forward a different interpretation of Aristotle's outlook in the tenth book, according to which moral virtue is not seriously downgraded and the continuity and coherence of the *Nicomachean Ethics* can be defended.[7]

---

little as it has by way of support in Aristotle's texts. And many commentators take it that Aristotle's contemplative life of book X is the moral life filled out with a quantity of theoretical activity: thus, for example, Stewart, Gauthier, Dirlmeier, and, most recently, Düring, agree on this at least. But for those who, like Düring in *Aristoteles* (Heidelberg: Carl Winter Universitätsverlag, 1966, p. 471), also admit that in this contemplative life "die *theōria* das Endziel ist," it follows at once (though they do not make this explicit) that the exercise of the moral virtues must be somehow a necessary means to this end. W. K. Frankena (*Three Historical Philosophies of Education*, Chicago: Scott, Foresman, 1965, pp. 34-35) is clear-headed enough to make this point directly.

[7] See Ollé-Laprune, *Essai sur la morale d'Aristote* (Paris, 1881), chaps.

According to these authors, when Aristotle identifies human flourishing with contemplative thought of some kind (*theōria tis*, 1178b32), or, more fully, with the activity of excellent contemplative thinking (1177a12-18) carried on through a complete lifetime (b25), he does not mean to be recommending a life ideal any different from the "mixed life" in terms of which *eudaimonia* is defined in the *Eudemian Ethics*. In this respect the verbal divergences in the definitions of *eudaimonia* in the two works are misleading; the *Nicomachean*, in referring only to *sophia* in its formula (*energeia kata tēn aristēn kai teleiotatēn aretēn*, 1098a17-18; *kata tēn kratistēn*, 1117a13; *hē [tou aristou] energeia kata tēn oikeian aretēn*, 1177a16-17), only means to single out the primary and decisive constituent of the mixed life, the constituent which possesses the quality of "happiness" directly and somehow conveys it to the rest.[8] Excellent theorizing is the ultimate end in the sense that it is the summit of human life: even though the best life for a human being is one devoted jointly to the moral and the theoretical excellences, nonetheless any reasonable man cares more for the theoretical than he does for the moral side of his life,

---

IV-V, esp. pp. 136-170; Gauthier, *La morale d'Aristote* (Paris: Presses Universitaires de France, 1958), chap. V, and, in Gauthier-Jolif, *L'Ethique à Nicomaque*, the commentary to books VI and X, esp. pp. 860-866, 891-896. In the text I follow what I take to be Gauthier's version, where it diverges from Ollé-Laprune's. It should be observed, whatever is to be made of the fact, that Michael of Ephesus appears to adopt what is at bottom the same interpretation: see, for example, in *Nic. Eth.* (Heylbut) 578, 19-37. But, as usual, he does not provide details or consider alternatives, so it is hard to be sure just how committed to this view he really is. (On Michael see further n. 16 below.)

[8] See Ollé-Laprune, p. 136: "Le bonheur est essentiellement dans la pensée pure"; p. 170: morally virtuous activity "n'est pas le bonheur même. C'en est un reflet, ou un rayon." Gauthier, *La morale*, p. 110: "La contemplation est une vie rationelle *par essence*, puisqu'elle est la vie de l'esprit s'exerçant à l'état pur, et elle est du même coup, puisque le bonheur n'est rien d'autre que l'activité de l'esprit, le bonheur *par essence*. Au contraire, l'activité de la sagesse (= *phronesis*) et des vertus morales ... n'est une vie rationelle, et donc un bonheur, que par *participation* ... l'activité des vertus morales ... émane d'elle (viz., la contemplation)" (his italics).

and although he accepts without complaint (but not without regret?) the limitations of the human condition which make the mixed life the best one, there is a sense in which contemplation is what he really lives for.[9] What he values in his life is the rationality it manifests; but it is his theoretical thinking that displays this quality in its purest and most direct embodiment, while rationality in practical thought is secondary and "derivative" in character. In short, in glorifying the life according to the intellect (*ho kata ton noun bios*, 1178a6-7), Aristotle does not reject the mixed life in favor of a retiring, contemplative life; nor does he mean thereby to announce a reconstructed conception of what it is to flourish, according to which intellectual values are made dominant, while moral activity is regarded as just a constantly necessary means to this dominant end. On the contrary, with the expression *kata ton noun bios* he refers to *one part* of the life of combined moral and intellectual virtue, the "intellectual life" in which the moral agent himself sees his own perfection and finds the "essence" (but not the whole) of his own happiness.

This interpretation, although it is couched in vague and rather metaphorical language (and is buttressed by its defenders with theories of questionable Aristotelian parentage),[10] does have a

---

[9] Cf. *EE* 1215b24-1216a10.

[10] For example, Gauthier's use of the notion of "participation" (see n. 8 above), which he apparently derives from Aristotle's remark (*NE* 1102b13-14, 26, 30) that one "part" of the human soul, though in itself irrational, participates (μετέχει) in a way in reason, namely, by following and obeying it. But Gauthier seems to forget that here Aristotle refers only to the passions (τὸ ἐπιθυμητικὸν καὶ ὅλως ὀρεκτικόν, 1102b30), and that he evidently contrasts them primarily not with theoretical but with practical reason (this being the capacity which is followed and obeyed): so that exercising one's mind in practical affairs would *not* be exercising reason only derivatively and by "participation," according to Aristotle's use of this expression, but directly and "in itself." It is the passions themselves, in obeying practical reason, that are said to be rational by "participation." Hence, when Gauthier says that practical reasoning is a "rational life" not "*par essence*" but only by "participation" he misapplies Aristotle's distinction between the two senses of "rational." And his own distinction is nowhere to be found in Aristotle. It follows that in maintaining that according to Aristotle the

certain interest. For it holds out the hope of a reasonably satisfactory meshing of the theories of the first and tenth books with what comes in between. To the extent that the intervening books recognize moral activity as an element in the best life (*eudaimonia*), this can be seen as a venially imprecise statement of Aristotle's considered theory, according to which, strictly speaking, *eudaimonia* consists only in theoretical activity, since on this theory moral activity does make up part of the ideal life and can be said to be "happy" in a derivative sense. Furthermore, on this theory one might understand the relations between the *Eudemian* and *Nicomachean Ethics* in an easy and not unnatural way: where the *Eudemian Ethics* defines *eudaimonia* simply in terms of the two types of specifically human excellence, the *Nicomachean Ethics*, taking account of intellectualist elements already present in the other work, sophisticates the theory by distinguishing between intellectual excellence as that whose exercise constitutes the "essence" of human flourishing, and moral virtue as that whose exercise constitutes flourishing only in a derivative way.

Nonetheless, I do not think that either this more sophisticated reading of Aristotle's argument in the tenth book or the cruder views it is meant to replace is ultimately adequate. Close examination of what Aristotle actually says will show why these interpretations must be rejected as well as point the way to a better one.

---

rationality of practical thought is a "derivative" form of rationality Gauthier, besides indulging in an obscure metaphor which would be very difficult to cash adequately (—derivative exactly how, and from what?), has no text of Aristotle on which to ground his interpretation.

More fundamentally, Gauthier interprets the identification of εὐδαιμονία with excellent theoretical activity not, as Aristotle's discussion of εὐδαιμονία in book I (resumed in X 7) implies it ought to be, as the specification of a whole scheme of life (an ultimate end), but as predicating a certain quality (the quality of *bonheur*) of a single element within such a scheme. But Aristotle's concept of εὐδαιμονία is fundamentally misrepresented if it is regarded as a quality possessed in varying degrees and at varying levels by different activities.

3. Aristotle's Preference for the Contemplative Life

In the sixth chapter of book X Aristotle returns to the topic of *eudaimonia*, having abandoned it at the end of the first book for discussions on "the excellences, the forms of friendship, and the varieties of pleasure." He reminds us at once (1176a31-32) that his interest in *eudaimonia* is motivated by a concern to discover "the end of things human." That is to say, *eudaimonia* is still explicitly being considered, as it was in the first book, as the ultimate end in view of which we are to do all that we do—a scheme or pattern of life, or, better, a life lived according to a certain scheme. In asking what *eudaimonia* is, therefore, Aristotle is asking which such life and which such scheme is the best. He begins by combining two points made in the preliminary discussion in book I (1097a30-b1, b24-25): *eudaimonia* is to be identified with an activity, or activities, that are chosen for their own sakes. There are many such activities: not only virtuous actions but also all forms of play and amusement are activities chosen for their own sakes. But *eudaimonia* cannot be made to consist in play because, among other reasons, play itself is chosen as a respite from more serious endeavors. These activities cannot then be made the organizing focus of a satisfactory life; only the exercise of the excellences can reasonably be assigned this role. Thus Aristotle arrives by a somewhat different route at his conclusion in book I. "For flourishing does not consist in this kind of pursuit, but in the active exercise of the excellences, as indeed was said earlier:" that is to say, a flourishing life consists in the exercise of the excellences in the sense that a flourishing life is one organized by keeping the pursuit of excellence and its active exercise constantly uppermost, and engaging in other pursuits only so far as they contribute to or are involved in these.

This general conclusion is sharply, and rather surprisingly, narrowed in the next chapter.

If a flourishing life is excellent activity, it is reasonable that it should be the activity of the highest excellence; and this would be the excellence of the best thing. Whether this is intuitive mind (*nous*) or something else that is thought to be by nature the ruler and leader and to take thought for noble and divine things, whether it is itself godlike or the most nearly godlike possession we have, the active exercise of this in accordance with its own excellence would be consummate flourishing (*teleia eudaimonia*). That this activity is a contemplative one has been said already.[11] (1177a12-18)

Now this is a most curious assertion. Why does Aristotle say that, given the general conclusion that the exercise of excellence is that in which *eudaimonia* consists, it is reasonable to identify *eudaimonia* with the exercise of a *single* excellence, that of the theoretical intellect? No argument is given for this statement, and offhand it seems a mistake. For, as we have seen, it amounts to saying that the best plan of life is to pursue constantly the single end of theoretical contemplation in preference to all else; and this would not seem reasonable at all to anyone who regards himself, as Aristotle seemed to do in the *Eudemian Ethics*, as not merely an intellectual but also an emotional being. For anyone who has this conception of himself, the moral virtues and their exercise would also seem an essential good to be aimed at in any suitable life. To plan explicitly for the satisfaction of the intellect alone would not be a reasonable thing, involving as it does treating these other satisfactions as indifferent at best. How then can Aristotle in so offhand a fashion affirm the opposite?

The immediately succeeding passage (1177a18-b26), in which Aristotle gives six reasons in support of his view, does not provide much illumination. For the reasons given seem only to support, at most, the conclusion that contemplative activity is the best among human activities: that *theōria* is the best, most continuous, most pleasant, most self-sufficient, most free and leisurely activity, and especially loved for its own sake,[12] certainly does not tend to show

[11] Aristotle has not in fact quite said this before; but he makes it clear in book VI (see esp. 1145a6-9) that σοφία is the highest excellence and that its activity is theoretical (cf. VI 7).

[12] What Aristotle actually says here is something considerably stronger, that only θεωρία is loved for itself. But this is both false and contradicted by

that this activity would reasonably be pursued as a dominant end in anyone's life. Yet Aristotle emphatically reaffirms this when he infers from these six considerations that "this (viz. contemplative activity) turns out to be consummate human flourishing, provided it is given a full span of life" (1177b24-25).

Intelligible reasons for holding this opinion begin to emerge only in the following passage. For the objection to his view which I cited just now rests on the assumption that a human person is to be conceived of as not merely an intellectual but also an emotional being; and it emerges here that Aristotle means to challenge this assumption. For he considers an objection based precisely on the claim that a human being is not suited to such a life, and replies by insisting that according to the correct view of what a human being is such a life is exactly appropriate. The *Eudemian* conception of human nature is rejected in favor of a new, intellectualist conception, and this provides the needed grounding for the intellectualist ideal of flourishing.

But such a life [*bios*] is too exalted to suit a human being. For it is not *qua* human that one lives in this way but insofar as there is in one something godlike. And the active exercise of this [godlike thing] surpasses the exercise of the other sort of excellence by as much as it surpasses the compound [*to suntheton*, viz., the living body possessed of emotions, sensation, etc.].[13] If, then, the

---

what Aristotle says elsewhere (e.g. 1097b2-4). The most that could fairly be said is that θεωρία is loved for its own sake alone, and not, like moral virtue, both for its own sake and for the good things it brings: hence, in summarizing Aristotle's argument I have substituted the lesser claim for the one Aristotle actually makes. But it is highly significant that Aristotle should here overstate his case (and repeat the point at 1177b18). For if my interpretation of the contemplative life is correct the stronger claim would seem to be correct, provided that the contemplative's attitudes are taken as the norm: the man bent on contemplation as his ideal does *not* love anything for its own sake except θεωρία.

[13] This interpretation of τὸ σύνθετον has recently been defended, against Gauthier's different view (*Ethique à Nicomaque*, 893-896), by Hardie ("Aristotle's Treatment of the Relation between the Soul and the Body", *Philosophical Quarterly* 14 [1964], 69-71, and *Aristotle's Ethical Theory*, pp. 76-77). Joachim understandably takes it for granted (p. 287). So far as I can see

intellect is godlike in comparison with the human being, so too the intellectual life is a godlike life in comparison with the human life.—But one ought not to follow those who advise that, being human, one should be mindful of human affairs, or that a mortal should be mindful of the affairs of a mortal, but one ought so far as possible to act as an immortal and do everything with a view to living in accordance with what is highest in oneself. For even though it is small in bulk it exceeds everything by far in power and worth. And it would seem that each person *is* this, if this is the authoritative and better part. It would be odd, then, not to choose one's own life [*bios*] but someone else's. And what was said earlier applies now: what belongs peculiarly to each thing is naturally best and pleasantest to it. So also for a human being the intellectual life [*bios*] is best, if this most of all *is* the human being. This life therefore is also the most flourishing.

But the life of the other sort of virtue is a flourishing one in the second degree. For the activities of this sort of virtue are typically human [*anthrōpikai*]. For we deal justly and bravely and in other ways virtuously *with* one another, preserving what is appropriate for each in business dealings, employments, and actions of varied kinds, and in the emotions: and these are all obviously typically human things. Some of them are even thought to arise from the body, and the virtue of character is thought to be much bound up with the emotions. Practical intelligence too is linked to the virtue of character, and this to practical intelligence, given that the principles of practical intelligence are in accord with the moral virtues, and rightness in the virtues accords with practical intelligence. Being bound up with the emotions, these would belong to the compound [that is, the living body possessed of emotions, sensation, etc.]; but the virtues belonging to the compound are typically human: so also, then, are that sort of life and that sort of

---

Gauthier's view (that the compound referred to here is a conjunction of two substances, a body and a soul) rests on nothing more than the determination to maintain Nuyens' now thoroughly discredited hypothesis concerning the alleged "*phase instrumentiste*" in the development of Aristotle's psychology. (See the article of Hardie just cited, and Irving Block, "The Order of Aristotle's Psychological Writings", *American Journal of Philology* 82, 1961). Failing that hypothesis, Gauthier has no basis for preferring his own to Hardie's, and my, interpretation.

flourishing. But the excellence of the intellect is separated [from the emotions]. (1177b26-1178a22)

I have quoted this long passage in full because on the correct assessment of it depends any hope we may have of understanding Aristotle's theory of flourishing in the tenth book. The first point to be clear about is that Aristotle is here comparing two distinct modes of life, one which he calls an intellectual life (*ho kata ton noun bios*) and one which he calls a moral life (*ho kata tēn allēn aretēn* [*bios*]). Gauthier, indeed, has argued that this is not so: according to him, Aristotle is not contrasting and ranking two separate modes of life, but two integral parts of a single mode of life. Thus, in Gauthier's view, Aristotle here has in mind a single person who has both an excellent intellectual life and an excellent moral-emotional life; he points out merely that it is fundamentally and essentially by virtue of the quality of his intellectual life that he can be said to be flourishing, while the side of his life in which he uses his mind in practical, as distinct from theoretical, contexts, though it can be said to flourish (because it is governed by the excellences of character and by practical intelligence), can be said to do so only "in the second degree." Practical reasoning is the less prized manifestation of the intellect; hence its flowering is only a secondary kind of flourishing, in comparison with the kind of flourishing attained by the intellect in excellent contemplative activity.

This interpretation is ruled out, however, by simple facts about the Greek word *bios*, which Aristotle uses in the quoted passage to refer to the two "lives" he is ranking. In English (and equivalently in French) it is common practice to speak of someone's intellectual life, or his social life, or spiritual life, or sex life. And we speak correspondingly of a community's political or cultural or artistic life. In these usages one refers to what are roughly synchronous parts or aspects of an individual's or a community's total life: thus one might say that Kierkegaard's spiritual life was uncommonly interesting, although he led a less extensive social

life than most members of his class. Now Gauthier seems to have
been led by these modern usages to forget that in Greek *bios*
cannot be used in this way:[14] it means always "(mode of) life,"
and in any one period of time one can only have one mode of
life.[15] One cannot be said to have both a religious *bios* and a
social *bios* on the ground that one's mode of life provides for
religious observances and social intercourse, as we might say
someone has an active religious life and an interesting social
life.[16] Hence, when Aristotle contrasts an "intellectual life (*bios*)"
with a "moral life (*bios*)," he cannot mean, as Gauthier's interpretation requires, the intellectual life and the moral life of a
single person. The Greek expressions can only mean two different
lives led by two different kinds of persons.

But precisely what two modes of life is Aristotle here
contrasting? The "intellectual life" seems relatively clear. As has
emerged earlier in the chapter, it is the sort of life led by someone
who concentrates on the development and exercise of his intellectual capacities, and makes such values not merely first but

[14] See Liddell-Scott-Jones, *Greek-English Lexicon* (9th ed., Oxford:
Clarendon Press, 1940), s.v.

[15] The same holds for societies. Thus Aristotle frequently speaks of a
city's life (e.g., *Pol.* 1265a21-28); but he never speaks, as we do, of the
workings of the political or cultural institutions of a society as its political
or cultural *life* (βίος). The expression πολιτικὸς βίος, applied to a city, as
in the passage just cited, means a way in which its life as a whole is organized,
and never its political life in the modern sense.

[16] The Greek word ζωή, whose basic meaning is "life" in the sense of
being alive, could be used to express some of these concepts. Cf. such usages
as that at *NE* I7 1098a1, in the following context: What then is the ἔργον
of man as such? Living (τὸ ζῆν) is something that other animals and even
plants do: but we are looking for something peculiar to man. Ἀφοριστέον
ἄρα τήν τε θρεπτικὴν καὶ τὴν αὐξητικὴν ζωήν: so we must exclude the
life of nourishment and growth.—Here the exercise of a certain life-activity,
the assimilation of food and consequent increase (or maintenance) of
physical size, is referred to as a "life" (ζωή): for complicated creatures like
ourselves, to be alive is a complex thing, and each of the different levels at
which our being alive shows itself can be called *a* life that we lead—notably
the life of nourishment etc., the life of perception, and the mental life are

dominant in his scheme of life. It is not entirely clear, however,
what else Aristotle might have thought such a life, if successfully
pursued, would contain. The contrast between this life and the
"life of moral virtue" might suggest that he thinks of the person
who leads it as devoid of moral virtue and indifferent to moral
and social interests. But this terminology is not decisive. For by
the "moral life" Aristotle might conceivably mean a life limited to
the pursuit of moral good, without independent provision for or
interest in intellectual matters—the life of the good but stolid
burgher. In that case the contrast he intends could be between a
life of combined intellectual and moral excellence and a life which
looks no higher than the virtues of the character for its organizing
principles. The former would be called an intellectual life by
contrast to this narrowly moral life, but would itself encompass
all the types of satisfaction obtained by the burgher, in addition
to its own special values. In support of this interpretation one
might bring in the allegation sometimes made by Aristotle's
interpreters, that he thought that the moral virtues and their
active exercise form an indispensable condition of the intellect's
flowering. For then, in the life dominated by intellectual pursuits,
Aristotle could nonetheless suppose that all the moral and social

---

all part of human life as such. See also *Met.* 1072b27, ἡ γὰρ νοῦ ἐνέργεια
ζωή. It is significant that Michael of Ephesus, who takes Aristotle's expression
ὁ κατὰ τὸν νοῦν βίος to refer to intellectual activities which he thinks ought
to supplement the moral activities which constitute the secondary, "political"
kind of flourishing (578, 16-25), introduces, and relies mostly on, the expression ἡ νοερὰ ζωή ("the intellectual life") to put what he takes to be Aristotle's
point. Obviously he felt that this sense of "an intellectual life" is naturally
expressed by using ζωή but not βίος. (When he does refer to ὁ θεωρητικὸς
βίος, he often seems to have in mind the total way of life of someone who
both lives a νοερὰ ζωή and exercises the moral virtues: see 592, 26-30, and
the conjunction ὁ θεωρητικὸς βίος καὶ ἡ νοερὰ ζωή at 590, 32 and 595,
20-21.) He even quotes Aristotle once (589, 35) as if he had identified
εὐδαιμονία with ἡ κατὰ τὸν νοῦν ζωή! See also his use of ἡ ἄλογος ζωή
at 579, 19 to refer to the "life of the emotions" as a whole, and his explanation
(572, 1) that Aristotle ὀνομάζει δὲ νοῦν τὴν λογικὴν ζωήν.

goods would be realized as well—incidentally, as it were, but realized nonetheless.[17]

But several indications seem to show that this is not how Aristotle regards the matter in the tenth book. Most important is the fact, mentioned above but not yet commented on, that in recommending the "intellectual life" Aristotle brings forward and emphasizes the idea that one ought to conceive of oneself as identical exclusively with one's pure intellect (*nous*). This is the more striking and persuasive of the two reasons he gives in favor of this life-ideal,[18] for if one identifies oneself wholly with one's intellectual capacities and refuses to accept the physical and

---

[17] It is often pointed out that according to Aristotle practical intelligence, and so moral virtue, acts in such a way as to foster the intellect's flowering (*NE* = *EE* 1145a8-9, *MM* 1198b12-20). But these passages do not themselves imply that Aristotle thought that the successful pursuit of intellectual values would involve one in moral virtue as well. For they do not show Aristotle holding that the intellect's flowering is *all* the φρόνιμος ultimately concerns himself with, nor do they imply that moral virtue is an indispensable, or even the best, means to this end. His point seems to be simply that if one is freed from irrational extremes of passionate desire, as the morally virtuous person is, then one important condition for the development of the intellect is achieved. But it does not follow that once the intellect has been developed moral virtue and its activities remain an essential condition for engaging in theoretical activities, nor that *precisely* that condition of quietude produced by moral virtue is absolutely necessary in order to develop the mind in the first place. A somewhat different one (say, one in which fewer and weaker passionate desires remained) might be preferable, even though the virtuous condition was effective enough (more effective, at any rate, than ordinary vices) in preparing the way for intellectual cultivation. And one should bear in mind that when in the *Politics* (VII 2 and elsewhere) Aristotle rejects the sort of "contemplative life" that Anaxagoras led for many years at Athens, where as a foreigner he was excluded from all participation in civic affairs, he obviously does not do so on the grounds that Anaxagoras would have got, on balance, more and better thinking done had he remained in Clazomenae and engaged himself fully in civic life there (or, alternatively, had he been born an Athenian and taken part in Athenian civic life). Yet this would have to have been his view if the interpretation being considered were correct. Plainly in rejecting the Anaxagorean ideal Aristotle counts other goods besides pure intellectual ones as basic constituents of the good life, and not merely as useful means of attaining intellectual goods.

[18] The other reason, that "even though it is small in bulk it exceeds

emotional capacities and needs which link one to other persons as essential and fundamental to what one is, then Aristotle's call to "act as far as possible as an immortal and do everything with a view to living in accordance with (the pure intellect)" makes perfect sense. If one adopts this attitude, and seriously takes it as an ideal for self-realization to cut one's volitional ties to one's physical and emotional nature, then of course one's intellectual interests will come to dominate. One will not think the other interests which might lead one to another scheme of life are true interests of one's self, and will, as Aristotle maintains, regard any choice of other goods—social, moral, or bodily—(unless as a means to intellectual activity) truly as choosing "not one's own life but someone else's." The identification of oneself, and thus one's true interests, with one's intellect and its interests thus means that one regards everything else as alien and having no independent claims on one's energies.

Now this fact has extremely important consequences: for such an attitude is obviously incompatible with moral virtue as Aristotle understands it. If one possesses a virtue, then, according to Aristotle, one performs the relevant acts for their own sakes, regarding them as good in themselves; but this one could assuredly not do if one thought that any value they might encompass was not of any direct interest to oneself.[19] The absence

---

everything by far in power and worth," is by itself a very poor ground for Aristotle's conclusion. For, as Aristotle argues in the *MM* (1.84a8-12), on which see above pp. 121 ff, it is a confusion to think that the best single thing there is is therefore, all by itself, a good thing to choose to make one's life of. But taken as a ground for identifying oneself with one's intellect (given that this choice of identity is a conceivable one at all) this comment, too, is not altogether without weight.

[19] See *NE* II 4 1105a28-33: "It is not enough, in order for actions that are in accordance with the virtues to be done justly or temperately, that *they* should have certain properties, but the person who does them must also have certain properties: first, he must act knowingly; next he must choose (προαιρούμενος) the actions, and choose them for themselves; and thirdly he must act from a firm and unalterable character (βεβαίως καὶ ἀμετακινήτως)." The contemplative will certainly fail to have the third property, and probably the second as well.

of moral virtue from the intellectual life as Aristotle here conceives it is confirmed by what he says, and fails to say, about it
elsewhere in the tenth book. In the eighth chapter (1178b3-7) he
says that "the theorizer has no need of such things (viz., the
external goods) with a view to his own activity, and they are really,
so to say, impediments so far as theorizing is concerned. But,
insofar as he is a human being and lives among other people, he
chooses to perform virtuous actions. Hence he will need such
things with a view to acting as a human being." It is important to
notice exactly what Aristotle says here. He says only that the theorizer may *perform* various virtuous actions—that insofar as he
remains involved with other people he may conform his conduct
to the requirements of the virtues. But there is a large difference
between this and *being* a virtuous person. For as Aristotle is at
pains to argue, to be virtuous one must not only do what the
virtues require, but also choose these actions for their own sakes
and as the expression of a fixed and unalterable character.
"Things are called just or temperate whenever they are such as
the just or temperate person would do; but it is not the person
who does these actions who is just or temperate, but whoever does
them in the way that the just and the temperate do."[20] And
Aristotle conspicuously avoids saying that his theorizer will *be* a
virtuous person. This is easily understood, since it is clear that
however often he may perform the just or the temperate or the
liberal deed, anyone who organizes his life from the intellectualist
outlook cannot care about such actions in the way a truly just or
temperate or liberal man does. He will not possess the social
virtues, or any other virtues, because he will lack the kind of
commitment to this kind of activity that is an essential characteristic of the virtuous person. He may, as Aristotle maintains,
have reason to act justly from time to time, or liberally, or
courageously, and so on; but he will regard such actions as forced
on him by involvements with others that he inescapably finds

[20] *NE* II 4 1105b5-9; cf. the passage quoted in the preceding note.

himself entangled in. He does in fact live among other men, and must therefore keep up satisfactory relations with them if he is to be free to devote himself as fully as possible to his intellectual work. But such just or courageous or liberal acts as he may perform are not *his own* acts; they are a concession to the human being—the living physical body—with which he refuses to identify himself, although he cannot avoid being in certain ways dependent on what happens to it for his own well-being.

The "intellectual life" discussed in the tenth book does not, then, involve the possession of any of the moral virtues. Aristotle does not put forward the theory that the development and continued exercise of these virtues is a necessary condition of the flowering of the intellect. He does not, indeed, discuss the question whether or not such a life would be compatible with positively vicious behavior on occasion, but he clearly implies that even if just or courageous acts formed part of it they would not be the acts of a just or courageous person. Hence, even in the tenth book he nowhere suggests the theory that moral virtues are necessary means to a dominant intellectualist end; virtuous *actions* may well be, but that is another matter entirely.

How then is one to interpret the other member of this pair of contrasted lives? It is described as a "life of moral virtue," and of course it is on this aspect of it that Aristotle's interests focus, since its provision for morally virtuous activities is the salient characteristic of this life, and that which distinguishes it from the intellectual life already discussed. But because his principal aim in these chapters is to explain and defend his preference for the intellectual mode of life he does not enter into the details of the contrasted moral life. This is unfortunate from our point of view, since it makes it difficult to be absolutely certain of the relation between the "moral life" of the tenth book of the *Nicomachean Ethics* and the flourishing life as this is conceived in the *Eudemian Ethics*. Is this "moral life" a life devoted exclusively to moral virtue, with no provision at all for intellectual excellences and their exercise, however circumscribed and limited? Or does

Aristotle have in mind, in effect, the *Eudemian* life devoted jointly to moral and intellectual cultivation? He does not make this clear; he discusses the second life and the rationale for preferring it only so far as it contains the moral virtues as fundamental values, and omits to specify it further, since for his contrastive purposes this is sufficient.

Given Aristotle's silence, however, one might with some justification be inclined to infer that the second life is as exclusively devoted to moral good as the other is to intellectual, that it is identical with the narrowly "political" or citizenly life mentioned in the first book of the *Eudemian Ethics*—the stolid burgher's life, as I described it above.[21] But if so then Aristotle will be maintaining that a narrowly philosophical life and a narrowly citizenly life are respectively best and second-best, without so much as mentioning the richer mixed life that he championed in the *Eudemian Ethics*. This would not be easy to explain. And three points about Aristotle's description of this second life seem to mark it off from that of the burgher. First, Aristotle nowhere says or implies that one who leads this life identifies flourishing simply with morally virtuous activity, whereas he does maintain that, on the other ideal, flourishing is made to consist in theoretical activity. Thus, although he mentions nothing besides virtuous activity as a fundamental good on this scheme, he does not describe it as a dominant good, as theoretical activity is clearly made dominant on the other scheme. Nor, secondly, does he say that in living the "moral life" one identifies oneself exclusively with one's physical and emotional capacities, as those who live the intellectual life identify themselves exclusively with their intellects. In this view a human being is conceived of at least as partly an emotional being (1177b26-31), and its proponents object to the simple identification of a man with his intellect, the godlike element in him. But nothing Aristotle says suggests that they adopt an equally restrictive conception which would forbid a

[21] *EE* I 4 1215a36, b3-4; and cf. *NE* I 5 1095b18, 22-31.

human being to identify himself in part with his pure intellect. And, thirdly, the call for the maximization of intellectual good ("so far as possible act as an immortal and do everything with a view to living in accordance with what is highest in oneself," 1177b33-34) finds no counterpart in the description of this second life: here, there is no corresponding injunction to maximize moral good.

In view of all this it seems reasonable to take the second life to be in fact the *Eudemian* mixed ideal. For the three points of the preceding paragraph, though admittedly negative, leave room for the supposition that the preference for the moral life is founded on the same broad commonsense conception of human nature as we found operating in the *Eudemian Ethics*, according to which both the intellectual and the emotional sides of our make-up belong equally essentially and fundamentally to what we are. And in adopting this view of human nature one is naturally led to the conclusion that the sort of life that would suit a human being would be one devoted jointly to both kinds of excellence. If this is correct, then Aristotle in calling this life a "life of moral virtue" names it after its distinctive aspect and does not imply that there is no provision in it for the intellectual excellences and their exercise. For although the intellectual life itself certainly will possess a much greater quantity of that kind of good in it than the "moral life" can possibly have (given that in the latter intellectual good is balanced, and so limited, against other types of good thing), the "moral life" will have its share as well.

It seems clear, then, that by the intellectual life which he pronounces "most flourishing" Aristotle means a contemplative life led by a person who takes no interest in family, social, or political life, although he will, as necessary, do his part in these spheres since his attainment of the maximum possible leisure for theoretical work depends upon doing so. There are also good (though somewhat less certain) grounds for identifying the moral life which Aristotle says flourishes in the second degree with the mixed life devoted to both types of excellence. What reason, then, does Aristotle give, or have, for ordering these two lives in this way? How does it come about that the conception of flourishing which he endorsed in the *Eudemian Ethics* and which he seems to presuppose throughout the main body of the *Nicomachean Ethics* is downgraded at the end of the treatise?

4. The Intellect as the True Self

It seems clear that what determines Aristotle's conclusion in the *Nicomachean Ethics* is the doctrine of human identity that he advances in the passage we have been considering. Once one accepts that one *is* his theoretical mind, then Aristotle's conclusion follows without difficulty. Our problem is to understand this doctrine of human identity and Aristotle's reasons for holding it. Aristotle only says here that the intellect is "what is highest in oneself," that it "exceeds everything in power and worth," and that it is "the authoritative and better part." He seems to infer from these points, especially the last one, that one ought to identify oneself exclusively with the intellect. In order to understand this idea and put it into its proper perspective it will be useful to trace it back through its appearances in other works of Aristotle to its origins in Plato's *Republic*.

The idea that a person is to be identified with his mind, rather than with his desires or emotions, let alone his body, appears with emphasis at various places in the *Republic*. Most notable, perhaps, is the passage in book IX (588b10-e1) in which Plato compares a man to a hybrid, consisting of a many-headed wild beast (appetite), a lion ("high-spirit"), and a man (the mind)—all grown together inside a creature with the outward aspect of a man. Here the representation of the mind by a man—a little man inside the large man—carries with it implications similar to those which we have seen Aristotle develop in the tenth book: the man that one is is identified with one's mind. And in the context Plato calls the mind the "best" (*to beltiston*, 589d7) and the "most divine" part (*to theiotaton*, e4). But what is striking about Plato's identification of a person with his mind, rather than his appetites or his "high-spirit," is that the mind in question is not merely concerned with knowing truths but also (and even more) with making decisions and governing the whole person. Thus at 590c Plato declares that undertaking menial occupations is unworthy because by doing so "one has a naturally weak best element, so that one cannot rule over the animals within, but only act as their servant, and can learn nothing but ways of flattering them." This conception of the mind is of course fundamental in the *Republic*, where, in introducing the three parts of the soul in the fourth book, Plato assigns to the mind the job of governing, having "foresight on behalf of the whole soul" (441e5) and "the knowledge of what is to the advantage of the whole community of the three" (442c5-7). Theoretical activities come in, but only because, for Plato, the practical knowledge which it is the soul's essential function to provide is only obtained by first mathematical and then philosophical investigations. In identifying the human being with his mind in book IX, Plato is plainly regarding the mind principally in its practical orientation.

Now it is noteworthy that in all the places in Aristotle, with the sole exception of our passage from the tenth book of the *Nicomachean Ethics*, in which this theory is stated, the human being is identified not with his theoretical intellect but either, as in Plato, with an undifferentiated mind regarded principally from the practical side, or else with the practical intellect itself.[22] The

---

[22] Besides the tenth-book passage, there are three others: *Protrepticus* frag. 6 Ross (B 59-70 Düring), and *NE* IX 4 1166a10-23 and 8 1168b28-1169a3. The two *NE* passages are discussed in the text and in n. 24 below. As for *Protrepticus* 6: in the first part of the passage (B 59-62), which culminates in the pronouncement that we are, either exclusively or especially "this part," viz. τὸ λόγον ἔχον καὶ διάνοιαν, Aristotle explains what part is meant by such phrases as ὅπερ κατὰ φύσιν ἄρχει καὶ κρίνει περὶ ἡμῶν (B 60) and ὃ κελεύει καὶ κωλύει, καὶ δεῖν ἢ μὴ δεῖν φησι πράττειν (B 61). So our identity is being made to consist, as in Plato, in that in us which decides and governs. The fact that later on in the passage (B 66-70) Aristotle discusses the ἀρετή of the mind and its proper activity in a way which emphasizes speculative aspects of the intellect (cf. B 69, referring to the knowledge in which this excellence consists, θεωρητικήν τιν' ἄρα φατέον

most interesting of these passages occurs in the ninth book of the *Nicomachean Ethics*, where Aristotle is making the point that a good man is not a lover of self in the standard, pejorative sense: he is not selfishly concerned exclusively or especially for his own comfort, pleasure, and material well-being. That is, to put it in the terms used in the last chapter to explain Aristotle's theory of moral virtue, the good man is not devoted simply and directly to the acquisition for himself of various first-order good things: he does not identify his own good with the possession, or the mere use, of any collection of these good things. But Aristotle insists that he is, in a different and more fundamental way, a lover of self.

At any rate, he takes for himself the finest [*kallista*] and best things, and gratifies the principal authority [*tōi kuriōtatōi*] within him and in all things obeys this. And just as the principal authority in a city is thought to *be*, properly speaking, the city (and the same is true of any other organized whole [*sustēma*]), so also with man. So the man who loves this and gratifies it is more than anyone else a lover of self. Also, a man is said to have self-control or lack it according as his mind [*nous*] is in control or not, which implies that each person *is* his mind; and people are thought to have acted *themselves,* and to have acted willingly,

---

εἶναι ταύτην τὴν ἐπιστήμην) is no difficulty. For frag. 13 (= B 46-51) makes it perfectly clear that in the *Protrepticus* Aristotle does not draw the radical distinction he later drew between theoretical and practical knowledge: as in Plato, the knowledge of the fundamental practical and moral principles is itself somehow a theoretical operation (cf. B 47, τὸν πολιτικὸν ἔχειν τινὰς ὅρους δεῖ ἀπὸ τῆς φύσεως αὐτῆς καὶ τῆς ἀληθείας, πρὸς οὓς κρινεῖ τί δίκαιον καὶ τί καλόν; B 51, τῆς ἐπιστήμης θεωρητικῆς οὔσης μυρία πράττομεν κατ᾽αὐτὴν ὅμως ἡμεῖς, καὶ τὰ μὲν λαμβάνομεν τὰ δὲ φεύγομεν τῶν πραγμάτων, καὶ ὅλως πάντα τὰ ἀγαθὰ δι᾽ αὐτὴν κτώμεθα). Naturally, he especially emphasizes its theoretical side, given his aim in the *Protrepticus* of exhorting people to undertake philosophical study. But the intellectual work in which he urges us to find our true selves is at the same time inescapably a practical activity, since it consists, among other things, in working out the ends of action. The important point to insist on here is that when he does explicitly state that we are identical with the intellect which performs this activity it is the practical side that is explicitly emphasized.

when acting by design [*meta logou*]. So there is no doubt that
each man *is* this, or is this more than anything else, and that the
good man loves this more than anything else. (1168b29-1169a3)

Aristotle gives two reasons here in defense of the idea that a
man should be identified with his mind. The first is contained in
the analogy between men and cities. This comparison apparently
rests on the idea that there is a supreme governing authority in
every city, to which all other state bodies stand as instruments for
the carrying out of its will.[23] In democracies, for example, the
assembly sets policy and makes the important decisions, while the
courts and the magistracies can be viewed as putting into effect
the assembly's wishes, expressed or implied; and *mutatis
mutandis* for monarchies, aristocracies, and so on. The idea that
we do (or should) identify a city with its central governing body
can perhaps be supported by various linguistic usages. News-
papers report that "the United States takes the view that no vio-
lation has occurred," where what is meant is that the American president, or his representatives, have taken that view. Kings
of countries can be, or used to be, referred to as "France" or
"Denmark", and so on. And in the case of armies, we do regularly say, for example, that "Wellington closed up the gap on
his left wing," when it was in fact soldiers under his command
who did the closing. But these and similar examples show, I
think, that the kind of identification which Aristotle had in mind
is only plausible where the organization in question has a strongly
hierarchical structure. There is no person or body with which one
might be tempted to identify the Congregational church, as one
might identify the Roman Catholic church with the Pope. A
second restriction would seem to be that the "authority" must be
a governing one, making policy and taking decisions for the whole

[23] The assumption that there is in every sort of political constitution a
supreme governing authority is made explicit at *Politics* 1278b8-14. That
the subordinate bodies are to be regarded as instruments seems to be implied
by what Aristotle says about human beings in *Protrepticus* frag. 6 Ross:
the soul rules the body, that is, uses it as an instrument (B 5a Düring).

membership: the blocks making up an arch may be organized round the coping stone, and the arch as a whole may be dependent upon it, but it would be a joke to identify the arch with the stone.

Interestingly, it seems clear that Aristotle's use of the analogy between cities and men in this passage conforms to these restrictions. For, as his second argument for the identification of a person with his mind shows, he is thinking of a person as identical with that in him which properly ought to decide what he is to do and which controls and guides his inclinations and desires in their job of moving his limbs and generating actions—in short, with his practical reason. The mind which is in control in the self-controlled man and out of control in the incontinent is the practical reason, whose virtue, *phronēsis*, is said in the sixth book to consist in issuing *commands* (1143a8). The rationale thus given for this identification is simply that where decision-making and initiative-setting is concentrated in the hands of a single faculty or single body it is fair to speak of the whole that is so organized as essentially identical with the decision-making power.[24]

Hence Aristotle's point about self-love in this passage is just that the good man loves himself more than anything else because—and in the sense that—he acts always as he knows he ought, finding his own good in that kind of action itself. It is, as it were, not the content of the action but its form that is essential here: when Aristotle says the good man "gratifies his mind" he means only that, whatever he does, he does it because he has decided upon it by reasoning; he does not mean that he forgoes

[24] The same is true, though perhaps less obviously, of the other passage of IX where the identity of a person with his mind is alluded to, 4 1166a10-23. What Aristotle emphasizes there is the harmony that exists in the virtuous man between his practical judgments, and practical opinions generally, and the impulses toward or away from action which arise from his emotions and appetites. Thus Aristotle says (a13-14) that the good man ὁμογνωμονεῖ ἑαυτῷ καὶ τῶν αὐτῶν ὀρέγεται κατὰ πᾶσαν τὴν ψυχήν: cf. VI 1139a29-31, where the proper condition of practical reason is said to be ἀλήθεια ὁμολόγως ἔχουσα τῇ ὀρέξει τῇ ὀρθῇ. The two things that agree with one another are the practical intellect and the passions.

dinner or sex in order to continue work on some intellectual problem or project (thus neglecting appetite in favor of "the pleasure of the mind"). These things the good man may well do on occasion, but when he does do them the gratification of the mind to which Aristotle refers here will show itself in his doing what he has decided by correct reflection he ought to do, and not in the pleasures he gets from the intellectual work. This is why Aristotle can feel himself justified in saying later on in the chapter (1169a18-26) that good men do many things for their friends, even if they must die in the process: their commitment to moral virtue involves them in the risk of death (say, in courageously defending a friend from attack), and because they see their highest good in virtuous action, they refuse to abandon this good for any other, even life itself. They insist on gratifying their minds, by obeying the moral principles enunciated by reason, rather than their inclinations and desires. Such men, in choosing those actions, certainly could not be said to be gratifying their theoretical intellects—since in choosing death they would be abandoning all hope of further intellectual activity.[25]

[25] The question may still remain, of course, how, on Aristotle's theory of the justification of moral principles, any such stringent moral requirement can ever be imposed. Aristotle seems simply to assume here that moral principles do require that one be ready to die for one's friends; but doubts about whether this is true, or whether Aristotle's theories allow him to hold it, do not call into question the correctness or coherence of the point he *is* making, namely that, given this assumption, even in choosing an action that brings death, one will be gratifying one's mind and choosing one's own good.

It was apparently chiefly reflection on what Aristotle says in this passage about self-sacrifice that led Ollé-Laprune to his interpretation of Aristotle's theory of εὐδαιμονία. Ollé-Laprune thought that if one takes Aristotle to hold that moral action shares, in a derivative way, the property that makes contemplative activity εὐδαίμων (namely, rationality), all would be in order with this passage: for according to Ollé-Laprune, Aristotle could then hold that in self-sacrifice a man does in a manner achieve that which he has been pursuing in pursuing contemplative activity as ultimate; his pursuit of that end need not lead him to prefer to save his own skin in order to do more and better pure thinking, instead of nobly risking death for his friend's sake. But this is plainly not so. It is obviously irrational to prefer a lesser ("derivative") manifestation of the end to a greater, if it should be impossible

In this passage, then, and the other passages cited, it is essential to the underlying rationale of this theory of human identity that the mind be thought of as what makes decisions and controls the action-producing apparatus of the person. It ought therefore to be found surprising that the *nous* with which we are urged to identify ourselves in book X is the intellect in its theoretical aspect alone, carefully distinguished not only from the inclinations and desires but even from the action-guiding activities of mind itself. Aristotle is explicit on this point. *Nous* is first (1177b28-29) distinguished sharply from *to suntheton*—the living body—and then the living body is assigned not only the virtues of the character, which belong properly to the passions, but even practical intelligence itself: these two, he says, are interconnected, and as a result both are bound up with the passions and belong to the *suntheton*. Only the virtue of the mind (*hē tou nou [aretē]*),[26] i.e., theoretical wisdom (*sophia*), is free from involvement with the passions and therefore not an excellence of the living body (1178a16-22). Practical intelligence is not, then, an excellence belonging to the mind at all, in the sense in which Aristotle here means to identify a human being with his mind.

The result is that even though Aristotle describes the pure intellect as "the authoritative and better part" (*to kurion kai ameinon*), as he had described the (practical) intellect in the passage from book IX as "the principal authority" in a man (*heautou to kuriōtaton*), he cannot draw upon the arguments

---

to achieve both, and I do not see how Ollé-Laprune's solution to the difficulty can get round the objection that this irrationality is precisely what he attributes to the good man in the situation of self-sacrifice. Aristotle's approval of self-sacrifice here can only be made sense of on the assumption that he is treating moral action itself as an independent, basic good, and not in Ollé-Laprune's way a derivative one.

[26] That it is ἀρετή and not εὐδαιμονία that must be supplied at 1178a22 is made clear by two considerations. (1) The main subject of the preceding sentence (a19) is αὖται [αἱ ἀρεταί], viz. the excellences of character together with practical intelligence. (2) Ἡ ἀρετὴ τοῦ νοῦ is required as understood subject of δόξειε ἄν in a24, immediately following. The fact that the nearest preceding feminine noun is εὐδαιμονία (a21-22) has no significance.

given in book IX to support the theory of human identity put forward in book X. In book X the aspect of mind that is in question is not the practical reason; hence the rationale given earlier for treating a person as identical with his mind cannot apply here. The pure intellect is not "authoritative" in the sense of exercising control over anything.

It appears, then, that Aristotle in the tenth book has given a sharp and unexpected twist to the conception, inherited from Plato, which identifies a human being with his mind. What can explain this development? The answer, I think, is simple. As we have just seen, Aristotle in the tenth book sharply separates the practical from the theoretical reason, associating the former with the *suntheton*, or living body, while making the latter a godlike thing apart. This way of thinking about the powers of what we call the human soul plainly derives from the theory of the *De Anima*. It is well known that Aristotle in the *De Anima* draws a sharp distinction between the highest intellectual powers and the other psychological and biological functions. The latter are in fact all psycho-physical functions of various kinds, and the soul which exercises them can be defined as the "first actuality of a (certain kind of) natural body having (certain) organs;"[27] these functions can neither exist apart from one another nor apart from a body whose actuality they are.[28] But the highest intellectual function is not connected in this way with the other functions nor with any body;[29] and, accordingly, the soul which exercises this function is not defined as the actuality of a body. It is, as Aristotle says at one place (413b26), *psuchēs genos heteron,* another kind of soul;[30] and, as he seems to say elsewhere (*De Gen. An.* 736b27-28, 737a10, 744b21), it comes into the body from outside (*thurathen*). There are difficulties about just where Aristotle draws

[27] *De An.* 412b5-6.

[28] *De An.* 412b7-9, 413a3-6, 413b27-32.

[29] Cf. 429b25-27: there is no organ for thinking, as there is for the other life-functions.

[30] Cf. also 402b1-3, 408b18-19.

the line between the psycho-physical and the independent capacities; at one place (413b25) he refers simply to the theoretical capacity (*hē theōrētikē dunamis*), without drawing any distinctions, as separate from the rest, but usually he says *nous,* the capacity of intuitive insight which only provides the foundation of all theorizing.[31] The question is further complicated by the theory of the *nous pathētikos* (*De An. III* 4-5), which seems to connect even some intuitive thinking with the body.[32] But wherever the line is drawn, the consequence of drawing it is to make human nature not a single complex thing. If one accepts this theory, then strictly speaking we have not one soul with many capacities, but two souls, one the actuality of a body and the other not—though Aristotle does little to explain positively what it is instead.

It is, then, the late and technical psychological theory of the *De Anima* to which Aristotle implicitly appeals in arguing the identification of a human being with his (theoretical) *nous.* According to the theory of the *De Anima*, a human being cannot correctly be thought of as a single complex creature, possessing physical, emotional, and intellectual characteristics of various kinds, all bound together and unified as parts or aspects of the soul which, being his form, makes him the creature that he is. Instead, the highest intellectual powers are split off from the others and made, in some obscure way, to constitute a soul all on their own. Which, then, of these two souls should one say is what makes a human being what he is? Which of the two creatures that, it now emerges, are joined together in any actual person, is he to be identified with? On the psychological theory of the *De Anima*, these questions can hardly be avoided; and once they are posed it is a foregone conclusion what answer Aristotle will make. All the associations which for him link the mind with divinity combine to make it seem obvious that strictly it is a man's

[31] As at 415a12, 429a10-14, etc.
[32] Cf. 429b10-22; and Rodier's comments *ad loc.*

intellect that makes him what he is and that therefore any choice of ideal for self-realization other than the maximum development and exercise of the mind would be low and unworthy. The theme of divine kinship, as we have seen, is already introduced in book X chapter 7, when Aristotle calls the pure intellect something godlike (*theion*); and it is picked up and elaborated in two passages of the following chapter. Aristotle claims that *sophoi,* because they specially cultivate their intellects, endear themselves to the gods and can expect, if any one can, to be well treated by them in return (1179a22-32). And he argues that the gods, whom everyone assumes to lead a blissful life, must be thought to be constantly engaged in theorizing, from which he infers that the same activity must constitute *eudaimonia* for human beings as well (1178b7-23). In all this, Aristotle contrives to make it appear both impious and stupid for anyone not to regard himself as a purely intellectual being: impious because in doing so one prefers to deny or reduce his kinship with the gods in favor of kinship with the lower animals, and stupid because he willingly foregoes the quasi-divine bliss that could have been his. In general, Aristotle seems to condemn any other conception of the self as showing lack of nerve and paltriness of aspiration: to settle for a less exalted conception is, he seems to think, a sign of smallness of soul.

5. Conclusion

The technical psychology of the *De Anima* thus encourages the idea that a human being is essentially godlike, and it seems that Aristotle simply works out the consequences of this idea in the theory of flourishing which, as we have seen, he advances in the tenth book of the *Nicomachean Ethics*. But although Aristotle by clear implication reaffirms the *De Anima*'s theory of the soul in the last book of the *Ethics*, he does not decisively reject as false the more commonsense conception which, refusing to separate the highest mental functions from the remaining human life-powers, regards a human being as at once and equally an intellectual and a social being. At least, this is so if the moral life which Aristotle counts as a flourishing one—though in the second degree—is, as I have argued, the mixed life of the *Eudemian Ethics*. For the conception of human nature which lies behind and justifies this choice is, as we have seen, precisely this commonsense view. It is only because this conception remains, after all, an acceptable one—perhaps simply because it recommends itself so firmly to common sense [33]—that Aristotle can continue in the tenth book to describe the mixed life as flourishing.

The upshot is that although in the tenth book Aristotle does adopt an intellectualist ideal, he does so only with important reservations. First, this ideal is explicitly associated with a quite particular conception of human identity. But this conception, which is made possible for Aristotle by the conclusions to which he is led in treating human intelligence in the *De Anima*, will hardly recommend itself to everyone, even though for Aristotle it is the most preferred conception because most in accord with his technical psychological theory. Hence, secondly, he does not reject out of hand as false and misguided the more ordinary conception of human nature as at once both emotional and intellectual. The mixed life to which this conception leads remains a flourishing one. Though, to be sure, its status as an ideal life is compromised by Aristotle's own preference in book X for the purely intellectual life, in counting it a flourishing life at all Aristotle shows that he regards it as an intelligent and worthy ideal. Thirdly, Aristotle makes it reasonably clear that it is the second ideal, and not the first, which the morally good person

---

[33] Cf. *NE* I 13 1102a23-26: the student of ethics must study psychological theory, but only so far as suits his ethical interests and without needing to go into technical details. If this means, as it is often taken to, that moral theory must rest ultimately on common-sense psychological assumptions, then Aristotle is only being consistent in insisting in book X on counting the "moral life" as εὐδαίμων—though he might with even more consistency have kept his technical psychological theory out of the discussion altogether.

aims at realizing. Moral virtue only forms a part of the second life, and plays no role at all in the first. The intellectualist is beyond ordinary moral virtues—though, equally, beyond ordinary vices as well. Aristotle does not put forward in the tenth book a revised account of moral virtue and the morally good agent which refashions the more ordinary conception of virtue in the light of the intellectualist ultimate end. Moral virtue remains in the tenth book, as earlier in the *Nicomachean Ethics,* and indeed as in the *Eudemian Ethics,* an ingredient exclusively of the mixed ideal.

These are significant reservations. For they show that in his most mature ethical theory Aristotle does not totally abandon the conception of human flourishing as a life organized so as to bring a great variety of different goods by being devoted to the exercise both of the intellectual and of the moral excellences. He continues to develop and expound this view on the assumption that it is this ultimate end which the person who possesses practical intelligence (*phronēsis*) and a virtuous character will pursue. But whereas in the *Eudemian Ethics* such a life is the highest ideal conceived, in the *Nicomachean,* in the final analysis, Aristotle both conceives and prefers another, intellectualist, ideal which it is fair to describe, with Rodier, as superhuman, by contrast with the more down-to-earth ideal of the *Eudemian Ethics.*[34] Many

---

[34] See Rodier's edition of *NE* X, p. 52 (= *Etudes de philosophie grecque,* p. 214). P. Aubenque, whose interpretation of φρόνησις as involving essentially the recognition of the limitations of the human condition (*La prudence chez Aristote,* Paris: Presses Universitaires de France, 1963) is congenial to the views for which I have been arguing, tries valiantly (pp. 169-174) to accommodate even the superhuman ideal to his conception of the φρόνιμος. But unsuccessfully: for although the recommendation, ἐφ' ὅσον ἐνδέχεται ἀθανατίζειν, does imply an awareness that one *may* fail to succeed fully in living an immortal's life, it makes no provision for the definite and fixed limits the recognition of which Aubenque otherwise, and quite rightly, makes characteristic of the φρόνιμος. Rodier is clearly right to hold that this ideal *is* superhuman, so that Aristotle does not think any φρόνιμος would or should pursue it: φρόνησις, a human excellence,

will find much to regret in this, and will accordingly find the
moral theory of the *Eudemian Ethics* the more interesting and the
sounder of the two. I am myself sympathetic to this assessment.
But even in the *Nicomachean Ethics,* as I have argued, the older
view, though in the end given a secondary position, continues to
survive for those who do not, or cannot, regard only their intellectual nature as essential to what they are.

---

obviously involves the acceptance of the second ideal, and Aristotle as much
as says this himself (1178a16-17).

I should point out that Rodier, in his excellent discussion of these passages
of the tenth book, anticipates me both in interpreting the two lives as
alternative ideals, and in appealing to the *De Anima*'s theory of the soul
for the ground of the distinction. See the Introduction to his edition, pp.
50-55 (= *Etudes* . . . pp. 213-217).

Appendix and Indexes

Appendix

Aristotle's Use of the Word Ἔσχατον

The adjective ἔσχατον (literally, "last" or "ultimate") appears in some seven places in *NE* VI-VII (1141b28, 1142a24, 26, 1143a29, 33, 35, and 1146a9) without a noun either expressed or obviously to be supplied from the context. Most translators seem to think that in cases like these it means "individual thing." At any rate, Ross translates "an individual act" at 1141b28 (Dirlmeier agrees, rendering "Einzelhandlung"), Gauthier gives "l'individuel" at 1142a24, and Ross and Gauthier have "the individual facts" and "les faits particuliers" at 1146a9. Strictly speaking, all these translations are wrong, of course; even if what is being referred to are individual things, facts, or actions, the word does not ever *mean* "individual," but always "last." But I do not think a case can be made that Aristotle even refers to individuals in any of these cases.

When Aristotle calls something "last" it is always against the background of some order or process of counting, some things being first in this order and others later or last. Often the order in question can be easily supplied from the context, or is clear from the noun that the adjective qualifies: thus the extremities of a thing are regularly called its ἔσχατα (i.e., the parts of the thing farthest from its center: *Phys.* VI 2 233a18 and often elsewhere, with a natural extension to extremities in time as well as place); the law of contradiction is called at *Met.* Γ 3 1005b33 an ἔσχατον because one does not go back beyond it to derive it from anything more fundamental; the heart is apparently referred to in *De Mem.* 2 451a26 as τὸ ἄτομον καὶ ἔσχατον because it is the basic organ of all perception, the last organ one comes to in tracing back the effects of sensory stimulation; the minor term of a syllogism is called the "last term," *NE* VII 3 1147b14, *Pr. An.* I 4 25b33, and the three syllogistic figures recognized by Aristotle are called at *Pr. An.* I 32 47b1-5 the first, middle, and last. Sometimes what is last is the last thing one comes to as one counts *in* toward a given point rather than outward from it, as e.g., at *De Gen. et Corr.* I 7 324a28 and elsewhere.

But though the counting principles, as well as the direction of counting, vary widely, as one would expect, there is one counting principle that is specially prominent because of its close connection with Aristotle's central metaphysical doctrines. To the uses of ἔσχατον in these contexts Bonitz in his *Index* (289b39 ff) draws special attention, commenting that "logice τὸ ἔσχατον significat id quod ultimum est descendenti a summis generibus ad res individuas." This statement implies that, for Aristotle, what is last as one goes down from highest genera through intermediate genera and species toward individuals is individuals themselves; and it is undoubtedly on this usage, so understood, that translators rely to justify their renderings of τὸ ἔσχατον in the *Ethics*. But this is a plain mistake.

(1) With only one possible exception, what Aristotle counts as last in this metaphysical order is never the individual, but always a species or genus (usually, of course, the lowest, indivisible species). Many passages can be cited to illustrate Aristotle's usage here: but perhaps most revealing is *Met.* K 1 1059b26, where Aristotle says that every science has universals and not ἔσχατα for its objects, but plainly means not individuals but ἔσχατα εἴδη (cf. b35-36, with the conclusion at 37-38; and 998b14-17, which is the corresponding passage of B, contrasts universal genera with τὰ ἔσχατα κατηγορούμενα ἐπὶ τῶν ἀτόμων). Again, at I 9 1058b10, τὸ ἔσχατον ἄτομον means the lowest, indivisible species (as Ross sees: cf. his note *ad loc.*). Finally, the letters, i.e., A, B, C, etc. (not, of course, *this* A, *this* B, etc.) are said to be the ἔσχατα φωνῆς εἰς ἃ διαιρεῖται (*Met.* Δ 3 1014a28-29), and similarly the ἔσχατον ὑποκείμενον in a given case is e.g. water (i.e., watery stuff, not *this particular* volume of water, 1016a23) or, in another passage, ἡ μορφὴ καὶ τὸ εἶδος (1017b24-26). So also, as these facts would lead one to expect, one finds the expression ἔσχατον εἶδος sometimes taking the place of the more usual ἄτομον εἶδος, as at *De Part. An.* I 4 644a25 (cf. 644a2 and 643a15-18). The only passage

I know of (I have looked unsuccessfully for others) where what is referred to as ἔσχατον seems to be something individual is *Met.* Z 10 1035b30, where ἡ ἐσχάτη ὕλη is contrasted with ἡδὶ ἡ ὕλη ὡς καθόλου and therefore seems to mean, e.g., this particular flesh and bones (the matter making up Socrates in particular). (But contrast *Met.* Λ 3 1069b35-1070a4, where the ἐσχάτη ὕλη is the stuff of which a thing is immediately made, e.g. bronze—and not *this particular batch* of bronze.) Hence, if in the passages from the *Ethics* τὸ ἔσχατον is to be understood against the background of someone descending in order from the highest genera toward individual things, the evidence indicates that by this expression Aristotle would mean the lowest species and not the individual.

(2) But what, after all, suggests that we should read these passages against this background? At the first appearance of τὸ ἔσχατον (1141b28) there is no suggestion of the logical and metaphysical interest in division and predication which forms the background for the passages just cited; the focus here is on a process of political deliberation resulting in a voted decision. In another of these passages (1143a35 ff) it is plain that the order in question is the order which practical reasoning takes: νοῦς is said to be employed in connection with the *first* terms in theoretical demonstrations and also with the *last* stages of practical reasonings. Surely, then, in the earlier passage about political deliberation, and in the passage translated on p. 34 above (1142a23 ff), the sense of "last" intended is "last in the order of deliberation." (These considerations, and especially the parallel to 1143a35 ff just cited, show that Bywater was wrong to excise ἐν τοῖς μαθηματικοῖς in 1142a28: the phrase is entirely appropriate, and without it one can hardly make sense of the passage, except by gratuitously and wrongly forcing upon it, having deprived it entirely of its connections to its context, the metaphysical background of an interest in generic division. And, as I have argued, even if it were read against this background, as it plainly should not be, the reference would not be to individuals but to specific kinds of things.)

If, then, "last" in these passages means "last in the order of deliberation" it does not refer to individuals, but, as I argue on p. 38 above, to specific kinds of things. The fact that "last" here must mean "last in the order of deliberation" was first recognized, so far as I know, by John Burnet (see his notes pp. 271-274 and section 22 of his Introduction, *The Ethics of Aristotle*, London: Methuen, 1900): my interpretation is much indebted to his, though I hope it marks an improvement in one respect (see Chapter I, n. 49 above).

Index

Action (*praxis*): contrasted with production (*poiēsis*), 2, 78; narrowness of A.'s concept of, 78-79n; and instrumental value, 79-80
Akrasia, *see* Weakness of will
Allan, D. J.: on deliberation, 2-4; on the practical syllogism and intrinsic value, 2-5; distinguishes two types of practical syllogism, 3, 47, 51n; on "false reasoning" that achieves a good, 11; on rules as major premisses of practical syllogisms, 25n, 56n; alleges separation of choice from deliberation from *NE* VI on, 47n; on practical syllogism as thought displayed in action, 55n
Anaxagoras, 162n
Anscombe, G. E. M.: on choice and moral character, 48n; on action as conclusion of practical thinking, 57; on "flourishing" as translation of *eudaimonia*, 90n; on A. on ultimate ends, 93n
Aubenque, P., on *phronēsis* and the contemplative life, 179n

Bendixen, J., on coincidence of terminology in *EE* and *Politics* VII-VIII, 143n
Bios, *see* Life (*bios*)
Bipartite end, 112, 119, 143, 144, 147, 166-167. *See also* Ultimate end

Bonitz, Hermann, on A.'s use of the word *eschaton*, 184
Burgher's life, 161, 166
Burnet, John: on text of *NE 1142a30*, 34n; on meaning of "ultimate in mathematics," 38n, 40n; on *phronēsis* as not involved in selection of ultimate end, 64n; on dialectic in *NE*, 69-70, 107; on meaning of *eschaton*, 186
Burnyeat, M. F., 73n
Bywater, Ingram, 40n, 185

Choice (*proairesis*): A.'s definition of, 6, 47n; not limited to explicitly calculated decisions, 7; and fully developed character, 47-48n
Common books, the: Jaeger on, 72-73; Platonic terminology in, 73n; reasons for attributing to *EE*, 73n
Compound, the (*to suntheton*), 157, 174
Contemplation, *see* Knowledge, theoretical
Contemplative life, the, 145; Gauthier and Ollé-Laprune on, 152-153; and moral virtue, 163. *See also* Intellectual life

De Anima, 175-176
De Bona Fortuna, 135n
Deliberation: and prudential reason-

187

between intellectual activity and *eudaimonia*, 151-153; on self-sacrifice, 173n

Owen, G. E. L.: on deliberation and geometrical analysis, 20n; on *NE* VII *3*, 50n; on dialectic, 67

Particulars (*ta kath' hekasta*): A. on errors in deliberating about, 28; whether species or individuals, 28-29; as species, 31

Perception: has types, not individuals, for its objects, 43n; and the practical syllogism, 50, 52; and moral virtue, 134

Phronēsis, *see* Practical intelligence

Plato: *Cratylus 390b*, 15n; *Gorgias 503d-505b*, 84n; *Republic 348b-350c*, 84n; *Republic 441-442*, 139n, 169; *Republic 348-352*, 145-146; *Republic 588-589*, 168; on the intellect as the true self, 168-169

Politics, compared with *EE* on *eudaimonia*, 143n

Practical intelligence (*phronēsis*): contrasted with mathematical ability, 31n; concerned with ultimates, 33-34, 37; compared with political wisdom, 34-36; and perception of ultimates, 41-44; and moral character, 61-62, 101; involves recognition of occasions for action, 63; involves selection of means to ends, 63; involves selection of ultimate end, 63-64; and moral virtue, on intellectualist assumptions, 101; gives defining criterion of moral virtue, 101-103, 114-115, 134-135; aims at goodness of action itself, 105, 111; defined, 110-111, 150n; in *EE*'s definition of *eudaimonia*, 117

Practical reasoning: compared with theoretical, 65-71; and means-ends calculation, 95-96. *See also* Deliberation

Practical syllogism: Allan on, 2-5, 25n, 47, 51n, 55n, 56n; and rule-instance reasoning, 3; not illustrated by specifically moral examples, 4-5; whether illustrated in *NE* VI, 4-5, 27-32, 45-46; and perception, 23, 26-27, 52, 58; whether the last step in deliberation, 23-24, 26-27, 32, 59; illustrated, 24-25; action as conclusion of, 25, 46, 48n, 57; rule as major premiss of, 25n, 56; defined, 25-26; general form of, 26n; not part of deliberation, 38, 44, 46; and intention, 46, 48n; as link between deliberation and action, 46-51; and weakness of will, 48-50; and appetite, 50-51, 56; not a form of reasoning, 51-55; and animal movement, 52-55; compared with theoretical inference, 55

Proairesis, *see* Choice (*proairesis*)

Protrepticus: frag. *6*, 112-113n, 169n, 171n; frag. *13*, 149n, 170n

Rackham, H., on *NE 1141b26*, 35n

Rawls, John: on teleological and deontological ethical theories, 87-88; on one's good as maximum satisfaction of desire, 97n, 132n

Rhetoric: on nobility, 78; on the components of *eudaimonia*, 122

Rodier, G.: on intellectualism in *NE* X, 150n; on the contemplative ideal as superhuman, 179

Ross, W. D.: on "parts" of health, 21n; on *NE 1142a24*, 34; on *NE 1141b26*, 35n; on *NE 1142a23-30*, 38n, 40n; on *NE 1143b4-5*, 42n; interprets A.'s ethical theory as teleological, 87n; on intellectualism in *NE* X, 150n

Rules: as major premisses of practical syllogisms, 25n, 56; A. rejects the possibility of detailed, 134

Index Locorum

List of Works Cited

Allan, D. J. "The Practical Syllogism," *Autour d'Aristote* (Louvain, 1955).

Anscombe, G. E. M., *An Introduction to Wittgenstein's Tractatus* (London, 1959).

———, *Intention* (Oxford, 1957).

———, "Modern Moral Philosophy," *Philosophy*, 33 (1958), 1–19.

———, "Thought and Action in Aristotle," Bambrough, 143–158.

Aubenque, P., *La prudence chez Aristote* (Paris, 1963).

Bambrough, R., ed., *New Studies on Plato and Aristotle* (London, 1965).

Block, I, "The Order of Aristotle's Psychological Writings," *American Journal of Philosophy*, 82 (1961), 50–77.

Burnet, J., ed., *The Ethics of Aristotle* (London, 1900).

Cooper, J. M., "The Magna Moralia and Aristotle's Moral Philosophy," *American Journal of Philology*, 94 (1973), 327–349.

Dirlmeier, F., *Aristoteles, Magna Moralia, übersetzt und kommentiert* (Berlin, 1962).

———, *Aristoteles, Eudemische Ethik, übersetzt und kommentiert* (Berlin, 1969).

During, I., *Aristoteles* (Heidelberg, 1966).

Farquharson, A.S.L., trans., *The Works of Aristotle*, vol. V (Oxford, 1912).

Frankena, W. F., *Ethics* (Englewood Cliffs, 1963).

———, *Three Historical Philosophies of Education* (Chicago, 1965).

Gauthier, R.-A., *La morale d'Aristote* (Paris, 1958).

Gauthier, R.-A., and Jolif, J.Y., *Ethique à Nicomaque* (Louvain, 1958–1959).

Grant, A., *The "Ethics" of Aristotle Illustrated with Essays and Notes*, ed. 4 (London, 1885).

Greenwood, L. H. G., ed., *Nicomachean Ethics Book VI* (Cambridge, 1909).

Hardie, W. F. R., *Aristotle's Ethical Theory* (Oxford, 1968).

———, "Aristotle's Treatment of the Relation between the Soul and the Body," *Philosophical Quarterly*, 14 (1964), 69–71.

———, "The Final Good in Aristotle's *Ethics*," *Philosophy,* 40 (1965), 277–295, reprinted in Moravcsik, 297–322.

Jaeger, W., *Aristotle*, 2nd English ed. (Oxford, 1948).

Joachim, H. H., *Aristotle: Nicomachean Ethics* (Oxford, 1951).

Joly, R., *Le thème philosophique des genres de vie dans l'antiquité classique* (Brussels, 1956).

Kirwan, C., "Logic and the Good in Aristotle," *Philosophical Quarterly*, 17 (1967), 97–114.

Liddell, H. G., Scott, R., and Jones, H. S., *A Greek-English Lexicon* (Oxford, 1940).

Monan, J. D., *Moral Knowledge and its Methodology in Aristotle* (Oxford, 1968).

Moore, G. E., *Principia Ethica* (Cambridge, England, 1903).

Moravcsik, J. M. E., ed., *Aristotle: A Collection of Critical Essays* (Garden City, 1967).

Nagel, T., *The Possibility of Altruism* (Oxford, 1970).

Ollé-Laprune, L., *Essai sur la morale d'Aristote* (Paris, 1881).

Owen, G. E. L., "Tithenai ta phainomena," *Aristote et les problèmes de méthode*, ed. S. Mansion (Louvain, 1961), reprinted in Moravcsik, 167–190.

Rawls, J., *A Theory of Justice* (Cambridge, Mass., 1971).

Rodier, G., *Etudes de philosophie grecque* (Paris, 1926).

Ross, W. D., *Aristotle* (New York, 1959).

———, ed., *Aristotle's Metaphysics* (Oxford, 1924).

———, ed., *Aristotle's Prior and Posterior Analytics* (Oxford, 1949).